THE DYNAMICS OF THE CIVIL AVIATION INDUSTRY

The Dynamics of the Civil Aviation Industry

A. P. ELLISON
Aviation Planning Services, Montreal
(formerly of Queen Mary College, London)

E. M. STAFFORD
Southampton University

SAXON HOUSE | LEXINGTON BOOKS

Published by

SAXON HOUSE, D. C. Heath Ltd.
Westmead, Farnborough, Hants, England

Jointly with

LEXINGTON BOOKS, D. C. Heath & Co.
Lexington, Mass. U.S.A.

ISBN 0 347 01019 9
Library of Congress Catalog Card Number 73—16546

Printed in Great Britain by Robert MacLehose & Co. Ltd, The University Press, Glasgow

Contents

HE
9776
E44
1974

List of tables

List of figures

Introduction

Civil aviation is rarely out of the news. It is an industry at the forefront of technological change, enabling movement at a speed unattainable by any other means of transport. Air disasters will always arouse comment, but increasingly interest is centred on its economic organisation. The increase in air travel, particularly for holidays in the sun, has awakened popular interest in air fares, charter availability and tour operator viability. Anger over the airport delay has replaced the old moan about the late train.

Lack of information concerning the industry's structure, the rationale of its organisation, and the effects of regulation have all contributed to the ignorance surrounding the discussions. It is an ignorance found among administrators, aviation engineers and politicians as well as the air-travelling public.

The industry is difficult to examine, reducing statements of policy into inoperative generalisations. The difficulty lies in the industry's widely spread international operations, for almost all countries have their own or designated airlines, with which they exercise national sovereignty. The labyrinth of bilateral negotations has often led discussions to centre on piecemeal problems and selected areas — the North Atlantic Route, the European market, the US domestic market and its regulation. An overall international view of the industry, covering the final consumer as well as the producer market has yet to be attempted. Such a study is essential, for the development of the individual country's aerospace industries are increasingly dependent on the final consumer market; on the number of travellers taking an air trip.

This is particularly so in the US, where the slowdown in the space programme and the withdrawal from Vietnam have left the aerospace industries dependent on civil aviation sales. With an average eighty per cent of their capital tied up in aircraft, airlines quickly pass from black into red if they forecast incorrectly their aircraft purchases. The Lockheed/Rolls-Royce débâcle illustrated the importance of civil orders in one of the leading USA aerospace manufacturers. It is over a decade since Lockheed were in the civil market with their Electra, yet one mismanaged civil project today can threaten them with liquidation.

The text addresses itself to two main questions. Firstly, have the airline industry's cycles been caused primarily by external forces, or by the response of the airlines to these factors? Secondly, what would the effect be on the stability of the industry by altering some of the present controls? These are questions of dynamics, and can be approached only if the structure of the civil aviation industry is correctly defined. Detailed prognostication, allowing an evaluation of any given policy change, further requires accurate, up to date information. These are stiff requirements, but necessary if the battery of econometric and control theory techniques are to be used and to have validity.

The study time period is 1954 to 1972, a period during which the advent of subsonic, supersonic and wide bodied jets has transformed both the airlines and aerospace industries. In recent years, the growth of non-scheduled traffic has eroded a number of the 'rules' which govern scheduled airlines' decisions. Despite these changes, the structure of the industry has remained sufficiently constant to allow useful generalisations. Data sources have been good, and when needed, helpful cooperation was received from airlines and aircraft producers.

Chapter 1 outlines, in necessary detail, the organisational and control structure of the world's airline and aircraft production industries. Chapter 2 sets out, in formal terms, the structure of the relationship between the airline and the aircraft industries examining the determinants of demand and supply in the final passenger market and their relationship to this industry's structure and regulation. Following chapters then take up specific aspects of the overall model, formalising and testing appropriate model forms. Chapter 5 includes a comprehensive survey of the world's stock of civil aircraft and explores the determinants of aircraft scrappings. The relationship between changes in passenger demand, technology, income, prices, and so on, are used in Chapter 6 to explain the behaviour of aircraft orders. The order delivery lag in civil aircraft is measured in Chapter 7, while Chapter 8 formulates and forecasts the behaviour of the used aircraft market. Chapter 9 brings together these various segments of the model, and places them into the overall model formulated in Chapter 2. Here the stability of the model is tested, and the implication of alternative policies are explored. Chapters 3 and 4 are slightly outside the model, in that they formulate demand models for individual rather than aggregate world routes. These models are then tested on UK domestic and international routes.

Finally, the first of many cautionary remarks. The data upon which the models are tested and parameters derived have been thrown up by particular institutional structures. Changing the industry structure, in order to improve say the performance of the industry, could conceivably lead to a set of data yielding widely varying parameters from those estimated in this study. The implication is that policy changes based upon explicit (or implicit) parameter values must carefully consider the influence that particular institutional structures have played in determining these values. Hopefully this is what we have achieved in this text.

A final note. The international nature of air transportation, and the concentration of aviation technology in a few industrial economies has meant that the industry's impact on international trade balances has been proportionately greater than on domestic economic activity. This has been highlighted by the 1973 Middle Eastern War and the ensuing Arab oil restrictions. The inability of industrial consumers to reduce demand in response to supply reductions, and the unity of oil producers in exercising their monopolistic powers has resulted in very high increases in oil prices. The vulnerability of many countries' balance of payments and the jet engines' conspicuously heavy consumption of fuel has inevitably led to flight reductions. These have been particularly marked on the North Atlantic route and the US domestic market. The jolt has been considerable, and like all economic sectors of the western world, the aviation industry is left wondering what the long run consequences will be for its future development. In real terms, the price of fuel can be expected to reach a much higher than expected level and to remain there. Aviation seems to be at a disadvantage, for its enormous post-war growth has been based on producing services with increased time savings at reduced real prices. In terms of the input of fuel per service produced, aviation is at a disadvantage compared to sea and surface transport. The relative increase in the cost of fuel will mean that future growth will be curtailed, and largely limited to increases among the present flying public. Aviation's offer of time savings will be at higher prices, and will be afforded only by the higher income earners. The heydays of expansion into new markets by reducing the real relative price of air travel are over. In sum, the industry is likely to grow much more slowly than in the past, a factor which adds to the urgency of institutional changes.

These developments took place after this study was completed. They were also unforeseen, providing a contemporary reminder that the largest sources of the industry's fluctuations have been from changes exogenous to the industry.

Acknowledgements

The authors would like to thank numerous aircraft manufacturers, including the British Aircraft Corporation, Hawker Siddeley, McDonnell Douglas, Boeing and Lockheed, for their help and assistance with both data and access to commercially commissioned studies of the aircraft market.

Particularly our thanks are due to: A. Nayler, Librarian of the Royal Aeronautical Society; M. E. L. Spanyol, Market Research Manager, Hawker Siddeley; the staff of Queen Mary College, London; J. A. Bispham, National Institute of Electronic and Statistical Research; P. Davey, graduate student, Queen Mary College; Professor John Wise, University of Southampton. Finally, many thanks to the staff of A.P.S. for their diligence in proof reading.

1 The Structure of the Civil Aviation Market

1.1 Introduction

'The structure of world civil aviation has been fashioned by many forces, amongst which economic logic has played only a modest part.'[1]

Edwards' pithy sentence pinpoints the difficulty and fascination surrounding the problems of the civil aviation industry. Fashioned out of narrow nationalistic ends, international air transport has grown within a maze of bilaterally negotiated agreements. Its control is cumbersome, competition is highly restricted and as yet only a small proportion of the population of even the most advanced economies have used air transport. Its present development nowhere approaches its potential. The possibilities in large underdeveloped countries are enormous, as is the growth of international traffic between advanced economies. For instance, the increasing economic and political unification of Europe should see the region's air growth catching and rivalling North America by the end of the present decade. However, these possibilities will only be realised if the technological advances are translated into lower costs and fares. This requires a market structure which is flexible enough to realise these potentialities by stimulating the efficient airlines, and removing the wasteful restrictions. These restrictions, worked out in international agreements, have often been motivated by a desire of countries to protect their own airlines, and at the same time to stabilise the industry. Stabilisation of fares and the curtailment of frequencies have in their turn aggravated instabilities elsewhere — the qualitative competition in the form of aircraft orders — the high peaking of orders, capacity and load factors. An understanding of the present structure,[2] its effects and the implications for the future are, therefore, essential if any meaningful policies are to be explored.

This chapter sets out a brief historical survey of the institutional development of the industry since the war. Later sections highlight aspects of the economic structure of the industry — growth, concentration, fares and financial structure — all of which are important background detail for the development of later chapters. Similarly, the final section deals briefly with the aerospace industries as such, and the importance of civil production in the overall output.

1.2 Civil aviation's institutional framework

The institutional framework within which international civil aviation operates was formed during the latter years of the Second World War. The Chicago Convention of 1944, the establishment of ICAO in 1945 and the signing of the Bermuda Agreement in 1946, formed a legal, technical and commercial framework which has remained largely unchanged up to the present.

The Chicago Convention reflected the age of postwar reconstruction, the need for renewed assurances to international cooperation. The reality of the situation was that countries had (and have) sovereign rights over their own air space; the basic process of international intercourse was likely, therefore, to be bilateral rather than multilateral. The Convention formulated the international rights of civil transport operators. These five freedoms,[3] as they were termed, were:

1   The right to fly over another state's territory without landing.
2   The right to land on another state's territory for technical reasons (e.g. fuelling).
3   The right to establish a route to another country and carry passengers in both directions.
4   The right to pick up passengers at a third country on return flight to the country of origin.
5   The right of a country to transport goods and passengers between two other countries.

Fifty two countries were signatories to the Convention, while today the number has risen to over 300. All signatories became members of the newly formed agent of the United Nations, the International Civil Aviation Organisation (ICAO), which was instituted to establish uniformity in the non-commercial aspects of civil aviation activity. All member states are represented in the Assembly, which meets every three years to review the work of the five supporting bodies (covering navigation to finance). Centred in Montreal, it provides technical aid to developing countries, and is the industry's clearing house on international, technical and safety matters.

The Bermuda Agreement likewise reflected another aspect of the postwar world — the strength of the US carriers in international civil aviation. Before the war the lead lay with the Europeans, particularly the UK, for they had developed the equipment and personnel for international air travel. The Second World War changed the situation. A strengthened USA and a much weakened Europe resulted in a change of roles and objectives.

The American carriers, espousing free enterprise with all the confidence that superior strength is able to give, petitioned for freedom from capacity and fare control. This met with opposition from the much weaker European carriers, who saw a threat to their existence. The compromise was the signing of the Bermuda Agreement between the UK and the USA which, for some considerable time, became the blueprint for other bilateral negotiations, and the establishment of the International Air Transport Association (IATA), which was to supervise, among other things, the fixing of international fares.

A reading of the five freedoms shows that it is the third, fourth and fifth freedoms which are likely to be subject to bilateral negotiations. Despairing of multilateral agreement, the USA entered a bilateral agreement with the UK at Bermuda, which established the policy of unrestricted frequency or capacity with respect to third and fourth freedoms. The Bermuda agreement established this principle by (a) allowing no predetermined frequencies or capacity, and (b) by allowing more than one national airline to serve the route.

This policy of unrestricted capacity, a policy in line with the US carriers' aim, was applied to many other bilateral agreements. However, as more and more countries reached independence and introduced their own airlines, bilateral agreements have been struck which deviate considerably from this policy. Indeed, many international routes are distinguished by the capacity controls which have been obtained by bilateral agreements. Financial pools, shared routes and partnerships mark many areas of international civil aviation.

The second part of the compromise was the recognition by the US that international flights would be subjected to fixed fares. The International Air Transport Association, a reconstituted version of the prewar International Air Traffic Association, was recognised as a suitable organisation to provide the machinery for reaching inter-airline agreements on fares. The agreed fares at IATA, when given governmental approval, were applied to international routes by means of the bilateral agreements. In most of the agreements were clauses making it mandatory for the respective airlines to agree fares between themselves, and for the agreed fares to be approved by the governments concerned before being put into effect.

The emerged structure is one based on bilateral agreements between countries, negotiated by national airlines and sanctioned by the respective governments. The authority to fix international fares is derived from these inter-government agreements, and it is the fare clause in these agreements which establishes IATA fixed fares. Thus, the IATA fixed fares spread multilaterally by means of bilateral agreements.

Set up in 1945, IATA has grown in size along with the general growth in the industry, such that in 1971 it has 118 airlines[4] as members representing some 89 per cent of all ICAO members' schedule traffic. Its aims, as set out in its founding charter, can be summarised as:

1   To promote safe, regular and economic air transport for the benefit of the people of the world, to foster air commerce and to study the problems connected therewith.
2   To provide means for collaboration among international air transport operators.
3   To cooperate with ICAO and other international organisations.

Financed by member airlines' revenue (levied in proportion to the amount of international traffic carried), its main activities are those of a clearing house for its members, and as a centre where fares are fixed.

For tariff purposes IATA divides the world up into three Conference areas: area I covers North, Central and South America; area II covers Europe, Middle East and Africa; area III covers the Far East and Australasia.

Routes traversing more than one conference meet jointly, the most important being the transatlantic routes (Conference Joint 12) and the Round-the-World Routes (Conference Joint 123). These conferences usually meet in the third quarter of the year. Fares are set for the first quarter of the year, running for a period of two years.

The fares fixed in these IATA conferences are with respect to scheduled fares; indeed the member airlines until recently were predominantly producers of schedule services. Although there has been considerable dispute[5] over the distinction between scheduled and non-scheduled services, the former fulfil common carrier obligations. These obligations are fulfilled by providing regular, reliable, widely publicised services which can be used by any member of the public. The cost to the carrier of providing such public services is that load factors are lower, and consequently costs are higher. The distinction between scheduled and non-scheduled services has, however, become increasingly blurred with the growth of non-business travel, for many of the so-called non-scheduled services satisfy practically all of the above requirements. Indeed, such is the regularity of non-scheduled flights on certain routes, that business traffic is substituting the (usually) lower priced non-scheduled service for the scheduled services.

Such developments are having wider implications. The growing strength of the non-scheduled market at the expense of the scheduled operators has thrown open to discussion the purpose and efficacy of IATA controlled scheduled fares. Scheduled services, as we have mentioned above, are costly to produce. In the first decade after the war, most airlines of the world, including US carriers, were subsidised by their respective governments. Fares were at uneconomic levels; to have removed price control and to allow open fare competition would have led to a direct subsidy war. The services of the less subsidized airline would have suffered, the common carrier duties would not have been performed. There perhaps should not have been such uneconomic airlines operating, but then this fault would lie with the general aviation policies of the governments concerned.

Up to 1952 scheduled fares were charged as if services were homogeneous. Standard rates were applied to routes irrespective of the type of aircraft employed or the standard of comfort provided. Obsolete aircraft in certain parts of the world charged lower rates, but on the whole a standard fare system operated. The first major inroad into the structure came with the advent of the larger propeller aircraft – particularly the later Lockheed Connies. The potential earnings of these aircraft, it was found, could be considerably increased by curtailing the unit space provided for passengers, and packing more onto any one flight. The provision of such smaller space led to the introduction of the tourist fare, delayed until 1952 because of the opposition from airlines not operating this type of aircraft. The next major change was again brought about by an advance in aircraft design. The jet's extra speed led initially to its having a surcharge imposed, the market now being divided according to speed and not available space. The surcharge did not last long, for it was quickly realised that the jets were not only faster, they were cheaper to operate than their propeller substitutes. Parity between jet and propeller aircraft was restored, except that the tourist fare now became the economy fare. Introduced in 1958, and varying from anything up to 40 per cent of first class travel, this fare became the standard scheduled fare.

On certain routes, particularly in Europe, fare differentials were introduced according to the time of day and year. On the whole, though, the need for unanimous agreement, made worse by the intricate connections between regions, meant the fare structure remained fairly homogeneous. The change from this simple structure to the present day jungle of differential schedule fares resulted from the competitive strength of non-scheduled competition.

Non-scheduled services or charters are essentially services where a part or whole of the aircraft is rented for one or several flights. The seat prices are often negotiated between buyer and seller, as distinct from the scheduled service, which has a published fixed, non-negotiable rate and is sold to any purchaser. The purchaser is more than likely a tour operator,

9

organising holidays which he sells direct to the public. The airline, whose plane he rents, is rather akin to the tramp ship owner. The price is determined by demand and supply in the market or pool; in other cases, the airline may have an agreement sometimes in the form of financial commitment, to the tour operator. The airlines in the United States and the UK grew to financial strength in the fifties from lucrative troop contracts and from the openings they were allowed on scheduled routes. Some of these airlines, termed 'supplementals' in the United States, are now of considerable size and financial strength.[6]

The most rapidly growing section of the charter market became the inclusive tour. Included in the tour, as well as the hotel accommodation, food, etc., is the price of the air ticket. As the market expanded, further divisions were made along with rules regulating their operation. At the present they roughly consist of four main groups:

1 *Single entity charters*, where a person or corporate body charters an aircraft for his or its own use.

2 *Affinity group charters*,[7] where an affinity or 'closed' group charters an aircraft for its own members.

3 *Resale charters*, where a person or a corporate body charters an aircraft for the purpose of reselling individual passages to members of the public.

4 *Inclusive tour charters.*

These categories of charter, particularly (1), (2), and (4), have been in the vanguard of the non-scheduled attack on the market. High load factors, reaping the economies of the jets, allowed for fares far below the rigid, cumbersome rates of the scheduled carriers. The counter attack of the scheduled carriers was to enter the charter business, and through the network of bilateral agreements, pressure governments into relating the fares in (4) to their own charter rates. Known as resolution 0–45, IATA authorised that members should not allow anyone who charters one of their aircraft to resell individual seats on that chartered aircraft at less than normal scheduled fares. Adopted by various countries (e.g. in the UK known as Provision One), this meant non-IATA inclusive tour operators have a minimum price attached which was not less than the lowest applicable fare for a scheduled service on the route in question. In many countries, and until recently, IT charter rates were constrained to this minimum, although they were often licensed unlimited frequencies.

In the case of groups (1) and (2) IATA has failed to control fares, and instead the battle has been fought by means of legal controls and the scheduled carrier's own reduced priced fares. The legal battle has been over the definition of an affinity group. This problem springs from the often artificial differentiation of the market. Initially used to enable well defined organisations and their members to enjoy non-scheduled travel, the potential growth of the market by means of lower fares stimulated the growth of all kinds of bogus organisations, merely set up to provide any general member of the public with a lower fare. Despite recent stricter law enforcement on the reselling of affinity seats to the general public, the black market is still continuing. The fact is the market in reselling is growing, owing to the large differences between scheduled and non-scheduled fares. The meagre resources of governments and the already over-stretched airport facilities further suggest the scheduled operators will obtain little protection from the renewed law enforcements.

The second attack has been to launch all kinds of promotional fares, aimed at enticing the potential charter passenger to use a scheduled flight. The most aggressive fares are what are known as the ITX fares, which are special excursion fares for tours and groups at substantially lower rates than the scheduled fares. These are bought by the consumer from his tourist agent, who makes up his customer's holiday by using an ITX seat. Along with this fare have come a range of concessional or promotional fares, discriminating according to the time of year, time of day, length of stay or the age of the consumer. Some of these have caused much disagreement among the airlines (see the section on fares below), the problem being that within any conference area, individual markets are quite different, yet the interdependence of fares is such that general agreement has to be sought before they can be implemented.

The loss of markets to the non-scheduled carrier, intensifying in the late sixties, has caused desperate measures to be taken. Some airlines have formed their own separate charter companies, others have formed companies outside IATA ruling so as to benefit from the freedom of afforded by various governments. The difficulty for the scheduled carriers is that, unless they can obtain strict law enforcement from governments with respect to affinity groups, capacity controls and some measure of minimum price control, then they are faced with non-scheduled competition at fares way below the agreed rates.

The result has been a searching re-examination of the usefulness of fixed scheduled air fares by the scheduled airlines themselves. The arguments [8] for fixed fares are usually contained in the following:

1 *Stabilisation.* The weaker airlines need the stability of agreed fares, for a fare war would lead to losses and possibly bankruptcies. Irregular ser-

vices would be the antithesis of the schedule service objective. If not bankruptcies, then a subsidy war.

2 *Safety.* Competition in fares would probably lead to drastic cost reductions, which would injure the reputation of the industry.

3 *Convenience.* Air services are international and if they varied from day to day this would hamper the planning of trips. Inconvenience to the traveller would be caused, possibly causing him to postpone the trip.

Of the three, perhaps the threat of a subsidy war and the convenience of known fares are the most respected arguments.[9] Even argument (1), however, is increasingly under attack, for at the recent IATA meeting in Lausanne (November, 1971) Mr Dargan (Aer Lingus) voiced the view of many member airlines when he suggested IATA should set minimum fares, related in some way to the cost of the carriers, then giving individual airlines the right to charge any fare above this minimum. Such minimum has been tried elsewhere in the transport industry. It has at least the advantage that it increases the freedom of scheduled carriers, although in a segment of the market where prices are elastic, freedom to reduce prices would have been far more effective.

The scheduled industry is at the crossroads. For the first time the industry is facing a recession and a declining share of the market due to non-scheduled carriers' competition. The latter has intensified the slump. The difficulty the airlines face is to adopt short run measures which will alleviate their finances without restricting the overall growth of the market. To restrict the growth of the non-scheduled market will be to thwart the overall development of the industry.

The general aspects of civil aviation policy will be left to Chapters 9 and 10. The remaining sections concentrate on the economic aspects of the airline operations within this institutional structure.

1.3 Market structures

1.3.1 *Passenger flows*

Despite its rapid growth since the war, and particularly during the 1960s, air transport is still concentrated in the economically developed world. As Table 1.1 shows, North American and Western European regions are the areas of densest air traffic flows. The large distances separating the advanced Antipodean and Japanese markets from North America and Western Europe give them a share of traffic out of all proportion to their population masses. It is over these long distances that air's advantages over

Table 1.1

Geographical distribution of traffic
(billions of revenue passenger miles).
Scheduled ICAO world airline traffic

Year	ICAO Total	US Domestic	Trans-Atlantic	Intra-Europe	US Caribbean and L.America	U.S: Trans-Pacific	Intra-Orient	Others
1960	67.5	32.2	6.5	5.5	4.6	1.7	1.2	15.8
1965	123.5	55.5	13.4	10.1	9.0	3.8	3.2	28.5
1970	240.0	102.7	26.6	17.4	17.6	10.0	9.8	55.9
Average annual growth (%)	13.5	12.3	15.1	12.2	14.4	19.4	23.4	13.5

Table 1.2

Distribution of traffic by stage length
(Scheduled international services of 111 airlines, March 1968)

Stage length km	Thousands of passengers carried	Passenger load factor	Passenger % of total (Passenger km)	Stages % of total	Flights % of total
1– 1,000	2560.8	47	16.7	48.3	63.9
1,001– 2,000	948.0	48	18.6	22.7	17.6
2,001– 3,000	442.1	51	14.4	10.2	6.5
3,001– 4,000	205.7	48	9.4	5.7	3.2
4,001– 5,000	1007.7	45	5.9	4.3	1.7
5,001– 6,000	248.1	45	17.8	3.7	4.1
6,001– 7,000	132.5	47	11.2	2.8	2.1
7,001– 8,000	37.8	46	3.7	1.5	0.6
8,001– 9,000	13.8	47	1.5	0.5	0.2
9,001–10,000	5.8	47	0.7	0.2	0.1
10,001–11,000	0.4	29	0.1	0.1	0.0
Total			100.0	100.0	100.0

Source: ICAO *Bulletin* December 1969

surface transport are felt to their full and, indeed, these have been the growth markets in the sixties.

As well as being concentrated in the Northern Hemisphere, air flows are also developed more fully on certain route types. In a recent ICAO study[10] of the top thirty five international routes, nineteen were in Europe and four in North America. As these figures suggest, the heaviest routes are over relatively short distances, around 1,000 to 4,000 km in length. However, as Table 1.2 shows, the enormous importance of the long North Atlantic routes (3,000–6,000 km) is such as to break the simple pattern of traffic flows tapering off with distance. The intensity of use of particular routes (Table 1.3) shows that one third of all passengers carried on international stages are accounted for by stages carrying less than 2,000 passengers. The sample was taken from the passenger flows during one month of 1968 on ICAO international routes. A surprising

Table 1.3

Traffic intensities on international routes (March 1968)

Passengers carried during the month in one direction	Percentage of stages	Number of flights per stage	Average number of passengers per flight	Average number of seats per flight
1– 2,000	83.4	14	35	81
2,001– 4,000	9.3	63	44	91
4,001– 6,000	3.2	113	43	92
6,001– 8,000	1.4	152	46	95
8,001–10,000	0.7	177	51	98
10,001–12,000	0.5	223	50	91
12,001–14,000	0.4	285	46	99
14,001–16,000	0.2	294	51	107
16,001–18,000	0.2	369	46	81
18,001–20,000	0.2	450	42	83
20,001–22,000	0.0	389	55	120
22,001–24,000	0.1	501	46	85
24,001–26,000	0.1	461	53	104
26,001–28,000	0.1	480	57	88
28,001–30,000	0.1	741	39	86
	0.1	735	51	86
Total	100.0			

Source: ICAO *Bulletin* December 1969

result of Table 1.3 is that no clear relationship emerges as to the size of the aircraft and the intensity of passenger flow. More predictably, however, is that the higher load factors tend to be positively related to stages with denser traffic.

A development of the market is that the 1960s has seen an increasing share of the market captured by non-scheduled traffic. In 1960 only 8 per cent of ICAO passenger ruling were accounted for by non-schedule traffic, in 1970 it had grown to 15 per cent. Although growing very rapidly in the long haul Eastern and Pacific routes, non-scheduled traffic's major markets are intra-European non-business traffic and the North Atlantic. Tables 1.4 (*a*) and (*b*) show the enormous growth of charter traffic on both these routes, such that in a couple of years time, at the present rate of growth, charter traffic will have reached parity with scheduled traffic on intra-European routes. Not all this traffic is carried by charter

Table 1.4

Scheduled and charter traffic

(a) Transatlantic traffic (passenger miles)

Year	Scheduled	Charter	Percentage Charter
1960	6.5	0.8	7.3
1965	13.4	2.8	16.2
1970	26.4	10.5	37.1
Average annual growth 1960–70 (%)	15.1	29.5	17.7

Source: IATA

(b) Intra-European, domestic and international (passenger miles)

Year	EARB Scheduled	Charter	Percentage Charter
1960	5.5	0.6	9.8
1965	10.1	3.2	24.1
1970	17.4	11.9	40.6
Average annual growth (%)	12.2	34.8	17.0

Source: The European Air Research Bureau (EARB)

Table 1.5

Share of charter traffic among IATA carriers (1970)

Airline	Charter traffic as percentage of total kilometers performed
Seaboard World	40.6
Braniff	21.0
Flying Tiger	31.7
KLM	15.6
Qantas	18.6
Northwest	13.1
American	7.1
Pan Am	11.2
TWA	5.9
United	4.9

companies or 'supplemental' carriers as they are called in the United States. Many scheduled carriers now run their own charter services, and as Table 1.5 shows, even the big US scheduled carriers have a substantial (and growing) share of their output in the charter factor.

World air traffic, despite its rapid growth, is still largely confined to the economically developed world, and even there it is still used only by a small proportion of the population. [11] Development has been concentrated on the short haul, densely populated advanced countries. The long haul North Atlantic, linking economically advanced North America and Western Europe, has made this the most important international route. The economic advancement of the USA has given this large country the lead in the civil aviation industry as a whole, and one which it is unlikely to lose in the near future.

The civil aviation industry as it enters the seventies is still underdeveloped. Certain areas have been extensively explored by the aircraft, but it has been disproportionate. The US citizen flies ten times more than the average European, [12] a figure reflecting the economic, geographical and political divisions of the two continents. It also reflects the technical development of the aircraft, which has specialised in long distances and speedy travel. So the large, untapped markets are the short haul trips linking densely populated centres. The aircraft's development has a long way to

Table 1.6

Market concentration: top ten airlines

Airline	Percentage share of ICAO traffic 1969
United	11.1
TWA	8.1
American	7.4
Pan Am	6.6
Eastern	6.2
Delta	4.1
Northwest	2.9
BOAC	2.8
Air Canada	2.7
Air France	2.5
	54.4

* Aeroflot is excluded

go before it encroaches on the car, bus and rail over these distances. Civil aviation's future development in fact revolves around the ability of technology to produce cheaper transport, and the industry's structure to respond to translating these advances into lower costs and prices. These two aspects of the market will now be examined.

1.3.2 *Market concentration and economies of scale*

Despite the ability of any nation to assert its rights and support its own airline, traffic carried by individual airlines is concentrated among a few American and European carriers. Ten airlines in the non-communist world account for 54 per cent of the world's (ICAO members) traffic, while the top thirty handle over 80 per cent (see Table 1.6). The top ten are dominated by US carriers, and not surprisingly, the US domestic market is highly concentrated (see Table 1.7).

This concentration in traffic is also reflected in equipment ownership. North American and European airlines in fact account for over half the turbojets in operation (see Table 1.8).

Such regional concentration is to be expected, in view of the distribution of the world's traffic flows. Perhaps less obvious is the concentration among a few airlines. This concentration, and it has remained stable for

Table 1.7

US market concentration (1969)

USA domestic	Percentage revenue (passenger miles)
Trunks	
Big 4	62.4
Other 7	30.6
	93.0
Local service	6.6
Intra-Alaska	0.1
Intra-Hawaii	0.3
	100.0

Table 1.8

Regional commercial operators' fleet (1969)

	N. America	Europe	Latin America	Far East	Africa	Oceania	Middle East	World total
Turbojets	1790	779	98	107	69	39	52	2934
Turboprops	498	407	123	166	69	91	27	1381
Total piston	669	480	645	262	221	108	78	2472
Total	2957	1666	875	535	359	235	157	6787

some twenty years, is as much a reflection of the industry's regulatory structure as it is of the inherent advantages accruing to large scale operators. Most airlines are state subsidised, enjoying the shelter of restricted competition and entry regulations, even in the United States, where direct state subsidisation is generally unacceptable, indirect subsidies — in the form of mail contracts — and entry restrictions, have played their part in shaping the ownership concentration.

With such an industry, the examination of economies of scale and optimum size — both the subject of interest to policy makers — is made especially difficult. [13] There are too few airlines subjected to similar economic conditions, even in the US, to provide sufficient data for statistical costing exercises. Airlines also produce many differing outputs, they are 'multi-firms'. They 'distribute' their own services, provide their own maintenance, produce their own catering, etc. The implication is that aggregating parts of the multi-firm together (e.g. maintenance function with air services function) leads to difficulties if an attempt is being made to relate costs to one particular output unit. Different costs of the airline, in other words, may vary with differing output units. Thus, maintenance costs may vary with engine miles, while operating costs may vary with seat miles. Ideally what is required is the extent of the relationship between the relevant output units and parts of the firm. The Edwards Report [1] (Chapter 6) explored these relationships in some detail, relying heavily on extensive airline interviews and inter-country comparisons. It came to the following general conclusion:

> ... the size at which an airline may be most successful varies substantially, depending upon the nature of the operations in which it is engaged. Almost certainly the most efficient organisation for long haul inter-continental operations is a large airline which can gain the advantages of operating a large standard fleet. How large depends on the geographical spread and importance of concentrated marketing effort. . . .
> At the end of the spectrum it may well be that the most efficient airline for operating in the air freight charter business is one which uses no more than three to four cargo aircraft. Between these two extremes there may be a wide range of optimum sizes for different types of airlines. [14]

The Edwards Report is here referring to airline size and the economies if any which accrue from this organisational size. While recognising the possibility of economies resulting from intensive operation of a homogeneous route structure, the Report was unable to marshal detailed statistical evidence in support of these suggestions. Straszheim [2] on the other hand, in his recent study of the international airline market, has attempted to account for these factors by constructing a costing model, using a selection of 31 ICAO airlines, in which he poses an 'expected direct cost function'. He developed his model in something like the following way. He considered input prices, route scheduling and utilisation and the route system as the major determinants of costs. By averaging over operating conditions he calculated the direct costs of operating the various aircraft types. Different utilisation, route structure and input prices were then used to explain direct costs deviations for the individual 31 airlines in the sample. These three factors appear to have accounted for the considerable deviations that were found, such that he suggested these factors rather than airline size were the major determinants of airline costs.

Plane choice and import utilization prove to be the important cost determinants. Small firms report higher costs mainly because they fly routes or are forced to choose planes less economical to operate than the big jets and fly over short stage lengths. Size thus affects costs in an indirect way that is different from what economists generally mean when they discuss scale economies since firm size *per se* is not the important variable. [15]

Edwards and Straszheim suggest economies do result from increasing the scale of output of a standard size of service. This allows the more intensive use of standardised fleets, one of the main sources of economies. On the evidence available, long haul routes appear to be cheaper to operate than short haul, although of course intensity of use is an important variable. In fact, the calculation of costs, particularly the marginal cost so loved by economists, is quite imprecise unless the output and the time horizon are carefully defined. [16] The basic supply unit is the vehicle trip over a given route. It is an indivisible unit, consisting of seats ranging from around forty to anything up to four hundred. The individual demand unit on the other hand is the air service — the passenger journey. Demand can therefore vary considerably, up to the point where extra aircraft are required, without influencing supply cost. In the short run, with a given fleet flying given miles, the airline adjusts supply by adjusting aircraft mileage; in the long run it is able to adjust the size of the aircraft and thus the composition of its fleet.

In fact, there have been technical reasons limiting the economies of scale expected from the aircraft itself. The economies that do exist in large scale airline organisations result not from the actual production unit, but from other aspects of the firm, such as maintenance, marketing and bulk buying. These tend to be most fully exploited with standardised fleets.

1.3.3 Air fares

The pattern of fares thrown up by the administration mechanism in both domestic and international markets reflects the composition, flexibility and objectives of these institutions. Although the forces of demand and supply have moved fares towards the market clearing equilibrium, [17] the restrictions on entry and the administrative objectives of price stability and income distribution (by means of cross-subsidisation) have also had their impact on the resulting pattern.

Domestic policies differ with the country concerned, for each has sovereignty over its internal flights. On the whole, policies of administered fares rather than openly competitive situations have been adopted. The result has been that fares have tended to be lower than on comparable international routes. Direct government subsidies and cross-subsidisation from international routes have been the means by which income distribution policies have been implemented. In fact, domestic aviation[18] has often been in the advantageous position of enjoying government subsidised airports and internal mail monopolies. Such advantages have not been enjoyed, however, without strong surface carrier opposition.

International air faces, as shown in section 1.2, are subjected to the unanimous voting rule, and adjustments are made only every two years. Change has been difficult, the ensuing compromises result in a fare structure which far from reflects the underlying costs of production.[19] Before outlining such relationships, it is necessary to describe briefly the general fare formulations on international routes.

When a routes fare is set, a maximum mileage is established, which is usually 20 per cent longer than the route mileage. Within this extra limit, the passenger may then choose an alternative route without an additional charge. For various distances outside the 20 per cent limit, additional surcharges are made. The restriction this places on the fares for sections of the route is one of the most crucial determinants of the international fare structure. The restriction is that when fares for a route are fixed, the sections which could be used as alternatives cannot be charged for in such a way that the fare for them adds up to less than the fare for the direct route. We shall deal with the implications of this 20 per cent rule below.

Other general rules concerning fares are that there are no discounts for return flights (abolished in May 1969), and that the tickets are valid for one year. Airlines failing to charge the authorised fares are subjected to heavy fines by IATA.

One of the most surprising outcomes of the international pricing mechanism has been the lack of price discrimination with respect to quality of service. The introduction of jet services illustrates some of the reasons why this structure has operated.

When jets were first introduced it was thought their operating costs would exceed those of the propeller aircraft, and so there was some economic rationale for the imposition of a surcharge on the faster but higher cost jet services. Such a structure was suggested in 1957 but in Paris (March 1959) IATA came forward with a short term compromise solution. It was for a surcharge on jet travel ranging from 5.8 per cent on economy class to 4.7 per cent on tourist class travel. This was approved by the CAB and it operated for a year. However BOAC supported by the UK Government proposed the introduction of cheaper economy fares on their

Table 1.9

Jet and turbo propeller fares (1960)
London-New York one way fare ($US)

(a) Jets

March 1960		1 July 1960	
520	DL	500	F
460	F	—	
335	T	270	E
272	E	175	SP

(b) Propeller driven

March 1960		1 July 1960	
500	DL	500	DL
440	F	440	F
320	T	250	E
247	E	160	SP

Key

DL	De luxe
F	First class
T	Tourist
E	Economy
SP	Special economy

Source: 'IATA sorts it out', *Flight*, 25 March 1960, p. 421.

Eastern, African and Caribbean routes, a proposal which their rival airlines rejected at the Honolulu Conference in September 1959. In effect an open war situation threatened, Britain being able to introduce lower fares because of the government sovereignty over cabotage services. In fact these lower charges were maintained into 1960. The case of the surcharge was again only a temporary agreement and it had to be reexamined in Paris in February/March 1960. The compromise was the retention of the quality differential, i.e. the jet surcharge, even though operating data must have shown the operating costs of jets to be lower than the propeller aircraft. There were no substantial cuts and instead there was an attempt to reduce fares by means of introducing promotional fares. Details of the fares agreed in Paris are shown in Table 1.9.

Thus the year old jet surcharge of roughly 5 per cent was built into the agreement which meant that jet first class travel and economy class travel were 12 per cent, and 7.5 per cent to 11 per cent higher respectively on jet services. In consequence, the higher cost, slower propeller aircraft were charging lower fares for their services than the less costly, faster jets. This clearly protected airlines with large propeller fleets and probably reduced the movement of aircraft out of scheduled operations and into charter services.

It is ironic that this short lived price differential should set fares higher for the lower cost service. The standardised fare structure has failed to reflect the differing qualities and cost aspects of aircraft services. The first class differential, for instance, which varies between 30 to 40 per cent of the tourist class fare, rarely reflects the higher costs of providing the higher comfort standards such as greater cabin space and personal service.

This rigid standardisation has been the result of the difficulty in compromising many different airline requirements, each with their own aircraft mixes, costs and passenger flows. The outcome has been non-price competition. Widely advertised services differences, pretty air hostesses, cabin decor, meals, in-flight entertainment, etc. have been some of the means by which the competing airlines have differentiated their product. Even here regulatory controls have operated, such that the size of a sandwich has been authorised, the screening of films banned [20] and the issue of free theatre tickets prohibited. The pressure to regulate such non-price competition has come from those airlines which felt the obligatory provision of such services was too expensive in relation to the increased demand it stimulated. The cost of these services is indeed high, as the breakdown costs in Table 1.10 indicate. These are the costs produced by Laker Airway in their application [21] to run a no-frills 'Sky-train' from Gatwick to New York. The proposed one way fares of $90 (summer) and $70 (winter) compared with economy fares during 1972 of $552 and $452 respectively. No doubt the higher load factors helped them to produce lower cost figures, but it is clear from their accounting the major cost deductions came from low advertising and service costs.

Two recent studies of European and North American routes also suggest that fares rarely reflect the economies of long haul routes. A CAB Study [22] of US routes in 1966, using a sample of the country's 43,000 markets, showed that there was only a moderate fare taper. [23] The relationship between fares for several classes of services in markets beyond 700 miles was uniform but for shorter distances many variations were

Table 1.10

Cost breakdown of 'Sky Train', the proposed Gatwick to New York service 1972–73

Annual costs per hour per flight:	B707(1972/73)	DC-10 (1973)
Direct operating costs	2,408.15	3,639.51
Aircrew costs	519.24	436.71
Cabin staff	163.79	256.73
Aircraft hire	1,123.44	5,716.70 (aircraft deprecia- tion)
Overhauls	1,216.32	1,810.00
Training and testing	41.18	103.00
A.R.B. fees	11.63	18.53
Ticket sales	54.94	113.93
Spares insurance	6.28	
Insurance	156.40	28.96 (Legal fees)
General Overheads	670.60	696.00
Advertising	109.89	273.23
Cost per flight	£6,481.86	£14,016.83
Average net fare	£65.219	£63.98
Passengers required to break even	99.4	219.4
Break even load factor (%)	62.9	63.6
Fare Charged during winter	£32.50	£32.50
during summer peak	£37.50	£37.50

Notes: The proposed service (rejected by the ATLB) was for a daily service between 1 May and 30 September and 4 flights per week during the rest of the year. Use was to be made of a 138 seater B-707-138B. No reservations were to be made, no cash transfers and no refunds. The second application was made, at the same fare, to run a 345 seater DC-10. The application was approved by CAA, with the stipulations that Stanstead Airport should be used, and that winter capacity must not exceed 189 seats.

Sources: *Flight International*, 28 October 1971, p. 674. *Flight International*, 27 July 1972, pp. 116–17.

discovered, often reflecting the level of competition on the route. The study computed costs of operation, noting the disparity between operating costs and fares, particularly on long haul routes. [24] Rosenberg [3] in his extensive study of the European fare structure found similar results, although generalisations are somewhat difficult in this market, owing to the mixture of many domestic and international sectors. Using a regression technique on 486 routes, he related fares per kilometre to route distance, frequency and differing geography. As Table 1.11 shows, there is some general taper of fares with (log of) distance, but very little relationship between high frequencies and lower fares.

Within Europe itself, a great number of differing fare levels exist, as Table 1.12 illustrates. Domestic routes, particularly in the Soviet Union, are on the whole lower in cost, while the major North/South routes over the Alps are extremely high, perhaps reflecting the lack of strong surface

Table 1.11

European international fare structure:
variation of fares per kilometre

Geographical area	Regressions	
All routes	$y = 70.5 - 12.2 \log x$	$R^2 = 0.23$
All routes	$y = 66.5 - 11.0 \log x + 9.1A + 12.9Z$	$R^2 = 0.33$
All routes	$y = 66.5 - 10.8 \log x + 9.1A + 12.8Z$	$R^2 = 0.32$
West – West	$y = 67.4 - 11.1 \log x + 14.5A + 6.4Z - 0.5Q$	$R^2 = 0.47$
West – East	$y = 90.7 - 14.7 \log x + 37.3A - 1.2Q$	$R^2 = 0.47$
East – East	$y = 76.5 - 12.4 \log x + 0.4T$	$R^2 = 0.45$

Terms:
y = fares per route kilometre 1967
x = flight distance
A = dummy variable for routes crossing the Alps
Q = grouped frequency variable
T = flights per week
Z = short routes

Eastern Europe was designated to consist of the following states: Albania, Bulgaria, Yugoslavia, Poland, Romania, USSR, Czechoslovakia, Hungary, E. Germany and E. Berlin.

Source: A. Rosenberg [3] Appendix 7

25

Table 1.12

European route groups: fare comparisons (1969)

Route groups	Index of average fares in economy class
Turkey – Western Europe	130 – 135
Short Distances over the Alps	136
Scandinavia – The Continent	125 – 130
Greece – W. Europe	110 – 115
Scandinavia – the UK	110 – 115
The London Area – the Continent	105 – 110
The UK – Italy	105 – 110
Within Scandinavia	105 – 110
The UK (excluding the London Area) – the Continent	90 – 95
The UK – the Iberian Peninsula	90 – 95
Within the Continent	90 – 95
Iceland – W. Europe	85 – 90
The UK – Eire	85 – 90
Holland – the Rest of the Continent	85 – 90
The Canary Islands – W. Europe	85 – 90
N. Africa – W. Europe	85 – 90
All fares to and inside Eastern Europe	100
Scandinavia – E. Europe	120 – 125
To and from the Soviet Union	115 – 120
To and from Yugoslavia	90 – 95

Index: 100 is for km/fares in Western Europe

Source: Rosenberg [3] pp. 56–57.

competition. However, any interpretation of relative fare levels has to indicate the effect of the '20 per cent rule' and the impact of lower domestic fares. As it is possible to travel by internal routes in reaching an international destination, the prices of individual segments have to make up to the full value of the authorised direct fare. Hence if a domestic segment is particularly cheap, the international segments linking the domestic route to the foreign country will be correspondingly expensive in order to make up the price of the ticket. This has been one of the reasons why there are high fares on the cross-channel routes and on the North/South European routes going through the domestic German market. Furthermore, the 20 per cent rule enjoyed by North Americans has meant virtually free travel inside Western Europe. In order to make up the lost revenue, fares on international Western Europe routes have accordingly been pushed up.

Despite these regulatory distortions, the effect of surface and more particularly charter competition can be seen from the fare levels. Anglo-Iberian and North African—Western Europe routes, two of the largest markets served by inclusive tours, have particularly low schedule fares. This development in the case of UK routes has been especially marked since 1968. The UK upheld resolution D—45 of IATA, regulating the minimum inclusive tour prices until 1968. From then onwards the minimum was set at 1968 prices and not at the newly negotiated rates, so in effect the minimum prices have been pitched below the scheduled fares. Furthermore, in February 1971 the Minister of Industry and Trade announced that for an experimental period from October 1971 to March 1972 that control was suspended over fares the prices of short holidays of seven nights or less. These involved flights between the UK and places in Southern Europe. For holidays exceeding seven nights, a reduction of one sixth of the minimum price was authorised. The impact on comparable scheduled fares has been considerable,[25] for as Maynard and Cooper [4] point out, 'There was a significant correlation of -0.8 between both normal schedule fares and the percentage of the market held by charter flight companies, and between the latter and special promotional fares.'[26]

The late sixties saw governments moving away from the IATA D-45 control, and allowing IT fares to find their own level in the market. In Scandinavia a time restriction was imposed (not less than seven days) but no fare control, while in the Netherlands the minimum inclusive tour charge was pegged at not lower than 75 per cent of the two way scheduled air fares on route distances less than 500 km, and 85 per cent for distances above 500 km.

The impact on the scheduled operators has been strongly felt, but concerted action has been sadly lacking. Instead of moving towards much lower schedule fares, the airlines have instead developed what they term 'promotional fares'. These have taken many forms, discriminating according to age — 'under 26' — time of the year and length of stay.

The most complicated outcome of these policies has been on the North Atlantic route. The many interested airlines and countries involved, its central link between the developed parts of the world, and the hetero-

Table 1.13

Atlantic fares: 1 April 1971–31 March 1973
(New York–London, round trip fares in $US)

Fare group	1971/72 $US	March 1973 $US
First class	782	842
Economy		
Peak	552	550
Basic	452	430 winter
Excursion		
14/28 day		14/21 days
Peak	382	412
Basic	322	349
29/45 day		22/45 days
Peak	332	313
Basic	272	
Group inclusive tour (15 passengers or more)		
Peak	302	
Basic	237	
Affinity group (in season)		
40 or more passengers eastbound 30 or more passengers westbound }	277	
Shoulder season (basic fare)		
40 or more passengers eastbound 30 or more passengers westbound }	217	484
Off season		
40 or more passengers eastbound 30 or more passengers westbound }	197	
Incentive group		
Shoulder season (basic fare)	217	240
Off season	197	

Sources: ICAO *Bulletin* May 1971 and *Flight International* 8 March 1973.

geneous market it serves have caused this route to be the centre of extremely involved airline negotiation. The proliferation of promotional fares on the route is shown in Table 1.13.

It is a market in which charter services have made particularly heavy incursions. The schedule airlines' method of combat, however, has been far from unanimously accepted by the participating airlines. The heterogeneity of the market has meant that what suits one airline may not suit another.[27] For the Irish and Israelis, reduced ethnic charters suit their market, but not so for the British and the Germans. On the other hand the systematically minded Germans have found fault with Britain's (i.e. BOAC's) advanced booking fare reductions, known as APEX fares. This caused considerable difficulty in the autumn of 1971, meetings having to be held at Lausanne, Montreal and Honolulu before an open war was

Table 1.14

Airline dispute over North Atlantic fares

(a) Autumn 1971

	BOAC fare proposal	Lufthansa fare proposal
Return fare ($US)	180 off peak 200 basic 235 peak	243 170 group inclusive
Validity	14–25 days	14 day minimum excursion
Advanced booking period	4 months	

(b) Spring 1973

	BOAC proposal APEX		US proposal TGC	
Return fare (£)	62	Jan. – June	79.40	Jan. – March
	76	June – July	91.80	April – June
	94	July – Sept.	119.35	July – Sept.
	76	Sept. – Oct.	91.80	Sept. – Nov.
	62	Oct. – Nov.	79.40	Nov. – Dec.
	94	Dec.		

averted. In principle, Lufthansa won the approval of the other airlines for its reduced fares (see Table 1.14), but the authorised fare of £200 [28] was somewhat higher than its proposed fare.

The compromises however are still over promotional and not basic fares. There are limitations to this policy, for recent evidence announced by US carriers suggest that these promotional fares, rather than attracting passengers off non-scheduled flights, are being substituted by their regular passengers. Some of this revenue dilution is substantial; TWA estimated that 47.7 per cent of its transatlantic passengers would normally travel first and economy fares. Actually only 34·5 per cent paid normal fares while 65·5 per cent travelled at discount rates.[29] Pan Am have had similar experiences, which suggests increased charter competition will only effectively be countered by much lower economy fares and or stricter controls on charter operators. The former is likely to be achieved at the expense of IATA's unanimity rule.

Despite the heterogeneity in the fare structures a general pattern has emerged. As Table 1.15 makes clear, international European routes fares are higher than North and South American but approximately the same as central American, Caribbean, African and Far Eastern routes. The combination of surface competition, subsidised domestic sectors and the 20 per cent rule have led to the European fares being much higher than those in the United States. On the whole, therefore, fares have been based on a value of service pricing system. On domestic sectors, however, lower fare levels have been maintained by direct and indirect subsidies.

1.3.4 *Airline financial structure*

Aircraft purchases account for the major part of the airline's capital, and they are growing in importance. Despite the concentration of new purchases in a few airline's hands, in financial terms the second generation of jet purchases is enormous. For instance, the American Air Transport Association estimates that this investment programme has amounted to $10·5 billion between 1967 and 1971. As we shall see, these heavy demands on capital have necessitated considerable restructuring of the airlines' financing, which in turn has contributed to the airlines' present problems.

Between 1945 [30] and the mid fifties, aircraft capital costs of between $\frac{1}{2}$ million and $1\frac{3}{4}$ million meant the airlines could borrow from commercial banks and by means of small equity flotations. Terms were usually from three to seven years, with seven years considered as a realistic life for an aircraft. The jet orders made in the mid fifties involved capital outlays

Table 1.15

International comparison of fares:
average international non-stop fares (1969)

Routes	Distance (km)											
	201 – 600		601 – 1000		1001 – 1400		1401 – 1800		1801 – 2200		2201	
	No	ore/km	No	ore/km	No	ore/km	No	ore/km	No	ore/km	No	ore/km
International												
All W. Europe	131	36.7	110	33.5	4	31.0	49	39.6	21	28.9	14	27.1
Between USA and												
Canada	7	30.5	5	22.7	4	20.5	2	20.6	4	19.4		
S. America					5	20.8			1	24.4	5	21.3
Africa	4	35.6	2	34.1	4	36.2	2	28.3	1	33.5	4	33.2
Far East			4	34.0	3	32.4	2	29.0	3	31.1	3	27.7
Central America and												
Caribbean	8	34.5	6	36.2	6	30.5	1	30.8				
Domestic routes												
All routes in tne UK, W. Germany, France, Spain and Italy	169	27.7	21	28.4	2	22.3						
USA	16	24.2	9	21.1	7	20.4	4	19.5	2	20.3	2	19.6
Australia	12	25.8	6	21.0	4	19.2			1	17.3		

Source: A. Rosenberg [3] Table 9, Chapter 5.

Table 1.16

Summary of the financial structure of the
US consolidated airline industry

Year	1955	'56	'57	'58	'59	'60	'61	'62	'63	'64	'65	'66	'67	'68	'69
Ratio of debt to operating profits*	1.9	3.2	9.4	7.6	9.3	20.8	67.2	10.1	6.1	3.9	3.2	3.9	5.8	10.0	13.8
Rate of return on investment†	10.0	8.9	5.2	5.5	6.2	3.2	2.1	5.7	1.5	9.8	12.0	10.9	7.6	5.0	3.3
Interest on long term debt $ million	10	14	24	33	45	66	93	111	106	104	112	126	149	221	346
Operating profits as percentage of revenue	0.08	0.07	0.10	0.13	0.10	0.04	0.01	0.09	0.16	0.25	0.31	0.25	0.16	0.09	0.07
Retained earnings and depreciation allowances as a percentage of net investment	0.32	0.29	0.29	0.25	0.22	0.20	0.18	0.18	0.20	0.20	0.24	0.24	0.23	0.21	0.20

* Long term debt.
† Net income before interest and after taxes as a percentage of net worth and long term debt.
Source: Air Transport Association of America.

of the order of $5 million which meant a higher capital cost. Capital costs could not be paid off as quickly, so in order to cover these longer dated loans the airlines used institutional lenders such as insurance companies. These provided the long term loans of up to fifteen to twenty years while the banks, by means of revolving credits over some five to seven years, dealt with the airlines' short term requirements. In order to service this debt load and to maintain debt/equity ratios within the 1·25–1·50 range the airlines made extensive use of convertible stock.

This changing structure is reflected in Table 1.16 and 1.17 where US and UK carriers' financial structures are displayed. These tables show how the low return on capital in both UK and US airlines, and the following proportion of retained earnings in the financing on net investment. Similarly, Tables 1.19 and 1.20 show how the flow of outside funds has increased in proportion to funds supplied by stockholders. This situation has been aggravated by the fall in earnings occurring at the same time as the increased capital charges on the new jet purchases in the late sixties and early seventies (see Table 1.18). In the USA for instance, the earnings of the major trunks dropped from $428 in 1966 to $151 million in 1969. The causes are various. The increased labour costs following an expensive strike in 1966, when five carriers were grounded for 43 days, added considerably to maintainance costs. The situation was further aggravated by inept pricing policies aimed at enticing traffic from the supplemental carriers. This resulted not in increased traffic, but in scheduled passengers

Table 1.17

Financial structure of the UK industry

Year		1962	'63	'64	'65	'66	'67
Ratio of debt to operating projects	Independents	—	10.0	7.0	11.0	2.3	30.0
Rate of return on investment	Independents	(0.6)	3.0	4.4	3.8	4.4	3.2
	Grand total	(1.4)	2.4	11.5	7.9	13.0	10.1
Interest on long term debt £m	Independents	0.3	0.3	0.6	1.1	1.3	1.7
Operating projects as percentage revenue	Independents	(0.6)	3.0	4.4	3.8	4.4	3.2
	Grand total	(1.0)	15.4	23.1	26.9	28.7	22.7

Source: The Edwards Report [1] Table 3.6, Appendix 14.

Table 1.18

Pre-tax profits of the big five American carriers ($1,000)

Year	1966	1967	1968	1969	1970	1971	1972
Airline							
Pan Am	117.0	90.9	62.5	−46.8	−48.0	−45.0	−30.8
Eastern	14.7	31.7	−15.9	− 3.2	5.0	6.0	19.7
United	63.1	108.1	77.3	81.8	−41.0	− 5.0	17.7
TWA	51.3	41.4	9.2	9.0	−41.0	3.0	43.0
American	85.7	78.2	45.0	58.7	−26.0	3.0	5.6

Table 1.19

US trunk carriers:
proportion of total assets* supplied by stockholders†

Year	1955	'56	'57	'58	'59	'60	'61	'62	'63	'64	'65	'66	'67
Average proportion (%)	51.0	45.9	42.1	38.0	35.7	26.2	27.0	24.4	26.0	28.0	38.0	32.0	32.0

* All other assets supplied by creditors.
† Stockholders assumed to have supplied:
  (a) book value of common and preferred stock,
  (b) capital surplus,
  (c) retained earnings.

Table 1.20

UK independent operators:
proportion of total assets supplied by stockholders

Year	1963	'64	'65	'66	'67
Proportion	48.0	48.0	43.0	37.0	37.0

Source: Edwards Report, Table 3.6 and Appendix 15.

substituting the new, cheaper fares. As a result revenue fell, costs rose and the earnings for the capital expenditure were not available. In the UK the undercapitalisation of the independent airlines was commented upon by the Edwards Report: [31]

> The most important conclusion is that the private sector of the airline industry is seriously under capitalised. The proportion of shareholders' funds to net assets employed has declined progressively from 48 per cent in 1963 to 37 per cent in 1967. There can be little doubt that this has been one of the reasons for some of the troubles of the private sector in the past few years.

However, one development in the mid sixties which has eased this capitalisation has been the widespread adoption of leasing. [32] The popularity in the USA came from the tax concession that could be enjoyed from leasing. Tax concessions were obtained on the investment, enjoyed by the purchaser, who could then pass this on in the form of lower (equivalent) interest charges. This was a cost advantage over the usual sources of borrowed capital. Generally, the term of the lease varied between ten and eighteen years, a term of financing which has increased in popularity. From the airlines' point of view the advantages are that capital can be employed for other uses – spares, inventories, sales promotion, etc. The total fixed capital costs for the equipment are fully deductible over the life of the lease, rather than at a lower rate over the life of the equipment, and the lease involves no dilution of control. From the lessor's angle the major portion of the lease transaction has the characteristic of an equivalent trust certificate, for the lender has not only the credit of the airline but also a first mortgage on the aircraft. Thus it has been possible to interest the small institutions particularly the smaller insurance companies in financing purchases where equity sources have been tapped.

The latest development in financing has occurred with the heavy costs involved in purchasing the Jumbo jets. This has involved some interesting long term loan arrangements. TWA for instance, followed by American, have successfully floated lease-related trust certificates. In the UK, BOAC announced [33] their capital requirements to be £680 million for the nine years starting in 1969, of which £545 is earmarked for aircraft purchases. While most of the jet financing was accomplished with government loans and equity, in three years' time BOAC estimate that more than half will be financed from outside financial institutions in the USA and Switzerland. The servicing of these large debts is somewhat uncertain. Bardley [13] has suggested leasing as a source of funds will diminish, owing to the removal of the tax concession the consequently higher interest costs, and instead a return to equity funds as a means of maintaining realistic debt ratios.

As they stand in the early seventies, the airlines look most vulnerable. It is a vulnerability springing from an unprecedented investment programme followed by a sharp downturn in the market's growth. In order to stabilise their position many of the US trunk carriers have formed holding companies, in which the airline has become the wholly owned subsidiary. Extensive investment has been made in hotels (e.g. Pan Am with its Intercontinental Hotels Corporation, TWA with its Hilton International hotels), a natural market for the airlines to become associated with. Such diversification may aid financial stability, but one characteristic of the new era is the increasing control passing into the hands of institutional bodies. Banks and insurance companies now control considerable sections of the major US carriers, [34] owner management having almost disappeared. It remains to be seen whether this will alleviate or hinder the financing stability of the US industry. [35]

1.4 Aircraft and the aircraft industry

The organisation of the civil aviation industry, in which public authorities provide and charge for airport space, has meant the airlines have been able to reduce to variable costs many of the costs which remain fixed for other transport operators. Consequently, the motive and carrying unit, the aircraft, has become the most costly and important purchase. On the demand side, aircraft are not only factor inputs but also a means of discriminating the airline's output. As we have indicated earlier such equipment rivalry is intense.

On the supply side, aircraft are the outcome of a long, intense and detailed production process. [36] The prices charged reflect the complexity and the competitive pressure in the industry. Research and development costs are heavy, production periods, from design to completion, are long – anything up to a decade. It is a labour intensive industry, of high cost, highly skilled labour. However, the latter is considered to enjoy increased productivity as the number of aircraft produced increases. Known as the learning curve, [37] it is held responsible for considerable cost reductions as production runs lengthen. The latter is important, for longer runs usually mean lower costs and quicker delivery, important considerations in the competition for airline orders. The price set depends upon many factors. The break-even run, itself varying but usually said to be around 200, is important, so also are the development subsidies given the manufacturer.

Table 1.21

Economic dimensions of the aeronautical system
of the US (1964)

Activity	Employment ('000s)	GNP Contribution million $
Civil		
Aircraft manufacture	76.25	1,010
Airlines	230.40	3,500
Airports	16.90	218
General aviation	122.40	1,870
FAA	45.00	729
CAB	.80	8
Weather Bureau	1.000	15
NASA (aeronautical only)	1.70	48
Total Civil aviation	494.45	7,398
Military		
Aircraft manufacture, research and development	556.01	7,370
Dept. of Defence payroll	1,000.00	7,430
Dept. of Defence purchases	100.00	1,500
Total military aviation	1,656.01	16,300

Source: US Senate Committee on Aeronautical and Space Science. Policy planning for Aeronautical Research and Development. Staff Report prepared by the Legislative Reference Services. Library of Congress. Document no. 90, 89 Congress, second session 19 May 1966, p. 89.

Reduced costs of learning and subsidised research and development mean lower overheads and lower prices. On the demand side, the price charged will reflect the place of the airline in the queue and its delivery requirements. Initial purchases, incurring the risks of 'running in', of being left with an orphan if no one else buys, usually obtain a concessional rate, as do airlines placing orders at times suitable for the manufacturer. Penalties for late delivery, trade-ins of used aircraft, concessions for old customers, etc. all affect the limits within which the final price sits. Aircraft prices sometimes cover a wide range, even for the same aircraft type.

Civil aircraft production is dominated by US firms. Of the present turbojet fleet of ICAO member airlines, 84 per cent were built by USA firms, the remaining 16 per cent by UK, French and Dutch producers.[38] This dominance extends also to aero engine production. The leading manufacturer, Pratt and Whitney, employ around 70,000, with an annual turnover of $2,350 million (1969). This compares with a turnover of $727·3 m (1969) by Rolls Royce, the largest European aero engine producer.

The relative sizes of the aerospace industries are shown in Table 1.23. Apart from the US producers who have maintained their predominance during the sixties, the UK, Germany, Japan, Holland, Sweden and Italy are the only other countries with industries of any size. Within these markets concentration is centred among a few producers. In the civil market, the USA industry has been dominated by two, McDonnell/Douglas and Boeing. Of the others, Lockheed and Convair have made unhappy

Table 1.22

Aircraft types with production runs
of more than 200

Type
BAC 1—11
BAC Viscount
B707
B727
B737
B747
DC—8
DC—9
Sud-Caravelle
Fokker F-27/FH/227

Table 1.23

Leading aerospace industries: workforce

Country	1960	1961	1962	1963	1964	1965	1966	1967	1968	1969
USA: aircraft manufacture ('000s)	167	669	707	650	620	619	751	825	849	
total aerospace (million)						1.15	1.30	1.40	1.41	1.35
UK ('000s)	293	304	294	272	268	260	250	256	252	249
France ('000s)		26.7	30.4	34.5	43.0	48.7	54.7	62.4	63.2	64.7
Germany ('000s)	24.0	20.6	26.0	28.0	28.3	28.8	30.7	32.6	37.6	39.5

Sources: *Flight International*, Aerospace Industries of America *Statistical Year Book*, and *Interavia*

excursions into this market, but have never seriously challenged the big two. In the UK, after the reorganisations during the late fifties and early sixties,[39] two large airframe producers emerged, BAC and Hawker Siddeley. France since 1966 has had an industry divided between a public and private sector. The former consists of two firms, SNIAS (Aerospatiale) and SNECMA, the chief French aero engine manufacturer. The private sector consists of three large firms, the Dassault-Breguet Group and MATRA, and the Thompson-CSF combine. In Germany four main groups dominate the industry, being the Dornier, MBB, VFW and the Motoren and Furbinen-Union Group. As in the small aerospace countries, these are large conglomerates, producing across a wide range of similar highly technical products, of which aerospace products are often only a small proportion. Similarly with Japan for, although some 25,000 are employed in the industry, the sales of the 26 aircraft divisions represent only 4·5 per cent of the total corporate sales of the parent companies.[40] In Sweden, where SAAB is the country's only air frame producer, the aerospace turnover is almost 20 per cent of the group, but employing only 6,000 out of a total workforce of 28,000.

Viewed in aggregate, the aerospace industries of the USA, UK and France are large and an important part of their national economies. See for instance Table 1.22, which shows that in 1964 the US Aeronautical system generated some $16 billions worth of expenditure, a figure in the region of 4 per cent of the US GNP. This expenditure is dominated by defence production, civil aviation being relatively small. However, changing government policies with respect to the US space programme and the Vietnam war have resulted in civil production increasing in importance, as Table 2.4, Chapter 2 illustrates.

Although defence products still predominate, the distinction between civil and military production is a blurred one. Lucrative defence contracts have been the basis upon which many civil projects have been financed and subsidised, for even the most successful civil aircraft productions have yielded relatively little return. Using 200 aircraft sold as a bench mark of a successful aircraft – the number beyond which high R & D overheads can be recouped – we see (Table 1.22) that only ten turbine aircraft have reached this total by 1971. In such a fickle market, military purchases play a particularly important role in providing demand during slack periods. Boeing and Douglas have both benefited considerably from US military purchases of the DC–8 and B–707. UK producers have similarly benefited from military purchases.[41]

The part played by government has also been indirect. While not using to the full its monopsonist power it has affected purchases by the control

40

it has exercised on national airlines. In Australia, for instance, the federal government authorises every procurement of equipment as part of its two airline policy. Both Ansett and Quantas have to make submissions to the government, yielding details of their proposed purchases, even though Ansett is privately owned. In France and Canada the governments have the power to control decisions by means of issuing licenses. In the UK, in order to support the UK aerospace industry, the government has on many occasions interfered with the state airlines' decisions to buy abroad. [42] In 1968, for instance, BEA announced its wish to purchase Boeing 727 and 737 aircraft, while the government advised the BAC 1–11 Srs 500 and the Trident 3Bs. In order to facilitate this changed decision, the government paid compensation in the form of a £25m interest free loan.

Even in the USA, with privately operated airlines, the CAB has seen fit to persuade its national airlines to buy American. For instance[43] in 1962 the Chairman of the CAB, Mr A. Boyd, warned Mohawk and Bonanza

Table 1.24

Relative performance of US and UK aerospace industries

Year	Average annual rates of return. Net income after tax on percentage of net worth (US)		Net income after tax in cents/dollars of sales		Profits as percentage of capital employed (UK)	
	Aerospace industry	All manufacturing undustries	Aerospace industry	All manufacturing industries	Aerospace industry	All UK industries
1960	6.6	10.6	1.4	5.5	9.4	13.5
1961	4.4	9.9	0.9	5.2	5.9	11.6
1962	12.9	10.9	2.4	5.5	7.0	11.3
1963	11.7	11.6	2.3	5.7	8.7	12.3
1964	13.1	12.6	2.7	6.1		
1965	15.4	13.9	3.2	6.4		
1966	15.7	14.2	3.1	6.3		
1967	13.4	12.6	2.7	5.6		
1968	13.9	13.3	2.8	5.7		
1969	11.2	12.5	2.5	5.4		

Sources: US First National City Bank of New York, Economics Department; UK Plowden [21] Table II, p. 129.

that their orders of BAC 1—11 would involve substantial risks, suggesting that the aircraft ordered were too large for the route. This was the view of the CAB not of the respective airlines, an opinion however which had the threat of subsidy removal if it was not accepted.

Despite considerable government support, the aerospace industries in the USA remained relatively unprofitable. As Table 1.24 shows, in both the USA and UK, the industry has, with few exceptions, failed to reach the average return earned by other manufacturing industries. In fact military projects have not been profitable, particularly in the sixties following the MacNamara policy which introduced fixed price contracts.[44] The result has been a contraction of the US industry, and an increasing move to shared costs in Europe. Joint production between international producers now dominates the European aerospace industry. Today there are relatively few major national programmes.[45] Whether international cooperation, shared skills and risks is the way to meet the American challenge remains to be seen. The test case will be whether the European airbus can make its mark against the Americans' DC—10 and Lockheed Tristar.

1.5 Conclusions

The airline industry as it enters the mid 1970s is at a critical stage of its development. Its growth potential is enormous, particularly in the non-business sector. The realisation of this potential, however, requires radical changes in the institutional framework within which the industry operates. Lower costs passed on in the form of lower prices will only be effectively achieved by a structure which stimulates the efficient airlines and penalises the inefficient. Open and unprotected competition among the schedule operators would be one of the most effective ways of achieving this goal.

Advocacy of open competition between international carriers has met with the same opposition long familiar to free traders. The responsibility lies with the conflict between nationalistic and international goals. Sovereignty over home territory has allowed nationalistic policies to be implemented. The sum total of these policies, often motivated by wider (nationalistic), economic and political ends has produced an industry subjected to rigid entry and price controls. Expensive qualitative competition has resulted, fluctuations in aircraft equipment have been considerable, on occasions outstripping the growth in demand and resulting in highly fluctuating load factors. Stability in price (and profits) has contributed to instability elsewhere. One important question, therefore, is how much is the present structure responsible for the industry's instability? Before this can be effectively answered, we need to know the areas and extent of these fluctuations. This is dealt with in the next chapter, where an overall plan of the subsequent chapters is presented. Later chapters explore the major sectors of the industry, relating primary demand, investment decision, the aircraft productive process and aircraft resales to the industry's structure as presented in this chapter. By exploring the impact of the structure of control on the industry's development we hope to obtain some idea of the likely impact of introducing policy changes.

APPENDICES

1A.1 UK inclusive tour prices to Southern Europe

Since 1967 minimum prices of UK inclusive tours (IT) have been progressively reduced below the levels of the corresponding scheduled air fares. In view of their success in attracting traffic, the government initiated an experiment which removed control altogether over prices of short inclusive tour holidays to the Southern Mediterranean for the winter season 1971/2.

The effect on the price structure to these resorts can be seen from Tables 1A.1 and 1A.2.[46] Table 1A.2 shows those routes in which scheduled services have been competing directly with the no-limit IT during 1971/72, while Table 1A.1 shows those routes on which cheap IT's have made little penetration. Columns 6, 7 and 8 of Table 1A.2 show that IT price ranges are considerable, nevertheless their impact on schedule fares, as the averages of the foot of both tables show, has been considerable. The largest difference is seen in the winter tourist class, where the scheduled routes show an average fare per mile of 5.17 pence to 3.91 pence on those routes competing with inclusive tours.

A study [28] of the impact of these lower rates suggested that, over the five months, the number of holidays sold increased by more than 90 per cent.

1A.2 The North Atlantic fare battle: the scheduled airlines fight it out

The following is an extract from an advertisement run by Pan Am in the winter of 1972/73: 'If you're confused over who has the lowest fares to the USA, nobody has the lowest fares to the USA.' Hardly informative,

Table 1A.1

Scheduled fares in which inclusive tours have little impact

London to	Distance (miles)	Summer 1971 Tourist single (£)	Summer 1971 Excursion return (£)	Winter 1971/72 Tourist single (pence/mile)	Winter 1971/72 Excursion single (pence/mile)	Summer 1969/70 Tourist single (£)	Summer 1969/70 Excursion return (£)	Tourist single (pence/mile)	Excursion return (pence/mile)
Amsterdam	230	14.25		6.20		12.50		5.43	
Ankara	2365	75.85	93.65			75.85	110.15		
Barcelona	701	28.65	38.50	4.08	2.74	26.90	35.90	3.84	2.56
Basle	436	25.45		5.83		22.10		5.07	
Belgrade	1049	47.10	67.65	4.48	3.22	43.80	64.80	4.18	3.09
Bilbao	567	26.55	38.45	4.68	3.39	26.15	35.65	4.63	3.14
Bonn/ Cologne	326	17.50		5.37		16.25		4.98	
Bordeaux	449	25.45	38.45	5.67	4.28	23.75	35.65	5.29	3.97
Brussels	211		14.65		6.94	12.85		6.09	
Bucharest	1563	61.90	82.50			58.95	54.15		2.95
Budapest	917	42.40	51.50	4.62	2.81	40.35		4.40	
Copenhagen	611	35.60		5.82		32.35		5.30	
Dublin	290	13.20	20.10	4.55	3.46	11.90		4.10	
Dusseldorf	307	17.50		5.70		16.25		5.30	
Frankfurt	400	22.45		5.61		20.85		5.21	
Geneva	457	25.45		5.57		22.10		4.84	
Hamburg	463	24.25		5.24	3.48	22.55		4.87	
Helsinki	1152	53.20	80.15	4.62	3.48	49.30	73.95	4.28	3.21
Istanbul	1554	72.90	89.50	4.69	2.88	72.90	105.30	4.69	3.39

Table 1A.1 continued

London to	Distance (miles)	Summer 1971 Tourist single (£)	Summer 1971 Excursion return (£)	Winter 1971/72 Tourist single (pence/mile)	Winter 1971/72 Excursion single (pence/mile)	Summer 1969/70 Tourist single (£)	Summer 1969/70 Excursion return (£)	Summer 1969/70 Tourist single (pence/mile)	Summer 1969/70 Excursion return (pence/mile)
Luxembourg	311	15.10	26.15	4.86	4.20	13.55	23.35	4.36	3.75
Lyons	455	24.70	37.25	5.43	4.09				
Madrid				4.8	3.5			4.6	3.2
Marseilles	603	29.00	42.25	4.81	3.50				
Milan	584	31.25	47.00	5.35	4.02	29.05	42.90	4.97	3.68
Moscow	1557	72.25	99.65	4.96	3.20	77.25		4.96	
Munich	580	29.15	43.75	5.03	3.77	27.10	40.75	4.67	3.51
Nice	635	32.25	48.00	5.08	3.78	30.10	44.20	4.74	3.48
Oslo	743	39.00	45.50	5.25	3.06	35.45	41.95	4.77	2.82
Prague	644	34.65	46.50	5.38	3.61	33.00	49.05	5.12	3.81
Reykjavik	1186	38.95	54.60	3.28	2.30	37.05	58.05	3.12	2.45
Rhodes	1735	75.40		4.34		72.50	112.80	4.18	3.25
Rotterdam	209	13.65		6.53		11.95		5.72	
Seville	1212	41.75				39.35	59.70		
Shannon	378	16.45	26.10	4.35	3.46	14.80		3.92	
Stockholm	908	47.65		5.25		43.30		4.77	
Toulouse	688	25.45							
Turin	559	31.25	47.00	5.59	4.20	29.05	42.90	5.19	3.84
Valencia	817	33.55	44.10	4.11	2.70	31.55	41.20	3.86	2.52
Vienna	784	39.10	53.35	4.98	3.72	35.85	55.75	4.45	3.55
Warsaw	910	49.65	65.00	5.46	3.57	47.25	69.85	5.19	3.84
Zurich	480	26.90		5.60		23.40		4.88	
Averages				5.17	3.52			4.78	3.39

Table 1A.2
Scheduled fares competing strongly with inclusive tour operators

London to	Distance (miles)	Scheduled fares (£)			Inclusive tours (£)			Winter 1971/72 (pence/mile)		Summer 1969/70 (pence/mile)	
		Tourist single	Excursion return day turn night	Excursion return turn night	3–4 nights	1 week	2 weeks	Tourist single	Excursion return	Tourist single	Excursion return
Alicante	902	37.05	48.05		15–23	20–35	35–50	4.11	2.66	3.87	2.48
Athens	1392	68.25	85.00	75.00	27–33	35–43	49–60	4.57	2.84	4.39	2.82
Berlin	591	31.60			21–27			5.4		5.0	3.2
Faro	1057	40.60	62.60			30–45	45–65	3.85	2.96	3.62	2.78
Gibraltar	1077	34.65	52.25	48.65		40–50	60–70	3.22	2.43	2.93	2.21
Ibiza						20–35	35–50				
Las Palmos	1796	59.95	82.25			57–75	80–110	3.3	2.29	3.3	2.12
Lisbon	966	38.75	69.90		21–27	43–50	70–85	4.0	3.62	3.9	2.82
Madrid	765	36.35	52.85	45.20	19–25	25–45	40–60	4.8	3.5	4.6	3.2
Malaga	1032	40.90	58.05	49.10	17–26		40–60	4.0	2.81	3.7	2.64
Malta	1295	37.40	57.50	41.40		39–55	52–68	2.9	2.21	2.7	2.11
Marrakesh	1712	51.50	75.55			47–65	84–99	3.0	2.2		
Naples	1002	44.35	65.85		23–29			4.4	3.29	4.1	3.13
Nicosia	2001	78.90	107.00	90.00			85–100	3.9	2.63	3.8	
Palermo	1118	49.20	71.25			30–50	42–60	4.4	3.2	4.1	
Palma	826	32.30	42.95		15–20	30–45	45–60	3.9	2.45	3.7	2.29
Paris	209	12.90		18.00	19–25			6.2	4.3	5.9	5.1
Rome	892	41.15	61.10		24–29	36		4.6	3.42	4.3	3.26
Tangier	1112	40.75	61.50	54.75		56–70	75–100	3.7	2.76	3.5	2.63
Tel Aviv	2222	90.95	116.45				99–109	4.1	2.62	3.9	2.52
Teneriffe	1599	80.30	108.4			50–75	70–100				
Tunis	1126	41.85	68.85		21–27	30–45	46–65	3.7	3.06	3.7	
Venice	705	35.75	50.55		21–27			5.1	3.6	4.7	3.4
Averages (pence/mile)								3.91	2.84	3.72	2.58

but a reflection of the disarray caused on the North Atlantic route by the failure of the scheduled airlines to agree on the level and form of promotional fares.

Despite meetings ranging from Geneva to Honolulu, IATA's scheduled operators failed to agree on a fare structure. On 1 February 1973 previously agreed fares terminated, leaving governments to negotiate bilaterally. The so called 'war' never really broke out, for in April 1973 the major airlines agreed to maintain the then existing scheduled fare structure, accompanied by an agreed 6 per cent price increase.

The dispute was interesting, because it illustrates the competitive pressure on the route which has changed, and will continue to change, the fare and service characteristics of scheduled operations.

The overriding market forces are seen in Tables 1A.3 and 1A.4. Charter operators, by obtaining higher load factors, were able to operate at lower costs than scheduled services. The removal of restrictions on group charters allowed these economies to be reached. The growth in charter traffic along with increased frequencies made these services all the more competitive with scheduled services. By the early 1970s, the services were highly substitutable, while the prices favoured the charter operators. The scheduled carriers' response to their rapidly declining share of the market was to devise promotional fares aimed at differentiating the market. They were particularly keen to differentiate between business and non-business traffic; to recapture some of the business traffic lost to the charter operators by means of providing lower fares, but under certain conditions. These conditions have been devised to differentiate the market. The difficulty has sprung from individual airlines having their own different views on what those conditions should be. The winter dispute of 1972/73 was the culmination of at least four years of diverging opinion among the major North Atlantic carriers.

Table 1A.3

Market shares of the North Atlantic passenger market
(percentages)

Carrier	1963	1965	1967	1969	1970	1971
IATA scheduled	84	84	83	73	74	68
IATA charter	14	11	9	10	8	10
Non-IATA charter	2	5	8	17	18	22
Total charter	16	16	17	27	26	32

Source: *Flight*, 2 March 1972.

Table 1A.4

Costs and revenue on the North Atlantic run

	1965/66	1969/70	1972/73
Mean sector length (km)	7,571	7,571	7,571
Fare levels (US cents)			
First class	6.3	6.6	7.2
Low class: Economy	3.9–4.5	4.1–4.7	4.0–5.2
Group fares:			
Public	3.2	2.7–3.1	1.9–2.6
FIT	–	2.4–2.8	2.1–2.8
Costs per available seat mile			
First class	3.55	3.35	3.15
Low class	1.70	1.60	1.75
Yields per revenue, passenger km.			
First class	5.55	5.50	5.70
Low class	3.20	2.80	2.65

Source: 'Agreeing fares and rates', IATA, January 1973.

The cause lies among the differing market conditions. Conditions which might suit one airline may not suit another. Unanimity, however, is necessary under IATA rules.

In 1972/73 the dispute centred around three sets of promotional fares, each with their own conditions and supported by differing airlines and governments. In brief, they were as follows:

1 APEX, an abbreviation for advanced purchase excursion. Under its condition, the traveller is allowed to book directly through an airline. An example is the BOAC Earlybird. It must however, be bought in advance – 90 days in the case of the Earlybird – and involves a minimum stay requirement of around 14 days.

2 IPEX, an abbreviation for immediate purchase excursion. No advanced booking is required, but there is no guarantee of a seat. An example of this fare is the Skytrain fare proposed by Laker Airways.

3 ABC, an abbreviation for advance booking charter, known as TGC or travel group charter in the USA. This ticket is purchased via a travel agent who in turn has to fill a minimum block of 40 seats which he buys directly from the airline. Other conditions are that it must be purchased 90 days in advance, and that it has a minimum stay requirement of 14 days.

BOAC pushed for a simplification of the fare structure by advocating the removal of the cheapest excursion fares and the introduction of advanced booking (APEX). Its policy appears to have been to carry 40 per cent of its traffic paying APEX, the remaining 60 per cent travelling by standard scheduled services. The lower APEX fares would have been supported by the expected higher load factors, and a stiff 25 per cent cancellation fee.

This fare did not meet with USA approval, nor did Lufthansa's lower standard fares. The CAB, the one time advocate of low priced scheduled services, supported the US carriers in their opposition. One of the US charges was that the fares were uneconomical, and could only be afforded by state subsidised airlines [29]. The fare levels were higher than BOAC's,[47] and did not receive the British Civil Aviation Authority's approval.

There were other dissenters in the dispute. Alitalia did not want ABCs, while the Scandinavian governments did. Unfortunately, SAS did not agree with its governments.

The adoption of the *status quo* can only be a short term compromise. IATA has no single policy, it consists of airlines who have their own policies. Under strong competition from the charters, the heterogeneity of the North Atlantic market revealed itself in these differing airline proposals. The long run outcome is likely to be the removal of the unanimity clause, for it has shown itself to be inappropriate to the needs of the scheduled market. Retention of the rule is likely to cause scheduled carriers to move more into the unregulated sector of the market, and at the same time to push their respective governments into capacity and price regulation of the non-scheduled sector.

Notes

[1]   Edwards [1] para. 13.
[2]   A number of books have been written which deal in detail with air's international structure. These are Straszheim [2], Rosenberg [3] and Cooper and Maynard [4]. These sources, along with Edwards [1] give a comprehensive picture of the industry's structural development, and they have been freely drawn upon. However, the industry is changing rapidly, particularly at the non-scheduled end of the market, such that it is essential to reemphasise the effects of certain regulations and to bring the recent policy changes into the broader institutional framework.
[3]   These rights do not cover cabotage routes which refer to internal

routes or routes connecting country with its dependencies. These services are under the authority of the 'mother' country.

⁴ The European (non-communist) countries' airlines not members of IATA are Loftleider (Iceland) and Luxair (Luxembourg). Royal Maroc (Morocco) is also a non-member.

⁵ For a survey of the legal discussion concerning the definition of scheduled services see Edwards [1], Chapter 5. Edwards' non-definition of scheduled services is contained in para. 222 (page 57): 'The essential feature of a common carrier schedule service is that the demand for such a service is "collective". By "collective" here we mean, not that it is required by everyone at the same time, but that a significant proportion of the community could be expected to take the view that it should be available if they wish to use it.'

⁶ See *Interavia* 11/71, pages 1251–125 where an analysis is made of the US supplementals.

⁷ Difficulties have arisen over the definition of an affinity group. The definition given by IATA of an affinity group is: A group which has principal purposes, aims and objectives other than travel and sufficient affinity existing prior to the application for charter transportations to distinguish it and set it apart from the general public, subject to the following conditions:

(a) No charter may be operated for a group: (i) the membership of which exceeds 20,000; or (ii) the membership of which exceeds 5 per cent of the population of the political unit (i.e. country, state, province, county, town or village, or the equivalent combinations thereof) from which the membership is drawn, whichever is less.

(b) the group's principal purpose, aims and objectives are pursued in practice and are not merely theoretical or fanciful.

⁸ For an up-to-date view of the virtues of fixed fares see the interview of Mr Reynolds (Assistant Director-General of Traffic, IATA), *Airline Management,* vol. 3, no. 11, November/December, 71, p. 24.

⁹ For an air examination of the stability of the UK industry – in 1930 when there was no fare fixing – see A. P. Ellison [5] p. 486–7. For a general discussion of the evolution of airline controls see L. Foldes [6].

¹⁰ ICAO *Bulletin* Dec. 1969.

¹¹ For an analysis of air passenger profiles according to age, income, occupation etc. see: (for the USA) The Port of N.Y. Authority: Aviation Economics Division 1965 [7]; (for the UK) The Roskill Report, Papers and Proceedings, vol. VII, [8];(for Europe) *Characteristics and Forecasts of Demand in Europe* [9].

[12]   See *Air Transport World* Oct. 1968, p. 7.

[13]   For a discussion of these problems, and the use of varying estimating techniques, see Ellison A. P. [10].

[14]   Edwards [1], Chapter 6.

[15]   Straszheim [2], p. 96.

[16]   In practice what the economist means by marginal cost is in effect average varying cost. See G. W. Wilson [11] Chapter 3. In many airlines, e.g. BEA, variable costs are those which vary with aircraft flights, and include fuel, landing fees and various engineering costs. Allocated and apportioned costs are those costs which can be related to particular aircraft according to their peak operation during the year, while apportioned costs are apportioned on the basis of aeroplane weight.

[17]   See Chapters 4 and 9 for a discussion of this point.

[18]   For an analysis of UK domestic fare policy see Chapter 4 and Appendix 4A.2.

[19]   For a detailed examination of the relationship of fares to costs see: Edwards [1], p. 166—8, M. Straszheim [2], Chapter 8, A. Ellison [5], p. 488—92.

[20]   In-flight films, pioneered by TWA, were banned at the October meeting of IATA in 1964. Under pressure from the CAB, using the agreement that the ban was detrimental to the US film industry, the films were reintroduced a year later but with only on payment of a surcharge.

[21]   Applied for in the autumn of 1971 — but refused — November 1971 by the ATLB. A later application in 1972 met with approval from the newly instituted CAA, but opposition from the CAB. It is hoped to be in operation in June 1973.

[22]   See CAB [12].

[23]   A regression run on jet (day coach) fares during September 1966 yielded: $y = \$6.44 + 5.721$ cents x. Where x = miles.

[24]   CAB [12] p. 5. 'Unit costs per mile vary inversely with distance. However, on the longest domestic distances the costs for route passenger miles, particular jet coach, tend to swing upward due to lower load factors. Unit costs reflect a greater taper than fares per mile.' The study found the unit costs of operation were at least 70 per cent higher on routes of 200 miles than on routes of 600 miles.

[25]   For a detailed examination of the impact of these reduced IT prices on BEA's schedule fares see Appendix A1.1 to this chapter.

[26]   M. H. Cooper and A. K. Maynard [4] p. 27 and 28.

[27]   For a brief summary of the 1972/73 winter dispute over North Atlantic fares see Appendix A1.2 to this chapter.

[28]   The cheapest agreed fare agreed to in Honolulu was £83 return (No-

vember–March) for a stay of 22–45 days. The fare will be £121 in the peak periods.

[29] See 'The supplementals fights to live'. *Interavia*, November 1971, p. 1252.

[30] For an examination of the postwar financing history of the US market see: W. Barkley Jr. [13], H. R. Harris [14], P. W. Charington [15] and J. E. D. Williams [16].

[31] Edwards [1] para. 149.

[32] For a survey of the history and economic implications of leasing see E. C. Cassell [17].

[33] *Flight International*, 21 August 1969, p. 270.

[34] See W. V. Henzey [18] and [19] for an analysis of the holdings of US carriers stocks under CAB rules there is a requirement that all holders of 5 per cent or more of stocks should declare the extent of their interest. In 1969, there were 18 such holders, 11 of them institutions acting on behalf of stockholders unknown to the airlines.

[35] For an adverse view of the role of institutional holdings of US carrier shares see S. Altschul [20].

[36] See Plowden [21] and Elstub [22].

[37] If L is the labour imput to the first unit and r the learning factor, the labour imputs to the second, fourth, eighth and nth (where $n = 2p$) aircraft respectively are $Lr, Lr^2, Lr^3, \ldots Lr^p$. See S.G. Sturmey [23] p. 956.

[38] ICAO Bulletin May 1971, p. 39. The main producers were Boeing 49 per cent and McDonald Douglas with 29 per cent of world production.

[39] In the UK in 1958 there were 14 airframe producers, in 1963 three, employing some 80 per cent of the industry's labour force. See K. Hartley [24] page 851.

[40] See *Flight International*, 14 October 1971.

[41] For instance, the percentage of total production accounted by military transport sales of some major UK aircraft are: Viking 18, Bristol 170, 50, Britannia 30 and Comet 25.

[42] See Edwards [1], p. 192.

[43] See *Flight International*, 20 December 1962, p. 968, and 7 March 1963, p. 328.

[44] For a discussion of the impact of this policy change on defence earnings see G. E. Berkley [25]. For a very interesting examination of the relative profitability of different national aerospace industries see J. V. Connolly [26].

[45] The major national programmes still existing are: Britain's RB 211, France's F1 & G8 Mirage, Exocet Air Torpeol and Ballistic Rockets, Germany's VTOL VAK 191 and Italy's Aerolotine G222.

[46] The authors thank Mr P. Davey, a graduate student of Queen Mary College (1971/72), for the completion of these figures.
[47] See Table 1.15(6).

References

1   The UK Committee of Inquiry into Civil Air Transport, *British Air Transport in the Seventies – The Edwards Committee Report*, Cmnd. 4018, HMSO, 1969.
2   M. R. Straszheim, *The International Airline Industry*, Transport Research Project, The Brookings Institute, 1969.
3   A. Rosenberg, *Air Travel within Europe*, The Swedish National Consumer Council, Stockholm 1970.
4   M. H. Cooper and A. K. Maynard, *The Price of Air Travel*, Hobart Paper 53, The Institute of Economic Affairs 1971.
5   A. P. Ellison, 'The Edwards Report and civil aviation in the 1970s', *The Aeronautical Journal*, vol. 74, June 1970.
6   L. Foldes, 'Domestic Air Transport Policy, Parts I and II', *Economica*, 1961.
7   Port of New York Authority, Aviation Economics Division, *Travel Patterns and Characteristics of Air Passengers originating in New York*, 1965.
8   Commission on the Third London Airport, *The Roskill Report – Papers and Proceedings*, vol. VII, 1970.
9   *Characteristics and Forecasts of Demand in Europe*, Aeroport de Paris, Société d'Etudes Techniques et Economiques ISETECI, March 1968.
10 A. P. Ellison, *Size and Public Passenger Transport Operators*, Queen Mary College Dept. of Economics Working Paper no. 3, 1969.
11 G. W. Wilson, *Essays on Some Unsettled Questions in the Economics of Transportation*, Indiana University, 1962.
12 CAB, *A Study of the Domestic Passenger Air Fare Structure*, 1968.
13 W. Barkley, 'Financing the airline industry – the seventies', *The Wall Street Transcript*, 30 November 1970 (p. 22452).
14 H. R. Harris, 'Financing the airlines in the jet Age', *Air Transport Conference*, General Life Insurance Co., Connecticut, November 1961.
15 P. W. Cherington, *The Status and Economic Significance of the Airline Equipment Investment Programme*, 30 June 1958.
16 J. E. D. Williams, 'Financing the fleets of the seventies', *Flight International*, December 1969 (p. 981).
17 E. C. Cassell, 'The financial policy of domestic trunk airlines concern-

ing ownership versus leasing of flight equipment', *Transportation*, vol. 10, no. 4, 1971.

18   W. H. Henzey 'Who really owns the airlines?', *Airline Managing and Management*, June 1970.

19   W. H. Henzey, 'Airline control, who has it?', *Airline Management and Marketing*, May 1970.

20   S. Altschul, 'Market swingers score off investors', *Airline Management and Marketing*, June 1970.

21   Plowden, *Report of the Committee of Inquiry into the Aircraft Industry*, HMSO, 1965.

22   Elstub Report, *Productivity of the National Aircraft Effort*, Ministry of Technology, 1969. Chairman of Committee: Mr S. John Elstub.

23   S. G. Sturmey, 'Cost curve and pricing – aircraft production', *Economic Journal*, 1964 (pp. 954–82).

24   K. Hartley, 'The mergers in the UK aircraft industry 1957–60', *Aeronautical Journal*, 1965.

25   G. E. Berkley, 'The myth of war profiteering', *New Republic*, 20 December 1969.

26   J. V. Connolly, 'Comparative cost and analysis', *Aeronautical Journal*, 1967.

27   P. Ray, 'Inclusive tours: the growth sector', *Flight International*, 21 September 1972.

28   M. H. Cooper and A. K. Maynard, 'The effect of regulated competition on scheduled fares', *JTE and P*, vol. 6, May 1972.

29   'The uncertain cost of flying', *The Economist*, 10 February 1973.

Further reading

30   *Agreeing Fares and Rates: a survey of the methods and procedures used by the member airlines of IATA*, January 1973.

31   *The Aeronautical and Space Industries of the Community (EEC) compared with those of the UK and the US*, 5 vols. 1971.

2 A Model of the Civil Aviation Industry

2.1 The industry cycles and their magnitude

The airline industry's market structure has in its turn attracted credit for stimulating economic and technological progress, while during times of financial stringency, it has been fiercely criticised for its rigidity. Praise and criticism seem to follow in proportion to the industry's prosperity. During a profitable 1968, the Air Transport Association of America confidently proclaimed:

> As envisaged by the statutory and regulatory scheme, the prod of effective competition among carriers to maintain and expand their market share has helped to produce an environment of business rivalry conducive to a high degree of venturesomeness, efficiency and ceaseless striving, through improved service, to satisfy the needs of the travelling public . . . .

Only two years after this statement of confidence in the regulatory structure of the US airline industry, the largest US carriers were petitioning the CAB for capacity controls in order to lift the industry's depression. The decade of the first jet generation ended in the late sixties, as it had begun, with a worldwide industry depression. Progress had been considerable and the industry was not slow to broadcast them to interested consumers. ICAO in 1968 [1] illustrated the advance led by the jet by showing that the average aircraft capacity (measured in tonne-km available per aircraft hour) had increased by a factor of 3.3 between 1957 and 1967. Larger, faster aircraft led to cheaper travel, such that the air transport of America's air travel value index[1] in 1970 increased by some 35 per cent over 1948. Increased speeds and falling prices, however, tended to be concentrated on international routes.[2] The growth achieved has been high, rarely below 10 per cent for any year over the last 20 years.

These trends suggest considerable advances, yet it is movement about the trend which create profits and losses and the ensuing publicity. Losses seem to attract most publicity, and particularly so in the US, where private enterprise airlines operate largely without the government support

55

Table 2.1: Air and shipping comparisons

Year	(1) Tanker rates	(2) Tanker deliveries as a proportion of total stock	(3) Aircraft deliveries as a proportion of aircraft stock	(4) Deviations from the *Economist*'s average rate of return			(5) USA	
				All airliners	All shipping	Passenger lines	Airliners	Shipping
1953		16						
1954		22						
1955		15	10					
1956	+92.7	14	15					
1957	+22.2	13	19					
1958	−31.0	15	16					
1959	+1.0	10	25					
1960	+4.1	9	26					
1961	−16.3	7	16					
1962	+6.4	7	14	−14.1	−11.6	−15.4	−4.3	+1.3
1963	+12.0	8	12	−9.1	−10.9	−15.3	−2.6	−4.4
1964	−0.8	11	16	−0.6	−10.4	−14.7	−0.8	+0.7
1965	−10.6	10	16	−5.5	−9.4	−13.2	−1.5	+0.2
1966	−25.0	10	20	+0.3	−9.4	−12.8	+1.0	+1.9
1967		7	27	−1.7	−10.5	−18.7	+0.4	+1.8
1968		9	34					
1969		12	14					

Note: The deliveries in columns (1) and (2) are expressed as percentages of the averages of the two adjacent stock measures. Both profit deviations taken from measured means deemed to give an approximation to the average rate of return in the respective economies. The USA data was taken from the average of non-manufacturing industries and the UK data from the *Economist* index in the Rochdale Report.

Sources:

(1) German. Trip charter tanker rates. All flags to and from ports in Antwerp (UN *Year book*). Percentage deviation from a 4-year moving average.

(2) Tanker deliveries measured in gross deadweight tons and taken from Table 5.10, p. 51 in Z. S. Zannetos: *The Theory of Tankship Rates*. Later figures taken from the *Chamber of Shipping of the UK*, British Shipping Statistics 1970/71.

(3) Deliveries and stock measured in capacity units.

(4) The shipping data taken from the Rochdale Report (Cmnd. 4337 May 1970) and the airline data from the Edwards Report.

(5) The USA data taken from the First National City Bank of New York series in profits and rate of return.

provided by national carriers elsewhere. This has led to generalisations that the industry is subject to extra large fluctuations. Such pessimism must be kept in perspective for there are often others who are less fortunate. Shipping in general, and its various specialised markets such as oil transportation, have shown larger cyclical fluctuations. Table 2.1 presents deviations from their trends of tanker rates and world air passenger rates. Of course, deviations from trends can be misleading, the selection of the trend being all important. Given this difficulty, there can be little doubt that tanker rates fluctuate much more than air fares, which is perhaps not surprising when air fares are strongly regulated. What is more revealing is the considerable fluctuations in capacity created by tanker deliveries. Although these do not rise as high as aircraft deliveries as a proportion of stock, such fluctuations in conjunction with considerable rate fluctuation present tanker operators with substantial cyclical problems.

Other segments of the shipping industry are subjected to equally dramatic fluctuations. For instance, tramp rates for over a hundred years have shown extremely large fluctuations.[3] In a sense the shipping industry is exceptional in its fluctuations, perhaps the reason why so many fine economic minds[4] have puzzled the cycles in the industry. Nevertheless, the shipping industry, still the means by which most of world international freight is transported, does place in perspective the magnitude of the airline cycles.

The airline industry, as Chapter 1 showed, is characterised by rigid price and entry controls. It is also subjected to exogenous shifts in demand and substantial changes in technology. Given a change in demand (e.g. a rapid rise in real income) or the availability of a faster and bigger jet, the qualitative competition ensuing is likely to take the form of equipment rivalry. Market shares will be fought for by airline managers fearful of providing services with out of date equipment. Peak ordering, leading to concentrated capacity increases will follow, producing combined movements in investments, load factors and profits.

Table 2.2 shows deviations about the trend of prices, load factors, profits and demand. The trend extraction for each variable is given at the foot of the table, and the variables are plotted in Figure 2.1. Note the similar movement in deviations from the trend in profits and load factors, although in later years differences can be observed. This has occurred largely because load factors have had a downward movement over the last 20 years. This negative time trend was removed, but it should be noticed that the trend differs from the break-even load factor. The latter is determined by airline efficiency and revenue changes, and these have changed considerably over time. The data indicates that from 1962 to 1965 load

58

Table 2.2

World air transport trends

Year	(1) Air fares	(2) Weight load factor	(3) Profits (percentage of operating revenue)	(4) Air demand (percentage deviation from a pro-portional growth trend)
1953		0.0		+13
1954	(0.6)	+0.2		+12
1955	0.4	+0.8	2.5	+16
1956	2.2	+1.6	2.3	+15
1957	1.6	+0.4	(10.0)	+14
1958	0.7	−0.2	1.8	+ 3
1959	0.9	+1.2	2.1	+14
1960	1.4	−0.2	1.2	+10
1961	0.7	−3.2	(2.0)	+ 7
1962	1.7	−3.2	1.4	+ 9
1963	2.1	−3.0	4.5	+12
1964	1.8	−1.8	7.5	+15
1965	2.0	−0.4	9.6	+14
1966	3.3	+1.2	9.5	+14
1967	2.9	−0.3	7.4	+17
1968		−2.0	5.3	+12
1969		−2.6	5.5	+11
1970		−2.0	5.4	+10

Notes
(1) Air fares taken from a 2 year moving average. Expressed in percentage terms. The bracket figures denotes a negative number.
(2) Weight load factor. A linear trend was removed. This was negative with respect to time, i.e. load factors have been falling over time. Expressed as differences and not as percentages.
(3) Profits related to operating revenue. These figures are operating profits, and are more meaningful than return on capital after taxes, in that many airlines are subsidised and exempt from taxes, etc.
(4) A proportionate rate of growth was considered appropriate. It was calculated by expressing the annual difference as a percentage of the average growth of the 2 adjoining years.

Sources: ICAO *Statistical Bulletins.*

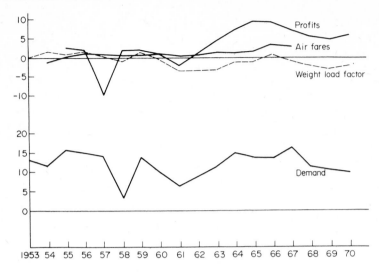

Fig. 2.1   World air transport trends

factors were below the trend, while profits were rising, yet the break-even load factor on the US market went down rapidly in those years from 60 in 1960 to 55 in 1965. The profit measure used, net operating profit as a percentage of operating revenue, shows considerable fluctuations, yet if we consider the profits of the UK and US shipping and airline companies, we see the airlines have been absolutely better off compared to all branches of the shipping industry during the 1960s, while in the USA the airlines have on the whole been subjected to less fluctuations.

As a proportion of aerospace manufacturers' sales civil aircraft have been small, of far less importance than military projects. This is brought out in the data on the aerospace industries of the US presented in Tables 2.3 and 2.4. The impact of civil aircraft projects has nevertheless been considerable, owing to the manner in which the airlines have handled their projects. Up to the mid 1960s it was acknowledged[5] that the only aircraft company having made substantial profits in the civil aircraft market had been Douglas. Certainly, the leading airframe manufacturers had suffered financially from the first generation jet programme. Up to 1960 Boeing had spent some $165 million development costs on the B707, and it was selling then below cost.[6] Lockheed spent $50 million in developing the Electra, and was out of pocket on the project by $16 million in 1959.[7] The worst losers were General Dynamics, with their CV-880's and 990's, having to write off some $425 million, leading to a $27 million loss in 1960.[8] The Lockheed company with its Tristar have had to rely on government support for their second generation jet project, while Boeing have

Table 2.3

Military aircraft sales as a percentage of net sales of the leading
US manufacturers

	General Dynamics	Douglas	Lockheed	Boeing	North American Aviation
1955	63.8	72.0	75.0	81.4	71.2
1956	64.1	61.3	71.6	77.5	59.8
1957	70.1	41.7	63.0	83.6	55.6
1958	70.1	34.9	51.1	84.2	40.9
1959	61.8	31.1	31.7	45.2	25.2

Source: Aerospace Industries Association of America.

committed themselves with long term borrowings totalling $700 million,[9] largely in order to finance their B747 programme.

The heavy development costs and the competition selling to often fickle customers has meant airframe manufacturers have been reluctant to engage in the civil market when safe military contracts could be won. Nevertheless, the sales of civil aircraft are growing in response to the downturn in the Vietnam war and the demotion of the space programme. The heavy capital requirements needed to complete a civil jet programme, and their increasing importance in the aerospace industry's diversification plans, suggest fluctuations in the civil air transport market are likely to be of increasing significance to the aerospace industry's performance.

2.2   Model development of the civil aviation industry: measures and interrelations

The aims of civil air transport regulation have differed over time and between countries. A commonly held view among airlines, however, is that unregulated competition would lead to unstable prices, interruption of services and airline bankruptcies.[10] The role of the common carriers, to provide regular and dependable services, would be undermined. The cost of service dependability has been regulated competition – schedule service monopolies, regulated price and service frequencies. As a result, competition for market shares has taken the form of service and equipment rivalry

Table 2.4

Market diversification of US aerospace companies as a percentage of sales

Date	1960	1961	1962	1963	1964	1965	1966	1967	1968	1969	1970	1971
Customer:												
Department of Defence	76	77	75	71	64	55	54	58	55	55	56	58
National Aeronautics & Space Administration and other government departments	2	4	7	13	18	22	20	15	14	20	12	13
Commercial aerospace	13	10	9	7	10	14	15	17	22	25	32	29
Non-aerospace	9	9	9	9	8	9	11	10	9	–	–	–

Source: Aerospace Industries Association of America.

which, in turn, has contributed to the considerable fluctuations in load factors and investment. A comprehensive understanding of the contribution of market structure, airline regulation and exogenous factors to the industry's fluctuations requires an understanding of their interrelationships. Similarly with predictions of policy changes, such as the removal of price controls, or with airline order forecasts. In order to be able to predict future demand for civil aircraft we need to know the determinants of primary demand, of the relationship between stock demand and primary demand, of the production lag between aircraft orders and deliveries and of the effect of aircraft deliveries on supply and demand in the final market. The effective use of such a model as a means of understanding the industry's growth and fluctuations requires consideration of model specifications, estimating difficulties, data sources, etc. In this section we shall introduce these sets of relationships, outlining their interdependence so as to produce an overall model of the industry. Individual chapters will then explore model formulations and estimations of various parts of the model, the concluding chapters bringing these estimates together and fitting them into the overall model.

2.2.1 *Demand and supply in the primary market*

Routes differ in character, having differing journey purpose mixes, social characteristics, etc. Estimates of primary (or final) demand on these routes, however, face a number of common problems.

First, there is the problem of specification, i.e. the selection of variables for use in explaining the demand for air travel. Secondly, there are problems of equation form. Elementary knowledge of statistical estimation can quickly show that differing specification and estimable forms can lead to a large difference in estimates of coefficients. If the econometric models are to have any validity, therefore, some theoretical explanation has to be given for the variables selected. Price and income are obvious demand variables, but 'qualitative' variables are more difficult to specify. Speed of travel, frequency of services, safety, etc. are variables which are likely to affect travel demand, but which are difficult to build into a model. Normally they are excluded, with the result that the estimates are biased (usually upwards).

Of those variables mentioned, frequency is one of the more important, owing to the effect its variations have on airport waiting times. The higher the frequency, the lower the waiting time, and thus the lower the total journey time. From an estimating point of view, it is difficult to include the variable in the demand equation. The problem can be overcome, however, by appreciating that airlines often adjust their frequencies at a given period of time in response to the output sold during the corresponding period of the previous year. Substituting in the lagged demand variable provides a means of representing frequency changes, and of obtaining estimable coefficients for them.

Price and income elasticities are often difficult to interpret owing to poor data, for income measures are rarely found for cities and there is the difficulty of using representative fare figures when the routes have complex fare structures. Another problem is caused by income elasticity coefficients which vary over time. Most studies use estimating equations in forms which lead to constant elasticity measurements, yet there is evidence to suggest that the income elasticity is not constant for air travel. For instance, the cross-section evidence on non-business travel presented in the Roskill Report showed a higher propensity to travel among higher income households. Evidence from UK and US studies also shows a threshold income level below which few non-business air trips are made.

Such information suggests that, as income *per capita* grows, and as the number of households above the threshold level increases, the demand for air travel will more than proportionally increase. To relate changes in income per head to changes in demand is to mask the important variable of income distribution. In order to include this variable, various evidence on income distribution in the UK was used on aggregate market data. This model and others have been developed in Chapters 3 and 4, dealing particularly with individual routes and route groups.

Of particular interest to the aggregate primary model is the extent to which air fares can be considered exogenous. Chapter 1 outlined some of the outcomes of the IATA fare fixing agreements, while Appendix 4A.2 of Chapter 4 notes the fares fixed in the UK domestic sector over the last sixteen years. An examination of these fares suggests that the fares fixed are not extraneous variables decided by the haphazard haggling of the airlines in the IATA enclaves, but variables responsive to the demand and supply conditions of the market. More precisely it is suggested that air fares are endogenous variables, functions of the load factors one or two years previously. Load factor is an expression of the extent of excess supply at the given fixed price such that, given the two year interval between fare fixing in IATA, it is reasonable to suggest that demand and supply two or one year previously are likely to have a considerable influence on the level at which air fares are pitched.

Air fares on international routes will, of course, be fixed for two years, when they again will come under review.[11] Given certain assumptions, supply of scheduled services will be infinitely elastic at the fixed price.

One assumption is that all the demand at the fixed price can be accommodated, and there are no discontinuities in the supply curve. A second assumption concerns the substitutability between scheduled and non-scheduled services. If we define total demand to include scheduled, charter and inclusive tour traffic, then the share of scheduled traffic at the fixed rate will depend upon the costs at which the non-scheduled carriers can provide the service. [12] It appears that there is considerable substitutability, for the share of IATA scheduled carriers is decreasing in the face of lower priced non-scheduled competition. For instance, Mr K. Hammarshöld, addressing the ICAO conference [13] in Vienna in June, 1971, pointed out that non-IATA charter traffic increased at an average rate of 58.1 per cent between 1964 and 1970, compared with 15.3 per cent for the scheduled airlines. The non-IATA share of North Atlantic traffic increased from 3 per cent in 1964 to 18 per cent in 1970.

The world demand functions are developed in Chapter 9, individual route estimates in Chapters 3 and 4.

2.2.2   Aircraft stock

In examining the supply of aircraft services we must remember that an aircraft is a durable factor imput. There is a distinction, therefore, between changes in aircraft stock and changes in the utilisation of aircraft stock. Under full capacity, supply will be determined by (net) deliveries, below full capacity it is likely to be elastic, and a function of the marginal cost of increasing output. Shifts in supply will be horizontal due to net additions, and vertical due to changing relative costs of production.

Accurate details concerning aircraft stock are essential, for aircraft stock is central to the supply in the primary market and to the determination of aircraft orders. Changes in stock utilisation result in changes in supply of aircraft services, changes in desired stock to changes in aircraft orders. The determinants of desired aircraft stock are derived partly from the final market, where changes in demand and supply affect expectations of future requirements and thus desired stock.

The aircraft stock constitutes many aircraft types, of differing speeds, capacities and ages. Consequently, simple aggregation of aircraft fails to give an accurate measure of the potential services that could be provided by the stock in any given period of time. Figure 2.2 for instance shows how aircraft stock, measured in aircraft numbers, differs from the same stock measured in capacity units. The latter is calculated by multiplying the passenger capacity of the aircraft by a utilisation factor which assumes around eight hours daily throughout the year. [14] Utilisation rarely reaches

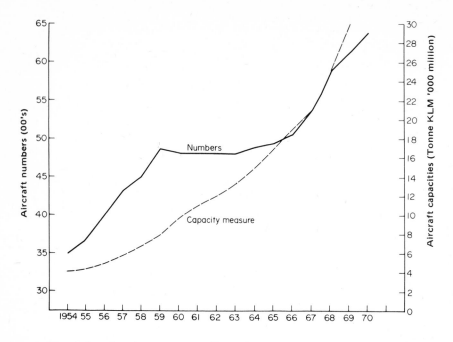

Fig. 2.2   Stock measures. Capacity and number of aircraft

this figure, affected as it is by aircraft overhaul requirements, fuelling stops, labour regulations, etc., all of which can be adjusted by the airline. As Table 2.5 shows, actual capacity supplied has rarely reached 70 per cent of potential capacity. The relationship between utilisation of stock potential capacity and real rates will be examined in Chapter 10.

2.2.3   *Aircraft orders, deliveries and departures*

The demand for aircraft is derived demand, the primary demand being for transport services provided by the aircraft. This derived demand is demand for a stock, not for the flow of aircraft deliveries, since the stock of aircraft is the factor in the airlines' production function and not the flow of aircraft deliveries.

Of special interest in explaining fluctuations in aircraft deliveries is the role of economic variables, technical change and the industry's structure. Changes in the price of aircraft, the price of factor substitutes (e.g. labour), the rate of interest and changes in expected demand are all likely to bring about changes in aircraft orders. So too is development in technology; the availability of faster, cheaper aircraft, a determinant in the timing of aircraft orders likely to be important in an industry which has

Table 2.5

Capacity and real prices

Year	(1) Air fares deflated by operating costs	(2) Utilisation of potential capacity	(3) Weight load factor (Capacity sold divided by capacity offered)
1953	98.2	63.0	59.6
1954	99.2	64.0	59.0
1955	101.0	68.7	59.5
1956	100.9	68.6	59.9
1957	97.4	69.1	58.4
1958	98.8	68.0	57.1
1959	100.7	65.0	57.1
1960	99.2	64.1	56.1
1961	96.6	59.0	53.0
1962	100.1	58.6	52.5
1963	103.3	59.2	51.9
1964	106.8	60.2	52.6
1965	109.1	62.2	53.3
1966	109.0	63.2	54.6
1967	107.8	79.7	52.5
1968	104.2	76.9	48.7
1969	104.4	81.1	47.5
1970	104.4	82.0	47.4

Notes

(1) Average air fares deflated by operating cost to give a real price.

(2) Potential capacity was obtained by multiplying the aircraft stock by the potential output obtained by the average aircraft. The latter tonne–km per aircraft hour was obtained for the individual years from ICAO sources, and multiplied by the potential number of hours an aircraft could be used in a year — 3.000 (i.e. 8 hours per day). The actual capacity supplied was then expressed as a percentage of the potential capacity.

(3) Load factor here relates capacity sold to capacity supplied.

Sources: ICAO *Statistical Bulletins*.

chosen to allow qualitative competition in place of price competition. The third aspect is the industry's structure. The purchasers of new aircraft are few in number, mostly airlines engaged in intense competition with one another. Equipment purchasers play an important part in rival bids for market shares, yet their orders are uncoordinated. The speed of response once a rival has ordered is often too rapid to allow an airline to consider the aggregate behaviour of the industry. Such an oligopolistic structure could itself be the cause of large order fluctuations. Explanations of the timing and magnitude of aircraft orders clearly requires consideration of these three factors before confident forecasts of aircraft orders can be made. These aspects are dealt with in Chapter 6.

The production lag between the ordering of an aircraft and its delivery is important because of the continuous need for forecasts of future demand. The longer the lead time, the proportionately greater the chance of error in the forecast. As Chapter 8 shows, lead times in civil aircraft production are long; longer than the average industry lead time, and consequently another source of the industry's relative instability. Equally the

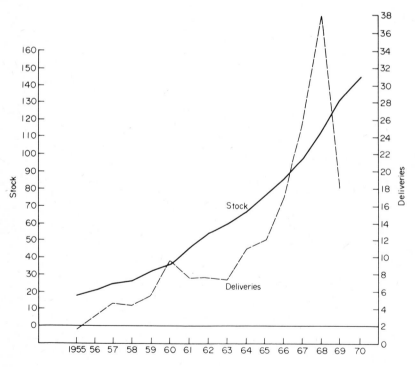

Fig. 2.3   Aircraft stock and deliveries measured in capacity units (tonne km '000 million)

variations between actual and expected lead times may also contribute to the considerable fluctuations in aircraft deliveries (see Figure 2.3).

Departures due to crashes are likely to be randomly spaced over an aircraft life, whilst scrapping is determined by economic variables such as operating costs and used aircraft prices. The same applies for temporary aircraft retirements, i.e. aircraft which have had their air licenses withdrawn. Chapter 5 examines these determinants of aircraft departures by studying in detail individual aircraft life histories, recording dates of deliveries, departures due to crashes, scrapping and retirements. In this way we are able to build an accurate measure of aircraft stock, distinguishing between active stock and retired stock, and measure of aircraft durability. For purposes of the aircraft order model a series of stock figures deflated according to aircraft life expectancy are calculated. Sales of aircraft from first hand owners are recorded, and related to used aircraft prices. A used aircraft market model is developed in Chapter 7 and used in a short term forecast of used aircraft prices.

2.3 Flow diagrams and functional forms

From development of elemental models it is found that a multi-loop structure of dynamic relationships exists, with exogenous variables such as financial indices, GNP, used aircraft prices, technological change, etc. It is convenient to avoid the explicit statement of functional forms, and merely to introduce the overall model in diagrammatic form with arrows indicating the dependence of variables between sub-systems. The overall model is thus viewed as shown in Figure 2.4. This indicates that the ordering process depends on, among other variables, output demand, and that the variables of this macro-view: $O_t, K_t, D_t,$ are in capacity units. The direction of the arrows indicates the dependence of stock K_t on the ordering policy O_t, demand D_t on stock K_t.

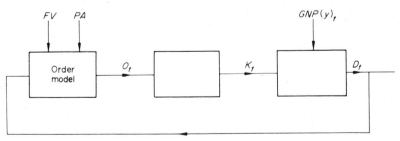

Fig. 2.4   Overall model

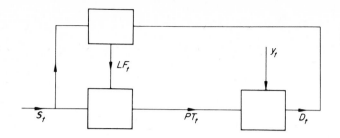

Fig. 2.5   Primary market model

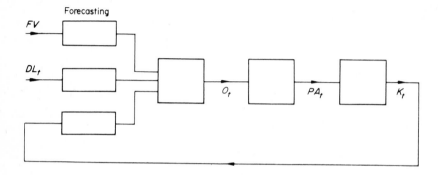

Fig. 2.6   Order/investment model

The same description may be used for the proposed factors influencing the elemental models, without reference to precise formulation, e.g. log or log/linear, etc., as follows. Each model is discussed at a later stage.

2.3.1   *Primary market model*

While endogenous to the primary market, the price structure is separately and explicitly retained in order to indicate how changes in the present institutional price fixing will affect output demand. Note, in Figure 2.5, that Y_t is the only truly exogenous variable.

2.3.2   *Order/investment model*

A number of model forms will be taken, including the concept of a moving desired equilibrium stock. FV_t, PA_t, in Figure 2.6 are exogenous variables.

70

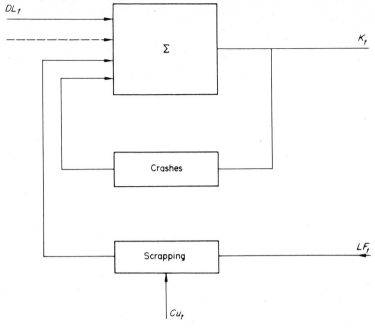

Fig. 2.7   Scrapping, crashes, replacement model

2.3.3   *A scrapping and crashes replacement model*

This model allows for the fact that other variables, as well as deliveries, affect stock (Figure 2.7). The only exogenous quantity in this model is CU_t, the used aircraft running costs.

Further elemental models are relatively trivial, e.g. the connection between stock K_t and supply S_t (see Figure 2.8a). It will also be deemed important to discuss the order-delivery situation, i.e. Figure 2.8b, in a section separate from the total order/investment model (Chapter 7).

2.4   Aspects of interrelations between elemental models

Several aspects of this study are novel. While sections of the aircraft industry have been investigated in the past, there has been little attempt so far to place such partial studies and their results within an entire feedback framework. Here we attempt to relate the primary and factor markets in a comprehensive manner, so as to be able to examine, for example, the stability of the industry with respect to price changes. Such an examination of

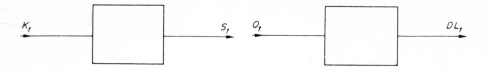

Fig. 2.8a   Stock model   Fig. 2.8b   Order/delivery model

the entire civil aviation industry will also provide the most comprehensive forecasting.

The conventional econometric measures of an industry are posed in monetary terms: in this study a continued effort is made to derive data in capacity (passenger seat kilometer) terms. The rationale for this is referred to in Chapter 5.

Further certain assumptions at each stage of the model-making incorporate new ideas: their validity is justified by the text and to a certain extent by the standard econometric tests. The total model is developed in the chapters following, to be summarised in detail in Chapter 9. As a first step in this process the importance of demand estimates of individual routes is considered.

Notes

[1]   This is obtained by dividing a real price index of air travel by an index of aircraft speed.

[2]   ICAO [1] Table 1.

[3]   See L. Isseris [2] who used a seven year moving average to remove the trend in tramp freight rates, showing that in percentage deviations from the trend were enormous up to the Second World War. For instance, the percentage deviation in 1900 was +26.6, in 1914 −69.4, and in 1918 +73.0. In the 1960s fluctuations have also been considerable, see Chart 8.3, p. 148 in the Rochdale Report on Shipping (1970).

[4]   W. R. Robertson, Koopmann and Tinbergen have during this century studied the fluctuations in the industry.

[5]   C. Murphy [3].

[6]   *Jet Airliners: Year of Decision* [4], p. 129.

[7]   C. Murphy [3].

[8]   R. A. Smith: *How a Corporation got out of Control* [5].

[9]   *Supersonic Transport Financial Planning Study* [6] p. 69.

[10]   See for instance, [7] and [8] for a discussion of airline regulation in general and UK regulation in particular.

[11] Domestic fares are on the whole less regularly reviewed. See, for instance, section 4A.2 outlining the changes in fares made in the UK domestic routes over the last 20 years.

[12] In the diagram below at price OP the schedule carrier will supply PSc the non-schedule operator's supply being SS. The quantity obtained by the non-schedule carrier would be OQ_1, Q_1Q being obtained by the scheduled carrier.

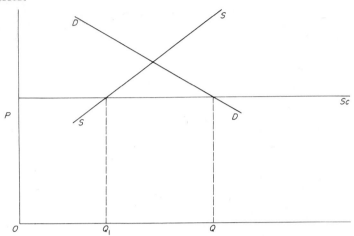

[13] See *Flight International*, 24 June 1971, p. 913.

[14] See Chapter 5, note 8, for a description of the method used by ICAO in calculating aircraft productivity.

References

1   ICAO Circular 89 – AT/15.
2   L. Isseris, 'Tramp shipping. Cargoes and freights', *Journal of the Royal Statistical Association*, vol. C1, 1938, p. 53–134.
3   C. Murphy, 'The plane makers under stress', *Fortune*, July 1960.
4   'Jet Airliners: year of decision', *Fortune*, April 1953.
5   R. A. Smith, 'How a corporation got out of control', *Fortune*, Jan. & Feb. 1962.
6   Supersonic Transport Financial Planning Study, *Contract No. FA-SS-66-33*, 16 May 1967.
7   L. Foldes, 'Domestic air transport policy', *Economica*, May & Aug. 1961.
8   A. P. Ellison, 'The Edwards report on civil aviation in the 1970s', *Journal of the Royal Aeronautical Society*, June 1970.

3 Air Passenger Demand Models

3.1 Introduction

Demand forecasting is a hazardous business, and particularly so in civil aviation.[1] Any technique which can improve the accuracy of forecasts will greatly aid the development of the industry, for demand fluctuations are a prime source of aviation's instability. If these fluctuations could be predicted accurately the consequences of wide demand fluctuations could be minimised, but this is rarely the case. Many of the causes of the fluctuations are outside the control of the forecaster, in other cases ignorance of the relationship between cause and effect is the source of inaccurate predictions. An approach to forecasting which is designed to overcome the latter, is the application of econometric models. Many of the econometric models in civil aviation are, as yet, quite primitive, yet much has been expected of them. It is necessary, therefore, to examine the limitations of these models if a balanced judgement is to be made of their worth. The forecaster needs to know the confidence which he can place on forecasts based on these models. This can only be achieved by having some understanding of the problems involved in formulating and estimating the models.

Such knowledge is not merely academic, but of interest to all participants in the complex structure constituting the civil aviation industry. For instance, one of the sources of dispute in the industry is the means by which governments exercise control. In most instances governments control those variables such as price and frequency which are assumed to determine passenger demand. Of course, there is some interplay between the price fixing bodies and the airlines, and the latter are not without influence, but the discretionary powers reside with the government appointed bodies. A knowledge of the magnitude of demand elasticities is therefore essential if government control is to be exercised in an effective manner.

Evidence on demand elasticities, particularly of individual routes, is still scanty, despite the increasing interest in Europe and in North America. This is not surprising, for while it is relatively easy to obtain data such as gross national product, it is far more difficult to obtain data on individual routes and sectors. The result has been the adoption of general policies,

75

such as across the board fare changes, which fail to take account of individual route characteristics. Such policies may be administratively convenient, but they can be injurious to the airlines, for not only may the growth of individual routes be harmed, but they may authorise unexpected fare levels. 'Across the board' changes, such as fare increases, are often designed to raise revenue, implying that the air demand price elasticity is inelastic. Failure to recognise such route differences can thwart the objective of the policy. However, in using individual route elasticities to yield extra precision, we should be fully aware of the limitations of these models.

This chapter sets out to develop demand models of air passenger behaviour. These in turn will be applied to routes and to route groups where appropriate. Our aim is twofold: to produce models which add precision to administrative policy and to forecasting performance. The problems of estimating these models will be examined in Chapter 4, Chapter 10 dealing specifically with forecasting. Emphasis in the following two chapters is placed on disaggregate markets – individual routes and route groups. The demand models and estimates for the world civil aviation model are dealt with separately in Chapter 9.

3.2 The demand for air travel

The demand for transport services is derived demand, depending upon the demand for transport trips. In turn the demand for a transport trip depends upon the contribution of the trip to the activity at the destination and upon the direct satisfaction yielded by the trip itself. Like other inputs, the elasticity of demand for a trip is a function of the elasticity of demand of the final product or activity, the elasticity of substitution between the trip and the other factor inputs involved in producing the final product and the proportion of the trip cost in the final product's price.

Dividing the purpose of transport trips into two groups, business and non-business, we can recognise the business trip as an input into the activity at the point of destination – a factor contributing to the production of utility yielding goods and services. The non-business trip, however, itself yields direct satisfaction, the demand for business trips being determined by the price of the trip and the difference between the marginal product of the businessman at his point of destination and at his point of origin, the demand for non-business trips by the price of the trip and the price and availability of complementary activities and attributes such as accommodation, weather, scenic beauty etc.

76

The demand for trips by a given mode is a function of the elasticity of substitution among trips by different modes. The modes themselves are seen as yielding satisfactions or utilities, these being produced by their individual characteristics such as comfort, speed, safety, etc. Given the prices of trips, optimum conditions are satisfied where the marginal rate of technical substitution between trips by the various modes equals their relative prices.

3.3 A classical demand approach

What might be termed the classical demand approach is to ignore the characteristics or quality attributes of commodities and instead to treat them as one dimensional. A train, car or aeroplane is treated as a commodity, and is not described or defined according to its quality attributes, such as speed, reliability, frequency, comfort, safety, etc.

With such an approach, the elasticity of substitution E_s measures the ratio of the proportionate change in the ratio of the number of passengers using (say) the air mode to a surface mode (say rail) to a given proportionate change in the ratio of their respective prices.

E_s would be defined as:

$$\left(d\frac{Q_a}{Q_r} \middle/ \frac{Q_a}{Q_r}\right) \middle/ \left(d\frac{P_r}{P_a} \middle/ \frac{P_r}{P_a}\right) \tag{3.1}$$

where Q denotes the number of passengers, a the air mode, r the rail mode and P the prices.

The logarithmic transform becomes:

$$E_s = \frac{d \log (Q_a/Q_r)}{d \log (P_a/P_r)} \tag{3.2}$$

A form suitable for estimation would, therefore, be:

$$\log \frac{Q_a}{Q_r} = \alpha_0 + \lambda_1 \log \frac{P_a}{P_r} \tag{3.3}$$

where λ_1 is equal to the elasticity of substitution, i.e. the value of the first derivative of equation (3.3) is equivalent to the definition of E_s given in (3.2).

From the traveller's point of view, E_s measures movement along a *given* indifference curve, in which real income and other variables remain constant. Given that the data is generated by aggregate movements in demand, it is unlikely that the community of travellers will remain on the same indifference curve. If this is the case, then the value of λ_1 will measure not only E_s but, for instance, the effects of real income changes. Consequently, the total derivative is inappropriate and instead a partial derivative including these other variables is representative of E_s:

$$\lambda_1 = \frac{\partial \log Q_a/Q_r}{\partial \log P_a/P_r}$$

There is one condition, however, which is hopeful. Morrissett [2] has shown that the partial derivative equals the total derivative if there are no effects from income and other variables, but they can also be equal *if the income effects on air and rail are equal and that there are no differential effects from other variables.*[2] The outcome of Morrissett's analysis is that if income elasticities for air and its competing modes display differential income elasticities, then there is reason to believe that the estimates of λ_1 are not estimates of the elasticity of substitution.

We shall examine the relationship between air and its competing modes to see the extent of this competition, and to see the suitability of elasticity of substitution models as predictors of modal split.

3.3.1 *Air and inter-modal competition*

The transportation market is, of course, extremely wide, the public/private transport division itself giving way to further subdivision according to journey purpose and class of travel. Is air travel a substitute for bus travel, is bus travel a substitute for car travel, are air and sea transport substitutes for business travel or only for non-business travel? The answers differ according to the route and countries concerned. Some general points, however, can be made.

1   In UK domestic travel air and rail appear to be strong competitors for business travel over 200 miles. This is shown by the strong competition between the two modes in the form of fares and frequencies. In many ways the situation resembles controlled oligopoly. Aspects of this market are examined in Chapter 4.

2   Rail appears to be sandwiched between road and air competitors, for it competes with road at the low income end of the market (non-business

journeys made by low income non-car owners), and with air for business travellers at the higher income end of the market. Rail and air are likely to be strongly affected by car ownership, in that the latter is a strong substitute for non-business travel (both in the UK and abroad).

3   In the case of international traffic, apart from rail/car journeys for vacation trips, the major competition comes from sea travel. Because of the speed factor, such competition is likely to be confined to non-business travel.

One method of examining this competition between sea and air travel is to consider the differing growth rates, and their variation over time. It could be postulated that in a strongly competitive market we would expect an inverse relationship between individual modal growth rates. In other words, when air grows, if it is a substitute for sea travel, then some of this growth is likely to be due to passengers switching to air. Standard deviations from annual growths for the main route groups are shown in Table 3.1. The lowest fluctuations are shown in the European market, the

Table 3.1

Air and sea competition

Route	Mean growth/annum			Standard deviation			Rank correlation Air/Sea
	Sea	Air	Total	Sea	Air	Total	
All routes *	4.1	15.7	8.4	3.4	8.4	3.6	Non-significant
European	5.0	13.9	9.5	3.1	5.3	2.2	Non-significant
Irish	1.4	12.0	4.9	6.7	8.6	3.0	Non-significant
North American	−8.7	17.8	12.1	6.8	8.1	6.4	Significant

* 1950−68: all the other routes are for 1958−68.

Similar studies were done for UK domestic routes and compared with bus traffic. Again, insignificant ranking was recorded.

highest in the North American. Furthermore, when rank correlations of these growth rates were made, only the North American route proved to be significant. In other words, this test would suggest that the market divides between the two modes, and that they are differently affected by economic forces. Rather than being substitutes, they are separate commodities.

In order to examine more closely this suggestion, elasticity of substitution estimates were applied to two route groups. Route group one consisted of all routes, 1958–68. Prices were obtained by dividing total revenue by passengers travelling, an inadequate measure, but nevertheless it was used. More acceptably, on route group two, North Atlantic, the length of estimate was longer (1950–66), and fares by both sea and air were obtained by weighting according to share in the market.

The estimates of λ_1 vary on the two routes. Furthermore, the income elasticities differ for each mode, suggesting that this is an inappropriate measure of the elasticity of substitution.

Our conclusion, therefore, is that modal competition is important, that fares and time changes should be considered in our estimatable models, but that elasticities of substitute models (and modal split models; see below for a discussion of these models and estimates in Table 3.2) are unsuitable.

3.3.2   *A different approach: the treatment of quality dimensions*

Classical demand theory has been the source of much that has been fruitful in microeconomics. Its treatment of commodities as homogeneous and one dimensional has been sufficiently close to reality in a large range of commodities to yield fruitful insights and predictive accuracy. But there are many commodities which are characterised by quality dimensions which do affect consumer choice and which need to be incorporated into demand theory. Early studies[3] provided a useful start into the examination of such commodities, but it is only recently that the ideas and techniques developed 20 years ago have been brought back into the main stream of demand theory.[4]

Such developments are of special interest when examining transport demand, for transport trips are provided by modes which are characterised by dimensions which do influence consumer choice: the consumer requires a mode which will accomplish the trip with reliability, speed, frequency, comfort and safety. These are dimensions, *qualitative attributes* of the mode which affect choice. To neglect these attributes would be to exclude important determinants of modal choice. Given these attributes, and given a market in which the suppliers of modes with differing attri-

Table 3.2

Results of elasticity of substitution models

Model: $\log\left(\dfrac{Q_a}{Q_r}\right) = \alpha_0 + \alpha_1 \log\left(\dfrac{P_a}{P_r}\right)$

Coefficients/Route	α_0	α_1	R^2	D.W.
1 London/all routes	-0.070	4.0	0.26	0.59
2 London/North Atlantic	0.75	1.44	0.47	1.14

Model: $Q_a = \alpha_0 + \alpha_1 Y; Q_r = \alpha_1 + \alpha_2 Y$

Coefficients/Route	α_0	α	R^2	α_1	α_2	R_2
1 London/all routes	-3.9	2.81 (0.11)	0.90	$+5.28$	10.79 (0.37)	0.98
2 London/North Atlantic	-14.8	3.5 10.38	0.78	5.6	$+0.14$ (0.13)	0.97

Model: $\log\dfrac{Q_a}{Q} = \alpha_0 + \alpha_1 \log P_a$

Route	α_0	α_1	R^2	D.W.
North Atlantic	11.4	-2.10 (0.18)	0.89	1.26

Q_a =	air	Q =	total passengers
Q_r =	sea	P_a =	air fare

butes have priced accordingly, the consumers of trips would choose modes, given the price, which they consider to have the most desirable attributes. In equilibrium, the bundle of attributes priced and offered by transport operators will be derived from supply and demand forces.

A commodity is, therefore, defined as a composite of measurable qualitative dimensions. For any such commodity q_i, there will correspond the different quality dimensions λ_{ij}.[5] In general, the number of quality dimensions λ_i will differ with the commodity. We shall be concerned with a subset of transport modes each with a similar number of dimensions.

The consumer maximising model proceeds as follows:

$$\max u = f(q_i,..., q_n, \lambda_{i1}, \lambda_{i2},..., \lambda_{in},..., \lambda_{j1},..., \lambda_{jn}) \qquad (3.4)$$

where q_i is commodity i

λ_{ij} is the j quality dimension of commodity i.

subject to $\quad \sum_i p_i q_i = Y$ where p_i is the price of commodity i $\qquad (3.5)$

and Y is the consumer's income.

Using Lagrangian multipliers, the following function is formed:

$$Z = u(q_i, \lambda_{ij}) + \phi \left(\sum_i p_i q_i - Y\right) \qquad (3.6)$$

Assuming[6] the quality dimensions are continuous and that there is no direct substitution between quantity and quality, if we set the partial derivatives of Z with respect to the quality dimensions λ_{ij} and the q_i equal to zero, we find that for each λ_{ij} we have:

$$\frac{\partial u}{\partial \lambda_{ij}} = \phi q_i \frac{\partial p_i}{\partial \lambda_{ij}} \qquad (3.7)$$

ϕ is, of course, the marginal utility of income. Equation (3.7) therefore states that, in equilibrium, the marginal utility of a given dimension equals the marginal utility of the income spent to obtain the increment of λ_{ij}.

It follows from equation (3.7) that the marginal rate of substitution for the same commodity i between quality dimensions m and n is proportional to the ratio of their (implicit) quality prices. That is:

$$\frac{\left(\dfrac{\partial u}{\partial \lambda_{im}}\right)}{\left(\dfrac{\partial u}{\partial \lambda_{in}}\right)} = \frac{\left(\dfrac{\partial p_i}{\partial \lambda_{im}}\right)}{\left(\dfrac{\partial p_i}{\partial \lambda_{in}}\right)} \qquad (3.8)$$

Similarly, for the mth quality dimension of the rth commodity with the nth quality of the sth good:

$$\frac{\left(\dfrac{\partial u}{\partial \lambda_{rm}}\right)}{\left(\dfrac{\partial u}{\partial \lambda_{sn}}\right)} = \frac{\left(q_r \dfrac{\partial p_r}{\partial \lambda_{rm}}\right)}{\left(q_s \dfrac{\partial p_r}{\partial \lambda_{sn}}\right)} \qquad (3.9)$$

Returning to the assumptions underlying this approach, we are faced with a number of problems. Firstly, what attributes does the consumer consider, and do these attributes yield utility or disutility? Secondly, can implicit prices of these attributes be obtained from consumer behaviour in the transport market?

Direct contact by means of enquiries is one means of finding the importance passengers attach to modal attributes. A number of such enquiries have been conducted on urban trips, see for instance Stopher [9]. As expected, speed, comfort and reliability were deemed to be important. Whether utility or disutility is derived from the trip itself is arguable. The problem has arisen from the search for a general model of behaviour. Some passengers enjoy making a trip for they derive satisfaction from travel itself. On the contrary, others find travelling in general, and certain trips in particular, irksome. The apparent drive to minimise travelling time, for instance, has suggested the attribute of time spent travelling is a disutility. The generalisation of this approach is to suggest that the traveller chooses that mode which minimises the disutility of travel. The dominating force resulting in the adoption of this approach has been the wish to obtain a measure of the value of time, sometimes causing highly restrictive constraints to be imposed on the utility function.

A method of calculating the weights to attach to the quality dimensions is to regress on the prices of transport modes these quality dimensions. The coefficients from say a linear regression would give directly the size of such weights.[7]

The use of this result for demand analysis can be seen if we examine a situation in which we have time series data of an air carrier on a given route. Suppose we have data for say 20 years, on demand, income, prices, speed, comfort, regularity and other quality dimensions of the mode. To regress demand on price, as is perhaps likely in the classical approach, would clearly lead to biased estimates. This can be shown by dividing up the observed price change of a commodity with observable quality dimensions into changes due to qualitative changes, and changes in price independent of such changes.

The price changes can be decomposed as follows:

$$d p_i = d \bar{p}_i + \Sigma \frac{\partial p_i}{\partial \lambda_{ij}} \, d\lambda_{ij} \qquad\qquad (3.10)$$

where p_i is the recorded change in price, $\bar{p}_i$ the change in price that would have occurred irrespective of any qualitative change, while the second

term $\Sigma \dfrac{\partial p_i}{\partial \lambda_{ij}} \, d \, \lambda_{ij}$ refers to the changes in prices due to quality changes.

Given p_o as a base price, and differing modes q_i, a qualitative change index could be constructed as follows: [8]

$$\frac{\underset{i}{\Sigma} \, q_{i0} \, p'_{it}}{\Sigma \, q_{i0} \, p_{i0}} = \frac{\underset{i}{\Sigma} \, q_{i0} \, \left[p_{it} - \underset{j}{\Sigma} \left(\frac{\partial p_i}{\partial \lambda_{ij}} \right) (\lambda_{ijt} - \lambda_{ijo}) \right]}{\Sigma_i \, q_{io} \, p_{i0}}$$

The inclusion of such a deflated price index could then be applied in an explanation of aggregate (i.e. across modes) demand between modes.

A problem arises, however, in the weights attached to λ_{in}, i.e. in the calculation of implicit prices for the qualitative attributes of the mode. The problem here is that the transport market is subjected to considerable price control.

It is true differences in prices reflect to some extent differences in modal attributes. The more comfortable first class compartments are charged a higher price, trips taken at an inconvenient hour are cheaper ('off-peak fares'), in some countries a ticket for the express train service is higher than for a stopper train. On the whole, though, the pricing restrictions have served to reduce the degree of discriminatory pricing. On international routes, services of faster jets are priced no higher than slower propeller aircraft, in the UK the price of the stopper train is the same as for the express. Non-price competition in fact has been a dominating characteristic of passenger transportation, a response to restrictions imposed on discriminatory pricing.

In view of these market imperfections, we are faced with the fact that the price charged for particular modes are unlikely to reflect the satisfactions yielded by the mode's particular attributes. It would appear that cross-section estimates of modal attributes regressed against fares will fail to give meaningful implicit prices. Consumers are not in equilibrium, their expenditure is not in proportion to the increase in satisfaction generated. Thus, the $\partial p_i / \partial \lambda_{ij}$ are likely to be too high (or too low) relative to their quality attributes. As we have seen in equation (3.9), in a market with unrestricted prices consumer purchases and $\partial p_i / \partial \lambda_{ij}$ will adjust until consumer satisfaction is reached. However, as is shown in the right hand side of equation (3.10), if the prices are restricted, equilibrium between the marginal rates of substitution and the 'prices' of the quality dimensions will be obtained by changes in the ratios of q_r to q_s. Thus, an overpriced commodity will be faced with a decline in its purchase, and this will be reflected in a decline in its weight in the index.

There are practical problems, however, of extracting changes in qualitative dimensions from market price changes. It could be reasonably argued that individual routes are themselves unique commodities, between which little substitution takes place. Significant trip substitutions between say London to Glasgow and London to Bristol is limited. To obtain statistically estimatable cross-sections of prices on a given route, even if all modes were included, is unlikely. To use cross-section estimates across a range of routes may be permissible, but there is the difficulty of obtaining passenger breakdown into classes, peak and off-peak, express and stopper. To use weighted fare averages defeats the purpose of the exercise.

Data limitations prevented the full utilisation of the approach outlined above. Nevertheless, as the next section shows, the emphasis on quality dimensions is upheld and introduced explicitly into the models.

Before introducing these models, it is instructive to examine earlier studies using some of these notions of quality dimensions.

One attempt using some of the ideas of this approach has been made by Baumol and Quant [10]. Their 'abstract mode approach', as they called it, viewed transport as a commodity with quality dimensions. The demand model developed estimates from an equation reflecting passenger choices for all modes. The modes are characterised by quality dimensions – speed, comfort, etc. – but these are defined relative to the value attained by the 'best' mode between the origin and destination in question. The assumption is that the passenger chooses a mode by comparing the performance of the particular quality attribute of a mode to the mode that is the best in this quality dimension. Thus, a car traveller considers the time taken to travel by car with the time taken to travel by air, the mode with the best speed attribute. This also implies that changes in quality attributes of a mode which are not the best (e.g. car travel time), have no effect on demand. The transport commodity is deemed to consist of the best attributes of the modes serving the route, modal choice being affected by changes in these best attributes relative to the mode's attributes.

The model estimated by Baumol and Quant is also interesting in the way they include a generation term. Their model is as follows:

$$D_{ijk} = \alpha_o \, (P_i)^{\alpha_1} \, (P_j)^{\alpha_2} \, (C^b_{ij})^{\alpha_3} \, (C^r_{ijk})^{\alpha_4} \, (H^b_{ij})^{\alpha_5} \, (H^r_{ijk})^{\alpha_6} \, (F^r_{ijk})^{\alpha_7} \, (Y_{ij})^{\alpha_8}$$

D_{ijk} = the number of trips between nodes i and j

P_iP_j = the populations of i and j
C_{ij}^b = the least travel cost between i and j
C_{ij}^r = the cost for the kth mode divided by the least cost
H_{ijk}^r = the travel time for the kth mode divided by the least travel time
H_{ijk}^b = the shortest travel time between i and j
Y_{ij} = the weighted average income at i and j.

As can be seen, the use of this model on cross-section data involved a 'penetration' component (similar to a gravity model), P_iP_j, and an income component. The model used the total values of the variables, and estimated on the logarithms. However, problems of cross-sectional estimation were observed, for as Quant and Baumol [10] observed: 'Although cross-sectional approaches of the type being discussed here often yield good correlations, they frequently result in very bad predictions of the future. This may occur because the parameters characterising the cross-sectional relation may change over time.'

We shall see in Chapter 4 that this problem of time varying coefficients has to be seriously considered when formulating forecasting models.

A direct approach to the estimation of modal choice using a general non-linear utility function to the quality dimensions has been given by Quant [11]. He assumes the individual disutility of modal choice has the form:

$$u = \alpha x_1^\beta x_2^\gamma$$

where x_1, x_2 are quality dimensions and where α, β and γ are random variables, varying across consumers, and independently distributed, having the exponential form:

$$f(\alpha) = a\, e^\alpha$$

The probability of an individual travelling by any one mode is defined as P, found by evaluating a joint probability integral. Assuming two modes, the fraction of travellers Q on each of the two modes i and j is given by:

$$Q_i = \frac{P_i}{P_i + P_j} \quad \text{and} \quad Q_j = \frac{P_j}{P_i + P_j}$$

Not only is the modal split defined, but changes in the modal split can be calculated (by changing the limits of the integration), and modal elasticities defined.

Letting D_i and D_j be the total traffic volumes on modes i and j, the modal split is:

$$M_i = \frac{D_i}{D_i + D_j} \text{ and } M_j = 1 - M_i$$

The modal split elasticity[9] of mode i with respect to price (f_i) is

$$E_{ifi} = \frac{\partial M_i}{\partial f_i} \cdot \frac{f_i}{M_i} = \frac{\partial \left({D_i}/{D_i + D_j} \right)}{\partial f_i} \cdot \frac{f_i}{\left(D_i/D_i + D_j \right)}$$

We shall now turn to the models which incorporate many of these concepts, and which have been built specifically to deal with aspects of the market served by air transport modes.

3.4 Model forms suitable for domestic and international air traffic

We have seen the nature of modal competition, and the competition between air/rail and air/sea. Our starting point, therefore, is that the reactions to competition of the operators reflects the true nature of modal choice as seen by the passengers. Hence in considering models for air (and rail and road transport modes) we assume two distinct travel goods, air/rail and air/sea.

Earlier research suggests that the demand for each of these sets of substitutable commodities are, in *total*, functions of:

1 Population and distance on each route.
2 Income effects (accounting for most of the secular shift).

Prices, times of each mode and its immediate competitor(s) account for short run demand effects.[10] If we attempt to describe traffic *differences between different routes*, or alternatively to estimate coefficients across cross-section data, we must include a 'generation' term. The traditional gravity model form:[11]

$$D = \frac{k \, (\text{Pop}i \cdot \text{Pop}_j)}{(\text{Distance})}$$

relates demand to population product and distance. An extended form due to Tanner is more appropriate for long distances

$$D = \frac{k\,(\text{Pop}_i \cdot \text{Pop}_j)}{(\text{Distance}_{ij})^n}\,exp[\,-\,\text{Distance}_{ij}\,]$$

A variety of these forms is tested in the next chapter and used in parameter estimation and forecasting.

In the last section we examined the consumer utility (or disutility) function, and discussed the modal dimensions which were included. Included in these quality dimensions were time, price and frequency. Let us examine the dimensions of time and frequency and see how they can be included in model estimates.

Of the several possible measures of journey time relevant to the individual's utility for air travel, we can consider:

1   Technical journey time (airport to airport), *Tr.*
2   City centre to city centre time. This will mean adding to *Tr* the two airport to terminal times, *Tcc.*
3   *Tr* or *Tcc*, together with *waiting time*.

3.4.1   *Frequency of service and waiting time*

This last measure, waiting time, is clearly relative to the item, 'frequency of service'. Let us consider some measure of this. We can either include

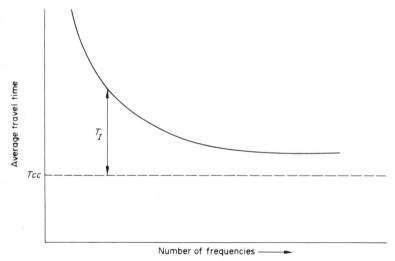

Fig. 3.1   Frequencies and travel time

frequency of service as a distinct qualitative attribute (as well as the technical journey time):

$$u = f^n \text{ (price, journey time, frequency of service)}$$

or else include it in the form in which it is actually perceived by the customer, i.e. some measure of waiting time:

$$u = f^n \text{ (price, journey time, waiting time)}.$$

We could even assume that waiting time has the same dimension and effects as journey time and add the two items together

$$u = f^n \text{ (price, total travel time)}.$$

This is the simplest approach if we consider the 'desire to travel' arises randomly over the day and that the total travel time includes the waiting time between services. This is illustrated in Fig. 3.1.

Hence, the average total travel time $= Tcc + T_I$
when Tcc = centre to centre time
and T_I = the average inter-arrival time
and $T_I = \frac{1}{2} TD/f$
where TD = period length
and f = number of services in period TD.

The variation in this waiting time and average travel time over the period of growth of an air route (where the offered numbers of flights change from 1/day to 12/day) is enormous, almost as to change entirely the character of the offered commodity. It is obvious that the frequency effect must be included in the demand estimate. The neglect of this effect, as we shall see, deprives many models of any meaning.

3.4.2 Structures of demand model

The above development of consumer utility and passenger travel suggests the following demand model for each mode; DK, on each route, ij:

$$DK_{ijt} = f^n (P_{kt}, P_{ct}, T_{tkt}, T_{tct}, T_{wkt}, T_{wct}, Y_t)$$

where P_{kt} = fare on mode K at time t
T_{tkt} = journey time on mode K at time t
T_{wtk} = waiting time on mode K at time t
Y_t = income
c refers to the competing mode.

We must now consider the extent to which this model can be identified. We shall leave the problem of inter-model competition and the possibility of simultaneous determination of prices and journey time until Chapter 3, and instead at this stage assume that the chances of such effects are remote. We will presume that any relationship between costs and innovation on the one hand and demand on the other hand are probably of a low order. It also seems reasonable to assume that income time series Y_t are exogenous — neglecting, therefore, the development of income in a city as a consequence of transport. Hence we assume that the demand relationship is identifiable in Y.

When we come to consider waiting time, however, we can see that, though frequency is a variable governed by the operator (and the licensing authorities),[12] it is also evident that changes in frequency over time relate to the *supply side* of the market and that this supply is related to *demand* in a very strong simultaneous relationship. In the case of domestic air travel the former Air Transport Licensing Board has used frequency licensing as a means of regulating supply, and of *stimulating* competition.[13] In the case of rail, road and sea transport offered frequencies have changed very little over the period examined, but on air, with very rapid growth on all routes, frequencies obviously relate to traffic demand.

Details of BEA operating behaviour (see Figure 3.2),[14] shows the strong, lagged relationship between supply changes (frequency changes) and demand changes. Furthermore, if we examine the time scale of filing applications for licenses, hearings, etc., it seems reasonable to postulate a supply relationship relating changes in frequencies offered to demand in terms of something like a one year lag.

Hence, even under these simplifying assumptions, the minimum description of the transport system from which we can estimate the demand on for *a mode* and *on a given route* is the set of three simultaneous equations:

$$DK_{ijt} = f\ (P_{kt}, P_{ct}, T_{rkt}, T_{rct}, T_{wkt}, T_{wct}, Y_t) \qquad (3.11)$$
$$T_{wkt} = f(\text{frequency } K_t) \qquad (3.12)$$
$$\text{Frequency } K_t = f(D_{k\,t\text{-}1}) \qquad (3.13)$$

For *forecasting* demand, the most acceptable approach is to substitute a form of the supply equation (3.12) and (3.13) into the demand equation (3.11), producing a reduced form equation with an autoregressive component. Demand at t is now a function of price, income and journey time at t, and also of demand at t-1.

In forecasting individual and aggregate routes, we must, of course, recognise that aggregate routes are likely to contain routes of differing maturities and, therefore, of differing frequencies. When we come to examine aggregate routes in Chapter 4 we must, therefore, deal with a number of variants of these model forms.

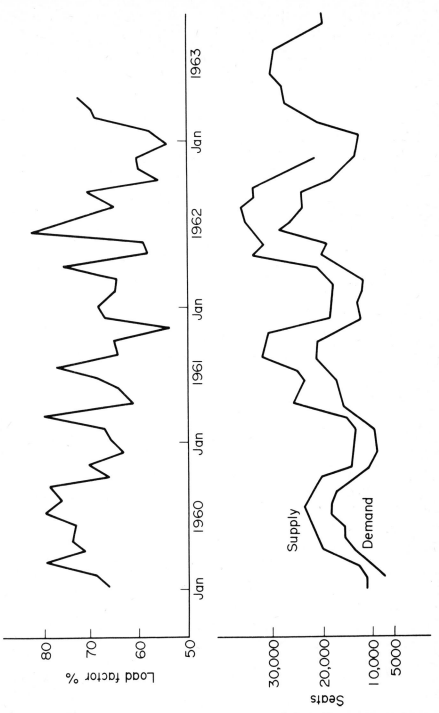

Fig. 3.2   Air supply, demand and load factor for a typical route

3.5 Conclusions

Partitioning the transport process, one can recognise the initial desire to travel, the determinants of this desire, the choice of destination and the choice of mode. A comprehensive passenger demand model would involve an explanation of this generation of transport desires, the origin and destination of flows and the modal choice. Over the long run, consideration would also have to be given to the simultaneity aspects in, for instance, the interaction of transport location, income generation and modal choice.

Data availability limits such a comprehensive scheme. Emphasis has instead been centred on modal choice, and on the consideration of the factors generating intercity travel. Special interest has centred on the interaction of service qualities and modal demand. It has been found that supply changes through frequency variation effect considerably waiting time. In turn waiting time and trip time are important determinants of modal choice, along with price and income.

The next chapter deals with the application of these models to time series data on various UK domestic and international routes.

Notes

[1] See A. P. Ellison [1] for a survey of some of the problems of forecasting air passenger demand with econometric models.

[2] Here we are assuming, along with the classical approach, that transport modes have no qualitative dimensions. In this case 'other variables' here refers to determinants of demand other than those qualitative dimensions such as the age or sex of the traveller.

[3] Some of the early work concerning quality dimensions in demand analysis was conducted by H. Theil [3], H. S. Houthakker [4] and H. S. Houthakker and S. J. Prais [5]. Similar work was also conducted on factor inputs. See H. Brems [6].

[4] Later work was developed in the sixties by K. Lancaster [7] and I. Adelman and Z. Griliches [8]. The latter approach is also the basis of the treatment of technological improvement in aircraft. This will be dealt with in Chapter 5, where models of aircraft orders are developed.

[5] See Houthakker [4], p. 156 for the use of this utility function.

[6] For the development of this analysis see I. Adeleman and Z. Griliches [8], p. 546–548.

[7] For example, $P_i = a_o + a_1\lambda_{ij} + a_2 \lambda_{ik} + \ldots + a_n\lambda_{in} + u_t$ when the a's are the weights and equal the respective $\dfrac{\partial P_i}{\partial \lambda_{ij}}$.

[8] Such an index has been used to deflate aircraft prices. See Chapter 5 for details.

[9] Notice that the modal split elasticity with respect to price will be less in absolute value to the size of the sales elasticity with respect to price.

Given $m_i = \dfrac{D_i}{D_i + D_j}$ let us denote this as $q_i = m_{iq}$ where $q \equiv D_i$ and D_j and $q_i \equiv D_i$

$$\frac{\partial q_i}{\partial f_i} = \frac{\partial m_i}{\partial f_i} q + \frac{\partial q}{\partial f_i} \cdot m_i \text{ and, therefore,}$$

the sales elasticity $\qquad \dfrac{\partial q_i}{\partial f_i} \cdot \dfrac{f_i}{q_i} + \dfrac{\partial m}{\partial f_i} \cdot \dfrac{f_i}{m_i} + \dfrac{\partial q}{\partial f_i} \cdot \dfrac{f_i}{q}$

i.e. sales elasticity = modal split elasticity + aggregate sales with respect to the ith price.

[10] See the next chapter for a discussion of these points.

[11] See Isard [12] Chapter 11 for a derivation and development of the gravity model.

[12] See Chapter 4: Domestic routes section.

[13] See for instance questions 546—550 in the second report from the Select Committee on Nationalised Industries: BEA October 1967.

[14] Supply and demand in Figure 3.2 are represented as seats supplied and demanded. This of course does not exactly represent frequency changes owing to developments in aircraft size and speed. The route example, however, was operated by Viscount 700s during the period observed.

References

1 A. P. Ellison, 'Forecasting passenger air demand', *Flight International*, 8 July 1971.

2 I. Morrisett, 'Some recent uses of the elasticity of substitution — a survey', *Econometrica*, 1953.

3 H. Theil, 'Qualities, prices and budget enquiries', *Review of Economic Studies*, 1951—52.

4   H. S. Houthakker, 'Compensated changes in quantities and qualities consumed', *Review of Economic Studies*, 1951—52.

5   H. S. Houthakker and S. J. Prais, 'Les variations de qualité dans les budgets de famille', *Economic Applique*, 1952.

6   H. Brems, *Product equilibrium under monopolistic competition*, Cambridge (Mass.) 1951.

7   K. Lancaster, 'A new approach to consumer theory', *Journal of Political Economy*, 1966.

8   I. Adelman and Z. Griliches, 'On an Index of Quality Change', *American Statistical Association Journal*, September 1961.

9   P. R. Stopher, 'Journey to work', Ph. D. thesis, University College London 1967.

10 W. J. Baumol and R. E. Quant, 'The demand for abstract transport modes. Theory and measurement', *Journal of Regional Science*, vol. 6, no. 2, 1966.

11 R. E. Quant, 'Estimation of modal splits', *Transportation Research*, vol. 2, 1968.

12 W. Isard, *Methods of Regional Analysis*, Wiley, 1960.

4 Air Passenger Demand Estimates

4.1 Introduction

The last chapter developed in a general way a number of demand models applicable to routes of differing characteristics. It is the purpose of this chapter to apply some of these models to particular UK domestic and international routes. Later chapters, particularly Chapter 9, will be devoted, in part, to estimating the movement in world passenger demand. Such an exercise is, of course, an integral part of the model outlined in Chapter 2. It is also useful and important to be aware of the demand characteristics on a wide range of individual routes and route groups. This, after all, is the level of disaggregation at which policy is often concerned.

Most of the information on which the models are tested is in the form of time series. Such data brings with it many problems. Added to the usual ones such as multi-collinearity, serial correlation and simultaneity are the civil aviation market's own characteristics. Its rapid growth and vulnerability to changes in economic conditions highlight the problems of trends and movements about trends. Special attention, therefore, is paid to short and long run responses to income and price changes, to methods of explaining secular trends in growth, and causes of fluctuations. Where possible, generalisations concerning the size of parameters and the appropriateness of certain model forms will be made. The approach, however, is to treat routes and route groups as unique, each with differing passenger characteristics, developments and histories. Such differences require different approaches and different models. Much of the discussion in fact will be concerned with examining the appropriateness of one or other model to routes of certain characteristics.

The data used in the estimates has been derived from diverse sources. The air data is largely in the form of time series observations, the estimated routes accounting for some 90 per cent of internal UK traffic, and the major share of the UK/overseas air traffic. In the case of civil routes, extensive time series runs on UK routes are not available. There is fairly extensive cross-sectional information available, and so it was possible to utilise a wide cross-section of aggregate two way annual flows for the year

1965. The road data utilised road passenger and private car details. Time series data, on a monthly basis, was obtained directly from the bus operators. The information covered four major UK routes. Private car data was thin, but the 1965 National Travel Survey covered car travel between a small number of city pairs. Cordons on a number of key points on major trunk roads provided estimates of annual inter-city flows.

Before embarking on an exposition of the estimating techniques, a number of cautionary remarks are needed. In order to ease statistical estimation, much of the data has been aggregated. Yet within these aggregated flows often lie distinct classes of traffic, with their own fares. Lack of consistent information and strong seasonal variations were often the reasons for the use of aggregate flows. Hence, data on fares, times, etc. used in the estimated models represent the averages of these variables, weighted by the relative time periods during which the various values were operative.

Two further simplifying assumptions were made. We have assumed that routes are largely independent, and consequently we have ignored assignment. Secondly, where possible we have introduced the competitive effect of closely competing modes, but the majority of the results relate demand to the particular modal characteristics.

4.2   Problems of estimation

The previous chapter outlined the theoretical underpinnings of passenger demand estimation and forecasting. In this section we shall examine the problems of estimating these models, and techniques of overcoming them.

The problems spring from the inherent nature of the data, particularly if the data is in the form of time series. The lack of control of the experimenter over the 'experiment' necessitates controlling the variables in ways which allow their impact to be estimated. Some of these problems overlap, but we shall roughly divide them into the following sections:

1   Structure of demand.
2   Multi-collinearity and interdependence of variables.
3   Trends; the long and the short run.

The next section will then examine methods of overcoming these difficulties.

4.2.1 Structure of demand

Some variables, such as population and other demographic variables can be termed 'static' in that they change very slowly over time. Other variables, such as time and price, change frequently and sometimes continuously throughout the time period. We must therefore consider some possible structures for the model: in particular assumptions about the dynamic nature of the partial responses.

The economic distinction between short and long run refers not to the rate of variation of the independent variables but to the response time period of the dependent variable to a change in one of the independent variables. Hence, in an assumed first order linear continuous relationship between demand and price the time constant response, T, is the critical factor.

If we test for the income coefficient of demand response by using a cross-sectional model, we will normally be testing an assumed

$$D = f^n (P)$$

relationship, as above, across a set of observations, where the demand (the dependent) and income (the independent) variables relate to the same period. The necessary assumptions, to obtain meaningful coefficients are that either:

1   The response is extremely fast (time constant, T, is small), or
2   That the tested independent variable (here income) has shown negligible variation on each route in the time periods immediately preceding the testing period compared to the variation between routes.

Similarly, if we know or could postulate with confidence, a long run response covering, say, two time periods or one period dead-time response we could show and allow for it in the model specification. For illustrative purposes of this point see Fig. 4.1.

The relationship between long run and short run elasticities can be illustrated by means of the following demand function:

Let $\bar{q}_t$ = the quantity demanded in long run equilibrium

q_t = the current quantity demanded

It is postulated that the current quantity consumed will change in proportion to the difference between the long run quantity ($\bar{q}_t$) and the short run quantity (q_t).

Therefore $$q_t - q_{t-1} = \alpha(\bar{q}_t - q_{t-1}) \qquad (4.1)$$

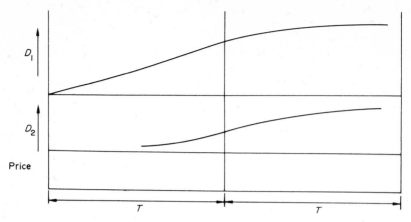

Fig. 4.1   Time response with effect to price

If we now suggest the following long run demand function

$$\bar{q}_t = aP_t + bY_t + c \qquad (4.2)$$

where P = price, Y = income (expressed in logs)

Substituting (4.2) into (4.1) yields

$$q_t = a\alpha P_t + b\alpha Y_t + (1-\alpha)\, q_{t-1} + c\alpha$$

In such an estimating equation the coefficient of the lagged quantity variable q_{t-1} will produce the value of α, allowing the long run price and income elasticities to be calculated.

In practice, the problem is to decide the length of time denoted by t. Evidence to a Transport Commission hearing suggested that British Rail consider that 12 months is required to register the full effects of price changes on demand. Evans [1] also used 12 months for a before-and-after survey of effects of electrification (changing journey time) on demand, suggesting that the full response is expected to be within this period. These are, however, insubstantial bases for specification.

4.2.2   Multi-collinearity and interdependence of variables

One of the major problems in estimation from time series data is the high degree of multi-collinearity in the data, leading to bias in the estimates. As we shall see when we come to examine the estimates in the sections below, the changes in the coefficients due to the inclusion of extra variables bears out the extent of this collinearity on many of the routes. If we wish to distinguish between price, income and time elasticities, this is a problem, for the significance of the coefficient estimates is seriously challenged. For forecasting purposes, the problem is perhaps not as serious, for if the collinearity remains the same over the projected period (e.g. income and price continue to move together as they did during the period estimated) the coefficient estimates have the merit of giving good, i.e. accurate, forecasts. If collinearity is not maintained, the problem remains. This question will be faced in the next section.

The problem of interdependence follows from inter-modal competition, where air/surface competitors are able to respond to competitive policies. For instance, suppose air operators lower fares, and within the period of observation (say a year) the surface competitor is able to adjust fares in response. The difficulty from an estimating point of view is the possibility of obtaining 'perverse' cross price elasticity coefficients from such a competitive structure. This is a possibility on UK domestic routes, where air competes strongly with rail. The problem is explored in the section below, but before doing so we shall outline the bias that such a structure is likely to induce.

Suppose the estimating equation relates the quantities demanded on air to the air fare and the rail fare. Given that air has administered fares, a reduction in say air fare will lead to a shift down the air demand curve, and an increase in output sold. The rail operator, on the other hand, would be faced with a fall in air travel price and, although rail and air are not necessarily supplying at the same price, the effect would be to force rail down its supply curve and to lower its price in turn. The observations in the regression would show a rise in the quantity of air seats sold, a fall in the price of rail, leading to a negative rail cross price elasticity. The greater freedom of rail to alter is fares (without the former control of the Transport Tribunal after 1962) is likely to cause its price reactions to be swifter than if it is constrained by administrative machinery, and furthermore, it has the greater possibility of becoming the price leader in this market. We shall examine the extent of these influences in section 4.2.4.

4.2.3 *Trends: the short and long run*

An examination of the behaviour of individual and aggregate routes over time in section 4.1 showed considerable differences in the behaviour of passenger growth. Most of the routes however displayed marked trends, some of them approximating to well known functional types. From an estimating viewpoint, the problem is to deduce the trend, and trend variables, from the short run effects, i.e. from those variables which cause short run deviations from the trend. For long run forecasts, it is perhaps with respect to the trend that interest centres, but if estimates of variables are required, such as price elasticities, a correct specification of long- (trend) and short run variables are required. It is here that the problems of distinguishing the trend emerge with the problems of multi-collinearity, in that the trends in passenger growth, fares and income are usually in the same direction. We shall explore ways of countering these influences, but before doing so we shall discuss possible forms of the long run trend.

As we shall see when we examine empirical studies of behaviour from cross-section studies, air travel has shown itself to be characterised by passengers who are in the higher income groups. Furthermore, growth can be expected to take place from passengers who are new to the mode. One obvious hypothesis when considering the growth of air travel is that much of the growth associated with the mode is the spread of transport as a 'new good'. This 'growth' might equally apply to the growth of the total quantity of passenger trips on a route or growth of the share of air among all transport modes. The assumption is that air transport as a new good is unknown to the majority, that its purchase is an innovation and will spread throughout the population over a time period. The rate of spread of this innovation will increase to a maximum and will then decline. At the end of this period, the market is saturated.

A very common function used in many empirical studies to represent this behaviour has been the logistic function [2]. The differential equation of this function can be written[1] :

$$\frac{dD}{dt} = a\,D\,(L - D)$$

where D = demand for travel and L = saturation level of demand for travel. Many of the empirical studies using this sort of model relate to consumer durables, such as motor cars, washing machines, television sets, where prior assumptions about saturation levels of the individual (or the utility to the individual of the good in question) can be easily made. Hence a saturation level of one washing machine per family can be confidently assumed.

For air travel, however, trends differ, and the basic trend of passen-ger flights cannot be said to be represented by a logistic or some similar function. If there is any one consistent growth curve, it is logarithmic and the only evidence for such is provided by US data.[2] Furthermore, periodic cross-section estimates in the UK and USA suggest that the number of flights taken per annum, particularly by the higher income groups, is increasing. There is little evidence, in other words, to assume a given upper limit of the number of air trips taken per annum. However, we shall return to the use of trend forecasting in the final section.

Referring to the trend and short run in a more formal framework, we can postulate the demand relationship in the following way:

$$D_t = F(X_t^i) + G(Z_t^i)$$

where X_t^i are short run effects and Z_t^i are long run effects. X_t^i. and Z_t^i are not restricted to be disjunct sets, and in particular no assumption is made that income is a variable with only long run effects. (We shall deal with such a model below.)

From an estimating viewpoint, the technique is a two stage estimating one, where the short run variables are specified, 'removed', i.e. estimated, and then the residual regressed upon the long run variables, whether long or short run, and the shape of the trend. Fisher [5] in his study of the decline of rail passenger traffic on one US route (Boston–New York) starts with the assumption that the long term trend in rail passenger movements is exponential. By taking first differences of logs of variables he removes the effect of this secular trend, and tests the short run responses of the model. In his model, income and fares (rail, air and bus) were short run variables, the trend then being explained by the growth in car stock.

Brown and Watkins [3] follow the Fisher short run form to estimate parameters of demand for air passenger traffic. An annual time series of 18 years (1948–1966) was used, not for any particular route, but for the entire US domestic market. The model, in which fares, income and time were designated as short run variables, treated air transport as a distinct commodity. No attempt was made to calculate the long term effects directly from the time series; instead a technique due to Nerlove [6] was used. Differences in traffic flows between routes were estimated separately using cross-sectional data of the major 300 city pair routes in 1960. The model included the following variables: fares, quality of service, distance, community of interest, the product of incomes in the city pairs and an index of sales promotion. The results of the study are contained in the summary of studies in Appendix A4.3.

In using this technique, which treats short run effects (of variables which are considered 'short run') as deviations from the trend, correct specification of the trend has to be made. Differences of logs implies an

101

exponential trend,[3] logs of first differences a linear trend. In view of the earlier examination of route growth in section 4.1, no particular trend can be assumed. The advantage of using the logarithmic transform is of course that the coefficient estimates yield constant elasticities, a most convenient form for forecasting. There are difficulties of such an approach. With a linear trend sometimes the first differences are negative (this is particularly the case for domestic and European routes in the period 1957/58, where there was a severe economic slump), in which case logarithmic transforms are meaningless.

There are other approaches which treat the trend in a similar fashion, except that the trend variables are specified *a priori*, and then removed, upon which the remaining variables are regressed. This approach removes the trend first of all, and then regresses the short run variables. For a theoretical treatment of this approach see M. R. Straszheim [7].

A similar approach is to estimate the trend variable from outside data, then remove this variable and proceed to regress the other variables on the residual. For instance, suppose we pose a model with constant elasticities, with three explanatory variables:

$$\text{price } (P), \text{ income } (Y) \text{ and air time } (T)$$

We have therefore

$$D_t = \alpha_o \, Y_t^{\alpha_1} \, P^{\alpha_2} \, T^{\alpha_3} \, U_t$$

where U_t is an error term.

If we take an outside estimate of income elasticity, i.e. α_1, from some study conducted on cross-section data, we can use it to estimate the remaining coefficients, α_2 and α_3, by regressing the residual on price and air time: $(\log D_t - \hat{\alpha}_1 \log Y_t) = \log \alpha_0 + \alpha_2 \log P_2 + \alpha_3 \log T_3 + \log U_t$

The estimate of the income coefficient in this example is important, for as we have mentioned above, we must be careful in our specification of trend factors. Firstly, we must make sure whether it is the main determinant of the trend, and secondly whether the coefficients we estimate can be assumed to be constant. There is reason to doubt the latter assumption, as we shall see.

In the UK over the last few years a number of studies have taken cross-sectional data of passenger behaviour, from which it is possible to calculate income elasticity. This supplements evidence derived from the continent of Europe [8], and the US studies [9]. We shall here concentrate on the more recent UK and Continental studies.

102

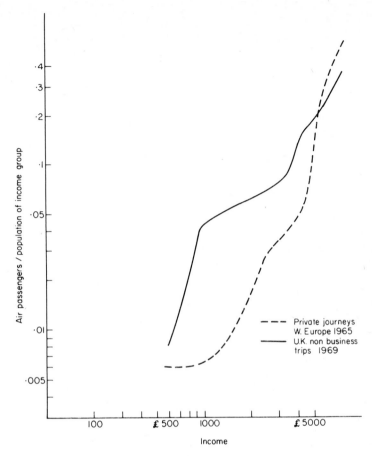

Fig. 4.2   Income elasticities, UK and Western Europe

The Roskill Commission has produced cross-section information of non-business flying passengers, the revised figures for which are displayed in Figure 4.2. The propensity to travel (the number travelling in each income group divided by the population within the income group) is related to the head of household income. This information can of course yield income elasticities, in this case the changes in propensity to travel being related to changes in income, the assumption being that a head of household in a given income group would increase (or decrease) the number of trips he would make if his income were increased (or decreased) and he found himself in the next income bracket. His behaviour would than approximate to the number of trips taken by those passengers in the higher income groups.

The interesting information yielded by the French and UK study is that

103

the income elasticity is not constant. In fact, it can be roughly said (see Fig. 4.2) that the higher the income the higher the income elasticity. The importance of this fact is that we cannot talk about a given income elasticity for non-business air travel. It can be shown [10] that as income increases (say at a constant annual rate, as is assumed in the Roskill forecasts) the income elasticity will itself change, owing to the varying response of the passengers within the range of income. Furthermore, there is evidence that the cross-section estimates themselves are subject to variation. This time varying nature of cross-sectional estimates is shown by the results of an estimating model of air passenger traffic tested on cross-sectional data for 3 years: 1954/5, 1959/60 and 1963/4.

The demand model tested was

$$\frac{D}{Pop_i \, Pop_j} \cdot PA = \alpha_1 \frac{(Y_i \, Y_j)^{\alpha_2}}{Pop_i \, Pop_j} \cdot (A_i A_j)^{\alpha_3}$$

where D = air passengers between cities i and j; Pop_i, Pop_j = populations of i and j; PA = air fare between i and j; and $A_i A_j$ = total airport movements at i and j.

The model estimated total expenditure on air transport on route ij as a function of income and total airport movements. The assumption was that a large part of the secular growth of air on any route relates to familiarity with their mode (excluding charter flights). The results obtained from the cross-section estimated for the 3 years were as follows:

	α_1	α_2	α_3
1954/55	−3.517	0.02	0.27
1959/60	−0.082	0.715	0.32
1963/64	1.45	1.34	0.37

The clear indication of the results from this model were that cross-sectionally estimated coefficients varied regularly over time. Hence, we require models which will characterise specifically this time movement. Without such models we can put little reliance on the cross-sectional estimates.

4.2.4 *Business and non-business income elasticities*

Any examination of income elasticities must first of all consider the (possible) differing elasticities with respect to business and non-business travel. The French airport study [8], after considering cross-sectional evidence, weighted the two groups, and used a constant income elasticity of 2. Roskill considered the difference between business and non-business travel by deriving propensities to travel for non-business travel from the cross-sectional estimate, and then related the number of business trips to the number of business men in the population. The average increase in the propensity to travel for business reasons between 1962–1969 was 8 per cent, and it has been assumed to increase at this rate in the future, until a ceiling level of 6 air journeys per person per year is attained. Thus, Roskill considered the two separate groups, business and non-business, and made individual forecasts.

The above methods are ways of treating the possible differing elasticities, but there are other ways which can be used which rely on roughly the same kind of information, and which from an estimating point of view are more convenient.

If we examine the cross-section survey data available [11], we observe that domestic and international travel is predominantly restricted to:

1   A set of social groups (largely managerial/professional) for business travel.
2   A set of income groups (upper income groups) for non-business travel.

In the case of domestic travel these observations hold for both the two most expensive modes, rail and air.

If we postulate the relevant income variable for non-business travel, we are then able to calculate the number of potential travellers above a threshold income. This can be illustrated by means of Figure 4.3. Denoting the threshold income as Y_0, we can calculate the number of the population with excess income as

$$N = \int_{Y_0}^{\infty} P(Y)dY.$$

assuming that the income distribution function can be defined. We shall discuss this calculation below.

We will then make the following assumptions:

1   That business travel is dependent on general economic activity for which we will take mean income Y_m as a measure.
2   That non-business travel is dependent on the number of potential travellers above a threshold income, denoted as N potential passengers.
3   That the threshold income is around £1,500/annum[4] and is constant over time. Evidence of this point is provided by data from the Family

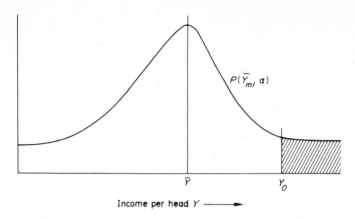

Fig. 4.3   Income distribution and threshold income

Expenditure Survey which shows that expenditure on travel as a whole as well as on the subsection including air is constant at each income level, over the entire period covered (see Mogridge's [12] study on car demand for confirmation of this point).

Given the cross-section data which clearly shows a threshold level of income for non-business travel, then the integral $N = \int_{Y_0}^{\infty} P(x).dx$ was calculated for each year of the time series for an assumed income distribution with constant variance and with a mean equal to the mean income Y_m for that year.

Confirmation of the constancy of the income distribution was taken by applying Pareto's function to income distributions between 1954–67. Pareto's 'law' suggests a function relating the percentage number income units above a given level, which can be represented as follows:

$$P(Y) = AY^{-\alpha}$$

where $P(Y)$ represents the percentage number of income units in excess of income Y. Here Y is the given income level and A, α are the parameters.

From this cumulative distribution function we can obtain the density function representing relative frequencies. In this formulation the given income Y is replaced by the threshold income, Y_0,

$$P(N) = AY_0^{-(\alpha+1)}$$

The parameters A and α were calculated for the years 1954–67 from Inland Revenue data [14] and the results confirmed earlier studies of Nicholson [15] and Mogridge [12] of the constancy of the parameter α.

106

We were thus able to calculate:

1 N for each year, representing potential non-business passengers.
2 Y_m for each year, the variable determining business passengers.

We could therefore proceed to enter the two time series Y_m and N separately, with a multiplicative demand function. However, if we take the ratio of N/Y_m and log each ratio, and then plot these ratios over time, we obtain a distribution as shown in Figure 4.4. As can be seen by the imposed line through these points, log (N/Y_m) with respect to time is linear. Hence, instead of entering the two time series separately, we can test the function $Y^{\alpha+Bt}$.

This function implies of course that the income elasticity will vary over time. The important implication of this is that a constant income elasticity is not to be expected over any lengthy period, as the characteristics of the travelling group are changing over time. Thus we obtain a 'point of time' income elasticity. This is consistent with the variation of the income elasticity changes over time which we have observed above. Furthermore,

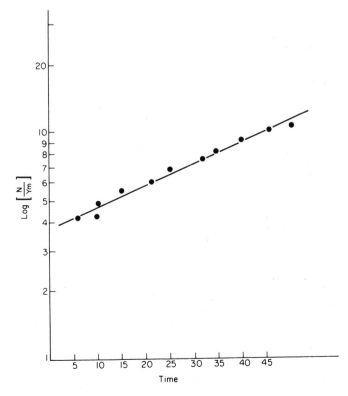

Fig. 4.4   log (N_t/Y_m) with respect to time

it neatly combines the two effects of business and non-business income elasticities.

It must be noted, however, that the formulation of the income elasticity in this form is purely a result of the integral limits and the time series behaviour of income over the period. It is therefore an historical observation.

We therefore have a number of approaches with which we can deal with the trend, and with the income effect in particular. One source of information is the Roskill Commission Report which divides the propensity to travel into various regions of the world, the derived figures from which are displayed in Table 4.1. This is a useful breakdown for it furnishes evidence of possible differing income elasticities on different routes, but the income differences are small. Despite these differences, an income elasticity for each route group has been calculated, the figure being derived from weights according to the percentage flying in particular income groups (see Table 4.1) on these routes.

With respect to business travellers' income elasticity we have mentioned above the assumptions made in the Roskill Report [5], and so if we use the Roskill figures on non-business travel, we shall have to estimate the respective weights to be apportioned to each type of travel on the various routes. The Paris airport study [8] came out with a figure of 2.0 as the combined income elasticity on inter-continental routes, while an estimate of the UK domestic routes for 1965 yielded an elasticity of 3.4. This consisted of the following model, regressed on twenty UK routes in 1965:

Table 4.1

UK propensities to travel (non-business)

Income/Route	Domestic and Ireland	Western Europe	North America	Rest of world
Up to £1,000	0.086	0.316	0.043	0.033
£1,000–2,000	0.142	0.513	0.063	0.071
£2,000–3,000	0.550	2.38	0.025	0.477
£3,000 +	0.637	2.67	0.382	0.552
Income elasticity	1.9	2.9	1.13	6.0

Source: Roskill Commission, vol. VII, para. 4.48.

$$D_{\text{air}} + D_{\text{rail}} = \alpha_0 \left(\frac{\text{Pop}_i \ \text{Pop}_j}{\text{Distance}^2}\right)^{\alpha_1} Y^{\alpha_2}$$

where D = annual passengers in 1965; Pop_i = population of city i in 1965; Y = income *per capita* of the cities in 1965.
This yielded the following results:

$$
\begin{aligned}
\alpha_0 &= 1.02 \\
\alpha_1 &= 0.632 \\
\alpha_2 &= 3.406 \\
R^2 &= 0.66
\end{aligned}
$$

The above discussion and results summarise the information and the coefficients we shall employ in the chapter. Before doing so, we shall briefly outline the models that will be estimated on the individual and the aggregated routes, and then in the next section we shall examine the data and methods of compiling the various variables.

4.2.5   Test models

We have mentioned the lack of uniformity in route and aggregate route growth over time. Consequently, we should not expect one particular model form to yield consistently satisfactory results. What we require therefore are models which account for the major determining variables, and methods of accounting for the trend.

The short run variables we shall include are air fare, competitive mode's fare, air time and air's frequency of service. As we have mentioned in Chapter 3, frequency of service is likely to be important in individual routes, less so in the cases of aggregate routes. We shall therefore examine separately aggregate and individual routes, making a distinction between those routes which have linear and exponential growth rates. In the former, logs of differences, in the latter differences of logs, will be appropriate methods of developing a two stage estimating model which treats short and long run elasticities separately.

The following models will be tested:

1   *Unrestricted*. In these models air traffic will be regressed upon income, fares and time.
2   *Two stage*. (a) In the first type of models short run influences will be examined, and then the long run variables accounted for:

$$\Delta \log \text{air demand} = \Delta \log \text{air fare} + \Delta \log \text{air time}$$
$$\log \Delta \text{air demand} = \log \Delta \text{air fare} + \log \Delta \text{air time}$$

Then the coefficients derived from these regressions will be used to generate a time series which will then be subtracted from the total number travelling. The residual will be regressed upon income, the form of the income elasticity being $Y^{\alpha} + \beta^t$.

(b) In the second type of model the long run trend will be removed first of all, using the income elasticity coefficients estimated from outside. The residual will then be regressed upon the short run variables — time and air fares.

3 *Individual routes.* These routes will include the term D_{t-1}, which as we have shown in Chapter 3, accounts for the effect of frequency.

4.2.6 *Data*

The independent variables have been obtained from disparate sources and methods. Dealing with income, the problem here is obtaining a detailed breakdown of income for regions and cities in the case of individual routes, and in the case of all routes, there is the problem of weighting. What weight should be given to the various countries or cities?

Dealing with the first point, a series of income indices have been calculated for UK cities, and these are described in detail in Appendix A4.3. With respect to foreign cities, no such study could be undertaken, so reliance has been placed on the income movements of the countries themselves. The second point concerning income weighting is difficult, but there is some evidence to show the particular direction of passenger flights. Survey data (see Ellison and Stafford [11]) has been available on travel origin on the major UK routes, showing rather surprisingly the extent to which London is a destination. For example the London/Liverpool route:

		Class of travel	
	Origin	First	Second
London/Liverpool			
Both directions	London	27%	23%
	Liverpool	43%	53%
	Elsewhere	30%	24%

As a result we have used income/head values for the domestic routes corresponding to the known origin of travel on that route.

In the case of overseas routes, the Board of Trade International Passenger survey gives the number of UK and foreign citizens travelling on the UK/foreign routes. For the aggregate routes in 1968 the following proportions were found to exist.

110

	Percentage UK
UK/France	54
Belgium	62
Netherlands	57
West Germany	54
Italy	80
Western Europe	72
Long haul	58
North Atlantic route	23

These weights have been used in the study.

Fares can be obtained in two ways. The division of total revenue by passenger miles, giving a fare per passenger mile. Another and more acceptable method is to obtain details of fares, and weight according to passengers in the various class groupings. The latter fare data has been used.[6]

Time data on domestic routes has been calculated by examining time changes on individual routes, and weighting according to route density. The time data on other routes was obtained by dividing aircraft miles by aircraft hours.

4.2.7 *Individual routes*

In this section we shall examine the results of applying the models developed in Chapter 3 to individual domestic and international routes. An institutional preface is required, however, if we are to evaluate the significance and reliability of these estimates, for as section 4.2.2 showed, the market structure within which estimates take place is as important in determining whether demand identification has been achieved, or whether price simultaneity exists. The latter is a potential problem in any air demand model including rail fares, for as we shall see, the freedom of charging allowed by rail on UK domestic routes may invalidate estimates in which rail fare is included as a variable.

Domestic air fares have been subjected to government control, direct or indirect, since the war. The Air Transport Advisory Council fixed fares during the period 1949 to 1960, subject to ministerial approval. From 1960 to 1972 the Air Transport Licensing Board authorised fare changes, and acted as a court when disputes arose between airlines and private individuals or regional boards. It was unable to show much initiative in introducing differing fare structures, and it was somewhat weakened in its authority by the power of reversal the minister had over its decisions.

111

The railways, on the other hand, have enjoyed for nearly a decade freedom of changing. During the fifties and early sixties (1953 to 1961) they were under the authority of Transport Tribunal, which had power to set maximum fares. This was removed by the 1962 Transport Act, which allowed the railways to charge fares which would cover their financial targets. No such freedom, however, has been given road transport operators. The licensing framework introduced in the 1930s has been largely maintained. The procedure is directed towards the reduction of 'wasteful' competition which was considered to exist between rail and road travel in the 1930s. One of the objectives of the licensing procedures was to control inter-modal competition, and the Commissions were given control of the choice of operator and the price charged. They were to fix fares so as to 'prevent wasteful competition with alternative forms of transport', and to consider 'the co-ordination of all forms of passenger transport, including transport by rail'.[7]

This brief survey of the institutional structure of the three modes shows that, with the exception of public passenger transport, important institutional changes have taken place. In the case of air, direct air competition has been authorised, although throughout the whole of the period air fares have been controlled by statutory bodies. Railways on the other hand had a maximum limit set on their fares between 1953 and 1962, while from 1962 onwards they have had control to regulate their own fares on particular routes. Of crucial importance therefore was the change made in 1962, which allowed the railways greater freedom of charging, for this in effect meant that from this year onwards, statistical estimation procedures would have to recognise that to estimate air demand functions with included rail price cross-elasticities would mean considering an unconstrained operator (rail) and a constrained operator (air or road). There is the possibility therefore of obtaining 'perverse' price elasticities.[8]

In order to examine the likely effects of such a market development, we shall turn to a detailed examination of the fares structure on all three modes before and after 1962. In this way we can discover the pattern of competitive behaviour, and the significance of this behaviour on the statistical techniques to be adopted.

An examination of the pricing behaviour of the modes, as indicated earlier in the description of the market structure, is handicapped in not having comparable data. This is because rail, of the three modes, at least up to 1962, had a rigid pricing structure, such that across the board changes, authorised in particular years, affected the prices charged on all routes. Air and road, on the other hand, are both characterised by less uniformity in control,[9] in that the respective price fixing bodies have

112

Table 4.2

Rail fares on competing air routes (September 1968)

Rail distance (miles)	Single, second class	Single, first class	Weekend return, second class	Period return, second class	Cheap day return
Under 100	3.39	5.18	4.86	5.41	4.06
101−150	3.51	5.20	4.77	5.26	4.06
Rail fares on air routes	3.49	5.67	5.37	5.70	4.36
151−200	3.45	5.53	4.87	5.33	4.12
Rail fares on air routes	3.56	5.66	4.52	5.69	4.23
201−350	3.27	5.20	4.44	5.14	
Rail fares on air routes	3.40	5.16	4.16		
350 and over	3.01	4.46		4.25	
Rail fares on air routes	3.07	4.59		4.53	

Comment: Surprisingly, many of the rail fares are higher on the air routes than on the group distance they belong to. This could be a result of the air routes being the 'high quality' traffic which could bear the higher charges. Hence the detailed examination of fares changes by rail and air operators on individual routes (see text).

Source: British Rail timetables.

issued fares for particular routes which sometimes have varied considerable from the average of all prices charged on the routes. Rail fare changes are documented in Table 1, Appendix 4A.1. All the fare changes note an increase, while an examination of Table 4.2, which contains the fares charged on some of the routes in the study, shows that up to 1962 at least, the standard second class fares were little, if at all, below the authorised maximum fare limit. Air fares, where they can be said to be 'across the board', have on occasion been lowered but comparison of the timing of air and rail fares shows the institutional constraints, in the form of licensing bodies, served to lag the inter-modal competitive pricing. (There is reason to be confident that up to 1962, the substitute mode's price could be included in the air or rail equation without this form of bias. However, there is likely to be high inter-correlation between them.) Road pricing has to be dealt with in a different way, because of the individual nature of its route pricing. The method adopted was to examine about 50 routes between London and regional centres, and to *calculate the standard single* fare per mile in 1960 and 1964, by which we could examine the nature and changes, if any, in the road pricing policy. This information was examined by means of scatter diagrams (not shown). They showed only a slight taper with respect to distance and hardly any discernible change between the two years. In view of the infrequency of bus fare changes, and their almost universal behaviour in an upward direction, it can be concluded that cross-elasticities of road price can be excluded throughout the whole period.

The period after 1962 leads to a less convincing conclusion. The across the board changes show 'reasonable' time gaps, but there is evidence that it was not with standard fares that the price competition took place; rather it was in the form of concessional fares. Evidence of this is provided in Table 4A.3, Appendix 4A.1 where documented for 1961 is the case dealt with by the ATLB on off-peak fare reductions. This was contested, unsuccessfully, by the railways, and it did show the concern of the railways at the effect of these concessional fares on their market. The response of the railways to air competition in 1968 (September) is shown in Table 4.2, where routes are grouped according to distance.

The form of this competition, as Table 4.2, varied from route to route. Two routes, the London to Glasgow and London to Newcastle did experience intense rail fare competition, particularly at the lower priced end of the market. On both routes since 1963 a price war over concessional fares has been maintained, with rail reacting promptly within the year to any price change introduced by air.

The significance of this is that we can use rail fares in air demand models up to 1962, but beyond this date there is the likelihood of bias. The fares we use in the annual models are aggregates of the seasonal fares, and weighted aggregates of the various class and concessional fares. The aggregation over the year of passenger movements will also contain simultaneity for, as we have suggested, inter-modal fare response between air and rail occurs within the year. A method of detecting the significance of such a market structure is to employ a reduced form estimating technique.

When passenger demand of the two competing modes has been assumed to be independent in prices in the current period, the procedure has been to estimate equations which have quantity demanded as the dependent variable, and price and income as the independent variables:

$$DA = KA + b_{11}PA + b_{12}PR + b_{13}Y + u \qquad (4.3)$$
$$DR = KR + b_{11}PR + b_{12}PA + b_{13}Y + u \qquad (4.4)$$

However, as we have just outlined above, there is the possibility that the prices of air and rail are simultaneously determined. Therefore, in order to derive elasticity coefficients which are statistically consistent, a reduced form method of fitting simultaneous equations was employed.

We posed therefore the following reduced form equations:

$$PA = KA + B_{11}DA + B_{12}DR + B_{13}Y \qquad (4.5)$$
$$PR = KR + B_{21}DR + B_{22}DA + B_{23}Y \qquad (4.6)$$

where P = price, D = number of passengers, Y = income, A, R are designated price and rail variables.

The relationship of the coefficients was as follows:

$$b_{11} = \frac{B_{22}}{B_{22}B_{11} - B_{12}B_{21}} \qquad b_2 = \frac{B_{11}}{B_{22}B_{11} - B_{12}B_{21}}$$

$$b_{12} = \frac{-B_{12}}{B_{22}B_{23} - B_{12}B_{21}} \qquad b_{21} = \frac{-B_{21}}{B_{22}B_{11} - B_{12}B_{21}}$$

$$b_{13} = \frac{B_{12}B_{23} - B_{13}B_{22}}{B_{22}B_{11} - B_{12}B_{21}} \qquad b_{23} = \frac{B_{21}B_{13} - B_{23}B_{11}}{B_{22}B_{11} - B_{12}B_{21}}$$

Equations (4.5) and (4.6) were run on the London to Newcastle and London to Glasgow routes for the years 1963–65 inclusive. The data was divided up into quarters, and seasonal dummies (d) were included.

The results for the London to Newcastle route were:

$\text{Log } PA = 0.59 + 0.007 \log DA - 0.04 \log DR - 0.05 \log Y + 0.06 \log d_1 +$
$\qquad\qquad (0.028) \qquad\quad (0.20) \qquad\qquad (0.33) \qquad\qquad (0.02)$

$\qquad\qquad\qquad\quad 0.08 \log d_2 + 0.03 \log d_3$
$\qquad\qquad\qquad\quad (0.06) \qquad\qquad (0.07)$

$$R^2 = 0.82$$
$$\text{D.W.} = 1.7$$

$$\log PR = 3.07 + 0.01 \log DA - 0.65 \log Y - 0.04\, DR + 0.06 \log d_1 + 0.03$$
$$\qquad\quad (0.01) \qquad\quad (0.22) \qquad (0.13) \qquad (0.01) \qquad\quad (0.04)$$

$$\log d_2 + 0.01 \log d_3$$
$$\quad\ (0.05)$$

$$R^2 = 0.87$$
$$DW = 1.69$$

The structural equations could have been obtained from the above results, and presented as below.[10] However, the results showed unacceptable signs[11] (negative income elasticities), and so the transformation was not completed. We concluded that with the test used, the simultaneity between rail and air fare was not shown to be significant. We therefore felt confident in proceeding to use air and rail fares in UK domestic routes without fear of such bias.

4.3 Statistical results

4.3.1 *Domestic routes*

The following short run models were estimated:

1 $\Delta \log D = f^n$ (Δ log price air)
2 $\Delta \log D = f^n$ (Δ log price air, Δ log price rail)
3 $\Delta \log D = f^n$ (Δ log price air, Δ log income)
4 $\Delta \log D = f^n$ (Δ log price air, Δ log price rail, Δlog income)
5 $\Delta \log D = f^n$ (Δ log time air, Δ log price air)
6 $\Delta \log D = f^n$ (Δ log time air, Δ log price air, Δ log income)
7 $\Delta \log D = f^n$ (Δ log time air, Δ log price air, Δ log price rail, Δ log income)
    where D = passenger demand.

The following domestic routes were tested for the period 1954 to 1966:

1 Aberdeen/Birmingham
2 Aberdeen/Edinburgh
3 Aberdeen/Glasgow
4 Aberdeen/London
5 Aberdeen/Manchester
6 Birmingham/Edinburgh
7 Birmingham/Glasgow
8 Birmingham/London
9 Birmingham/Manchester

10 Edinburgh/Glasgow
11 Edinburgh/Manchester
12 Edinburgh/London
13 Glasgow/London
14 Glasgow/Manchester
15 Glasgow/Inverness
16 London/Manchester
17 London/Inverness

As can be seen from the estimates shown in Table 4.3, the results are highly unstable, many perverse signs being recorded. This is, of course, mainly due to the exponential growth being an inaccurate assumption to make concerning the behaviour of the trend on domestic routes. Furthermore, the removal of the two observations spanning the halt in air traffic growth in 1958[12] does not lead to any meaningful change. Obviously, the assumptions of the model must be changed.

Our procedure from now on is to cut back the number of our routes to those which are of most importance in the domestic sector — namely the London/Glasgow, London/Edinburgh, London/Manchester and London/Newcastle. These routes account for a large proportion of the total number of passenger movements, and they are likely to continue to in the future.

These routes have been characterised by high growths, and considerable rail competition. Indeed the introduction of speedier rail services on the London/Manchester route in the mid sixties halted and actually reversed air growth on this route (this may also be the case when the electrification of the London/Scottish routes is completed in the mid seventies). The growth of frequencies is considerable, particularly on the London/Newcastle route, and so it is appropriate to examine the effects of frequency changes on passenger demand. These results (see Table 4.4a) show the right signs, although air fares are on the whole less significant than income elasticities. (The elasticities are read off directly, for log transforms were performed on all routes, and proved to be the superior model over the linear version. Compared with the first differences of logs the elasticities show larger coefficients, as would be expected, for these coefficients represent the longer run response of passenger demand, rather than the short run response which is caught by the first difference model.)

The demand elasticities for road transport, shown in Table 4.4 (b) and (c) suggest that own price elasticities are elastic, income inelastic. Low income elasticities can be expected from a mode of transport used largely by the lower income groups. Again another predictable result is the low

Table 4.3

First difference model results on domestic routes

Model	Route:	1	2	3	4	5	6	7	8
1	PA	−10.46	−0.28	−18.8	−0.59	−2.08	−0.12	−1.25	0.08
	R^2	0.09	0.004	0.16	0.06	0.02	0.002	0.06	0.001
2	PA	− 9.3	−0.36	−14.0	−0.8	0.01	−0.05	−1.29	0.10
	PR	− 3.2	2.70	− 6.3	−0.9	−7.35	−0.53	−5.66	−0.78
	R^2	0.09	0.41	0.22	0.10	0.16	0.006	0.21	0.01
3	PA	− 8.1	−0.90	−18.4	−0.56	−2.94	−0.50	−1.49	0.02
	Y	−28.1	−4.22	0.75	−0.20	5.63	−5.05	−5.04	1.03
	R^2	0.25	0.38	0.16	0.06	0.05	0.14	0.10	0.02
4	PA	− 6.8	−0.88	−14.3	−0.77	−0.76	−0.51	−1.56	0.04
	PR	− 3.5	2.34	− 6.4	−0.96	−7.09	0.09	−5.83	−0.70
	Y	−28.2	−3.60	−0.85	−0.12	4.64	−5.08	−5.56	0.95
	R^2	0.26	0.67	0.22	0.10	0.18	0.14	0.26	0.03
5	TA	− 9.25	−1.5	0.83	−0.16	2.58	−1.00	2.42	
	PA	− 6.55	−0.4	−19.68	−0.64	−2.62	−0.88	−1.32	
	R^2	0.19	0.14	0.17	0.07	0.07	0.23	0.09	
6	TA	− 8.6	−0.12	1.18	−0.13	2.41	−0.81	2.06	
	PA	− 4.5	−0.89	−21.2	−0.62	−3.35	−0.97	−1.53	
	Y	−27.0	−4.1	− 2.7	−0.08	5.05	−3.10	−4.58	
	R^2	0.34	0.38	0.17	0.07	0.09	0.28	0.12	
7	TA	− 8.58	0.34	1.73	−0.10	3.11	−0.81	3.29	
	PA	− 4.47	−0.89	−18.0	−0.82	−1.06	−1.00	−1.63	
	PR	− 0.3	2.39	− 7.1	−0.94	−7.88	0.18	−6.46	
	Y	−27.05	−3.93	− 6.1	−0.04	3.78	−3.16	−4.88	
	R^2	0.34	0.68	0.24	0.10	0.24	0.28	0.31	

Model		Route: 9	10	11	12	13	14	15	16	17
1	PA		-0.34	5.82	-0.31	-0.09	-0.59	-0.28	-0.19	-2.16
	R^2		0.004	0.16	0.02	0.004	0.19	0.01	0.01	0.21
2	PA		-0.897	5.86	0.41	-0.08	-0.69	-0.15	-0.16	-1.99
	PR		-3.30	2.13	0.25	0.87	-2.37	-1.25	1.38	-1.83
	R^2		0.34	0.16	0.02	0.125	0.51	0.08	0.19	0.22
3	PA		-0.28	6.09	0.17	-0.34	-0.60	-0.10	-0.09	-2.54
	Y		-0.19	-10.10	-0.4	-0.89	0.27	-0.95	-0.90	-2.33
	R^2		0.004	0.18	0.06	0.25	0.19	0.023	0.07	0.29
4	PA		-0.52	6.17	0.27	-0.31	-0.7	0.27	0.23	-2.31
	PR		-3.38	2.95	0.24	0.64	-2.4	-1.64	1.32	-3.77
	Y		-1.23	-10.72	-0.40	-0.79	0.7	-2.05	0.74	-3.00
	R^2		0.351	0.190	0.06	0.31	0.52	0.13	0.23	0.34
5	TA		-0.61	1.08	0.19	-1.4	-0.27	-0.09	-0.55	
	PA		-0.37	6.27	0.29	0.05	-0.67	-0.30	-0.11	
	R^2		0.06	0.17	0.02	0.17	0.22	0.01	0.02	
6	TA		0.68	1.52	0.47	-1.14	-0.26	-0.16	0.11	
	PA		-0.70	6.80	0.12	-0.29	-0.67	-0.09	-0.10	
	Y		1.05	-12.9	-0.46	-0.78	0.09	-1.14	0.94	
	R^2		0.07	0.20	0.07	0.36	0.22	0.02	0.07	
7	TA		0.58	1.65	0.51	-1.09	-0.10	-0.36	0.11	
	PA		-0.88	6.96	0.23	-0.26	-0.73	0.35	0.14	
	PR		-3.29	4.00	0.29	0.58	-2.39	-1.88	3.20	
	Y		-0.13	-14.07	-0.47	-0.70	0.69	-2.64	2.17	
	R^2		0.40	0.217	0.07	0.416	0.52	0.16	0.48	

Variables:
PA = air fare
PR = rail fare
TA = travel time by air
TR = travel time by rail
Y = income

119

Table 4.4a

The autoregressive model

Model: Demand (air) = (income) + (fare air) + (time air) + $(Demand_{t-1})$

Route	Elasticities Constant	Income	Price	Time	$Demand_{t-1}$	R^2	D.W.
London/ Manchester	−1.46	4.07 (1.3)	−0.20 (0.47)	−1.95 (1.9)	−0.26 (0.52)	0.97	1.50
London/ Edinburgh	−7.3	1.62 (0.8)	−0.15 (0.47)	−0.7 (1.18)	−0.47 (0.26)	0.99	1.57
London/ Glasgow	18.7	1.69 (0.9)	−0.32 (0.50)	−3.19 (1.2)	−0.05 (0.02)	0.97	1.90
London/ Newcastle	1.32	0.43 (1.31)	−1.83 (0.58)	−0.12 (0.60)	−0.31 (0.05)		

Note: The standard errors are given in brackets.

cross air price elasticity. These results confirm the earlier assumption that air and road passengers form two distinct groups, between which little substitution takes place.

The bus elasticities were conducted on annual time series data 1954—66.

4.3.2 International routes

International civil aviation is characterised by fare fixing agreements, sanctioned by IATA, which from an econometric point of view has meant that the demand for air travel can be identified.[13] The problems of identification, experienced in the last section with respect to domestic travel, are therefore removed. We shall not here go into an institutional examination of this market, except to note that air is largely competing with sea travel as the alternative mode, owing to the island nature of the UK.

The routes tested consist of a high proportion of the traffic carried on the aggregate route groups:

1 *North Atlantic*: New York.
2 *Long haul*: Sydney, Johannesburg, Nairobi, Tel Aviv and Beirut, comprising 30 per cent of the route group traffic.

Table 4.4b

Bus elasticities

Model: $DR = \alpha_0\ PR^{\alpha_1}\ TR^{\alpha_2}\ Y^{\alpha_3}$

Route	α_0	α_1	α_2	α_3	R^2
London/Glasgow	21.3	−1.09 (1.19)	−6.05 (1.12)	+1.03 (1.2)	0.95
London/Edinburgh	16.6	−1.38 (0.23)	0.42 (0.35)	+0.49 (0.29)	0.87

Table 4.4c

Bus elasticities

Model: $DR = \alpha_0\ PR^{\alpha_1}\ PA^{\alpha_2}\ Y^{\alpha_3}$

Route	α_0	α_1	α_2	α_3	R^2
London/Glasgow	12.5	−1.47 (0.25)	+0.04 (0.48)	+0.80 (0.13)	0.85
London/Edinburgh	19.6	−2.1 (0.55)	+0.06 (0.51)	+0.12 (0.17)	0.85

DR = demand road
PR = bus fare
TR = time by road
y = income
PA = price air

3 *European*: Paris, Amsterdam, Frankfurt, Rome, Zurich and Brussels (the top 6 routes), comprising 50 per cent of the total.

The period covered by this time series data is 1957−67, and the following models were tested:

1 log (passengers) = log (fare) + log (income)

2 $\log$ (passengers) = $\log$ (fare) + $\log$ (income) + $\log$ (passengers) $t-1$

3 $\log \Delta$ (passengers) = $\log \Delta$ (fare) + $\log \Delta$ (income)

4 $\log \Delta$ (passengers) = $\log \Delta$ fare + $\log \Delta$ (income) + $\log \Delta$ passengers $t-1$

The following variations were tried on the long haul routes owing to the (expected) importance of time savings on these routes:

5 $\log$ (passengers) = $\log$ (air fare) + $\log$ (income) + $\log$ (air time)

6 $\log$ (passengers) = $\log$ (income) + $\log$ (time)

The results of these estimated models are contained in Tables 4.5 and 4.6. Not all the models have been estimated on every single route; an examination of the trend often showed certain models to be inappropriate. Model (1), the straightforward inclusion of fare and income variables, shows the problem of multi-collinearity by producing varying coefficient signs, a number of the routes having positive (though insignificant) price elasticities. Model (2), the one developed at length in section 4.2.3 and including the frequency variable, performs well, having on the whole the right signs. There is the suggestion though of autocorrelation. In order to help remove this, first differences were taken (model 4), but although this helps to improve the *D.W.* statistics, some of the coefficients have unacceptable signs.

Summarising the results, income elasticities are on the whole higher and more significant than price elasticities, while frequency changes, affecting waiting time (as shown in Chapter 3), have higher coefficients on the long haul routes, as would be expected. Furthermore, as Table 4.7 shows, time elasticities are high (although not always statistically significant) on the long haul routes.

4.3.3 *Aggregate routes*

Aggregate routes refer to groups of individual routes, often including routes examined in the last section. One advantage of their size is that the income measures used in individual international routes can be used with more confidence. Roughly, the approach has been twofold, following the theoretical development in section 4.2.3.

The first approach has been to take the income elasticity coefficients obtained from various sources, and given in Table 4.1. These have been considered as long run variables, they have been regressed on the route data, and the residuals regressed on air fares, the fares of competing modes and air time. The second section of models have utilised the relationship found in the UK economy of the relationship between the number of people

122

above a threshold income and the behaviour of national income over time. In these models the short run variables have been regressed against passengers carried, the generated time series from these coefficients then taken away from the passengers carried, and this residual regressed against Y^{bt}. The latter model was estimated on those routes with a high proportion of UK travellers. These consisted of total UK routes, and the Irish route group.

The results are contained in Tables 4.7, 4.8a and 4.8b. Of Table 4.7 we see a number of differences in the explanatory power of the models. The two most acceptable results are those for long haul and continental route groups. In both cases the most acceptable models, i.e. those with acceptable signs, are of the form of model (2) in which extraneous income elasticities have been used. The long haul price elasticity is significant and greater than 1, as one would expect from the earlier individual route estimates taken on the routes comprising this route group. Model (2) performs less well on the other route groups, while the first difference model (model 1) performs badly on all route groups. The price elasticities are all positive, although few are significant.

Table 4.8(a) gives a number of short run variable models which have been variously tested on those routes with a high proportion of UK travellers: satisfactory results were obtained on both Irish and UK total routes, and so the second stage was conducted on these routes. In the case of total UK domestic routes, data was extended to include the period 1954–68. The short run models giving the best fit were (4) and (2). The coefficients obtained from these regressions were then used to generate passenger demand figures which were deducted from actual passenger numbers. The residuals were then regressed on Y^{bt} to obtain coefficients which are displayed in Table 4.8(b). The encouraging result on the total UK domestic routes is that, given the value of $t = 14$ in 1968 (1954 being year one), the value of the income elasticity is 2.8, which coincides almost exactly with the coefficient obtained by the Roskill team on their cross section data. The Irish route gives a lower income elasticity and a less satisfactory fit.

4.4   Survey of other studies

Most studies of demand have been conducted on aggregate national data, particularly the US domestic market, individual route estimates being less frequent. Most have been time series studies, often using expenditure data and consequently deriving expenditure elasticities.[14] However, increasing-

Table 4.5

International individual route models

Models/Route	Constant	log fare	log income	Constant	log fare	log income	log passenger demand $t-1$
London/Brussels	−2.2 $R^2 = 0.66$	+3.5 (3.3)	2.09 (0.6) D.W. 2.4				
London/Zurich	2.1 $R^2 = 0.98$	−0.29 (0.39)	1.74 (0.16) D.W. 2.16	4.9 $R^2 = 0.97$	−1.30 (0.79)	+1.59 (0.4) D.W. 1.08	−0.24 (0.29)
London/Frankfurt	0.47 $R^2 = 0.16$	+0.70 (0.7)	+0.78 (0.69) D.W. 1.65	−0.63 $R^2 = 0.99$	−0.17 (0.61)	+1.08 (0.76) D.W. 1.6	−0.68 (0.24)
London/Paris	0.102 $R^2 = 0.92$	−1.19 (0.13)	1.36 (0.47) D.W. 1.47	0.11 $R^2 = 0.97$	−1.25 (0.16)	+1.79 (0.3) D.W. = 2.05	−0.23 (0.8)
London/Rome	0.89 $R^2 = 0.98$	+0.41 (0.4)	+1.64 (0.93) D.W. 1.47	0.96 $R^2 = 0.98$	+0.22 (0.50)	+1.16 (0.79) D.W. = 1.53	−0.25 (0.44)
London/Amsterdam	0.24 $R^2 = 0.35$	−0.30 (0.86)	1.12 (0.84) D.W. = 1.9	0.14 $R^2 = 0.24$	+1.81 (2.17)	+1.69 (1.37) D.W. = 0.97	0.46 (0.60)
London/New York	9.4 $R^2 = 0.95$	−2.19 (0.36)	+0.39 (0.64) D.W. = 2.0	−0.91 $R^2 = 0.99$		−0.30 (0.10) D.W. = 2.0	+0.26 (0.28)
London/Sydney	4.8 $R^2 = 0.81$	−2.97	+3.11 (2.8) D.W. = 2.6	14.9 $R^2 = 0.8$	−5.53	+1.64 (1.7) D.W. = 1.7	−0.24 (0.14)
London/Johannesburg	−2.45 $R^2 = 0.81$	−1.21 (2.8)	+3.11 (2.8) D.W. = 2.6	−9.90 $R^2 = 0.99$	−1.27 (0.66)	+4.12 (0.18) D.W. = 3.11	−0.72 (0.12)
London/Nairobi	5.1 $R^2 = 0.91$	−1.12 (2.4)	+2.29 (2.09) D.W. = 1.34	20.81 $R^2 = 0.98$	−1.17 (2.6)	+0.77 (2.9) D.W. = 1.01	−1.69 (2.1)
London/Tel Aviv	−28.3 $R^2 = 0.9$	+0.19 (1.5)	+7.9 (1.8) D.W. = 1.3	−26.7 $R^2 = 0.98$	+0.47 (0.61)	+7.35 (0.77) D.W. = 1.7	−0.01 (0.59)
London/Beirut	−13.87 $R^2 = 0.97$	−1.09 (1.81)	+6.09 (1.88) D.W. = 1.57	−14.5 $R^2 = 0.98$	−0.40 (1.2)	+5.9 (1.6) D.W. = 2.01	−0.37 (1.22)

Note: Standard errors given in brackets.

D.W. indicates Durban Watson statistic.

* denotes that the model was of first differences of logs.

Constant	log Δ fare	log Δ income	Constant	log Δ fare	log Δ income	log Δ passenger demand $t-1$
			10.1	−3.1 (2.1)	+1.17 (0.58)	−0.18 (0.65)
			$R^2 = 0.98$		$D.W. = 2.22$	
			0.84	1.83 (0.85)	+0.59 (0.56)	−0.12 (0.27)
			$R^2 = 0.49$		$D.W. = 3.09$	
−1.67	−0.19 (0.66)	3.29 (0.24)				
$R^2 = 0.9$ $D.W. = 1.54$						
0.20	+0.15 (0.37)	+0.85 (0.56)	0.28	+0.21 (0.50)	+0.84 (0.81)	−0.11 (0.6)
$R^2 = 0.33$ $D.W. = 1.59$			$R^2 = 0.28$		$D.W. = 1.32$	
2.7	−1.06 (0.15)	1.95 (0.74)	9.6	−1.37 (0.14)	+2.40 (0.19)	−0.26 (0.77)
$R^2 = 0.99$ $D.W. = 1.48$			$R^2 = 0.99$		$D.W. = 2.56$	
*0.08	−11.8	+0.29	4.89	−1.13 (5.1)	0.44 (0.60)	−2.87 (2.1)
$R^2 = 0.81$ $D.W. = 7.0$			$R^2 = 0.90$		$D.W. = 2.0$	
*0.1	+1.17 (5.0)	−1.55 (8.6)	0.135	−7.29 (9.9)	11.5 (7.8)	−0.79 (0.33)
$R^2 = 0.01$ $D.W. = 2.61$			$R^2 = 0.38$		$D.W. = 0.75$	
*0.032	−0.12 (0.88)	+3.69 (1.8)	0.8	+1.4 (1.3)	5.0 (2.5)	−0.68 (0.43)
R^2 0.38 $D.W. = 1.9$			$R^2 = 0.4$		$D.W. = 2.52$	

Table 4.6

Individual long distance air routes

Route/ Models	Constant	log (air fare)	+ log (income)	+ log (air time)	Constant	+ log (income)	+ log (air time)
London/ Nairobi	5.1	−1.05 (2.8)	+2.2 (2.29)	−0.04 (0.58)	−3.0	+2.9 (1.21)	−0.12 (0.51)
	$R^2 = 0.98$ D.W. = 1.32				$R^2 = 0.91$ D.W. = 1.31		
London/ Tel Aviv	25.8	−1.21 (0.85)	+0.20 (1.9)	−2.75 (0.58)	9.8	+2.2 (1.36)	−2.4 (0.58)
	$R^2 = 0.98$ D.W. = 2.9				$R^2 = 0.98$ D.W. = 2.4		
London/ Beirut	6.036	−1.022 (1.26)	+3.04 (1.6)	−1.39 (0.94)	−3.15	+4.05 (1.02)	−1.39 (0.45)
	$R^2 = 0.98$ D.W. = 2.33				$R^2 = 0.98$ D.W. = 2.24		

Table 4.7

Models with extraneous income elasticities

Route group	Constant	log Δ income	log Δ fare	Dependent variable log (passenger − income elasticity)	Constant	log Δ fare
Long haul	+1.29	+0.04 (0.21)	+0.39 (0.20)		+9.8	−1.2 (0.4)
	$R^2 = 0.47$ D.W. = 1.04			$R^2 = 0.88$ D.W. = 2.61		
Continental total	+3.0	+0.47 (0.69)	+0.60 (0.58)		+3.02	−0.22 (0.80)
	$R^2 = 0.13$ D.W. = 2.30			$R^2 = 0.46$ D.W. = 2.3		
Other domestic	+3.2	+0.57 (0.82)	+3.20 (4.01)		−3.4	+3.2 (3.2)
	$R^2 = 0.14$ D.W. = 2.8			$R^2 = 0.21$ D.W. = 0.21		
Channel Islands	+4.6	+1.0 (0.3)	+0.32 (0.52)		−4.1	+2.1 (3.00)
	$R^2 = 0.41$ D.W. = 3.50			$R^2 = 0.32$ D.W. = 1.11		

ly evidence is being obtained from cross-section studies. An impression of the range of such studies is shown in the table contained in Appendix A4.3, in which descriptions of methods and results of a representative number of studies (of rail and bus studies as well as air). Such information allows us to compare the estimates derived in this study with comparable routes elsewhere.

An examination of studies conducted on US aggregate domestic route data suggests that own price elasticities are elastic. In the case of Moore and Wallace [30], their estimates suggest asymmetrical responses, i.e. less price elastic responses for fare decreases than for fare increases. An acceptance of these US fare elasticities is shown by Straszheim [7] who uses an elasticity of 2 in his *a priori* model. With regard to rail cross price elasticities, few of the studies include the variable. Houthakker and Taylor [26], however, suggest that 'rail price is important'. Income elasticities are estimated to be greater than 1, but less than price elasticities in practically all of the studies. In Europe, the Paris Airport Study [8] suggested non-business fare elasticities were greater than business price elasticities (1.0 to 1.5), while income elasticities were also larger for non-business trips, the aggregate being 2.0. The income elasticities were obtained from extensive

Table 4.8a

Two stage aggregate group models (first stage)

Route/models	(1) Constant	log Δ air fare	(2) Constant	log Δ + (air fare)	log Δ (air time)	(3) Constant	log Δ + (air fare)	log Δ (air time)
Domestic total	3.5	−0.94 (0.60)						
	R² = 0.19 D.W. = 1.8							
Long haul total	1.75	+0.226 (0.36)	1.76	+0.227 (0.24)	−0.026 (0.24)	0.024	+0.399 (0.59)	−1.85 (0.69)
	R² = 0.106 D.W. = 1.42		R² = 0.108 D.W. = 1.38			R² = 0.4 D.W. = 2.1		
Irish total	1.5	+0.20 (0.56)	−14.34	−2.9 (1.3)	−0.84 (6.3)			
	R² = 0.01 D.W. = 1.39		R² = 0.76 D.W. = 1.65					

Route/models	(4) Constant	log Δ air fare	log Δ + rail fare	(5) Constant	log Δ + air fare	log Δ + rail fare	log Δ time
Domestic total	3.77	−0.96 (1.8)	+0.21 (5.2)	2.68	−0.86 (0.62)	+0.17 (0.47)	+1.007 (0.89)
	R² = 0.21 D.W. = 1.7			R² = 0.32 D.W. = 1.64			

Table 4.8b

Two stage aggregate group models (second stage)

Route/Model	(Passenger − Short run variables) =	aY^{+bt}	
Domestic total *	−0.28 +0.2t log Y (0.09)		$R^2 = 0.71$ $D.W. = 2.8$
Irish total[†]	+0.001 +0.14t log Y (0.06)	$R^2 = 0.59$ $D.W. = 1.8$	

* model (5) above selected as the short run first stage model.
† model (2) selected as the short run first stage model.

cross-sectional studies, and showed increasing propensities to travel the higher the income of the household.

The price elasticities calculated on aggregate data in this study were generally high on domestic and long haul routes, but the standard errors were also high. Income elasticities were often greater than price elasticities.

Now that these points of difference between the estimates on aggregate routes have been made, it is relevant at this point to mention the likely biases that could possibly have entered into the estimates. Four possible likely biases could have been introduced, which have not been explicitly dealt with. Firstly, extraneous estimates of income elasticities often neglected to consider the effects of changing elasticities over time, and as we have seen in section 4.2.3, the extent of this change can be quite significant. Secondly, the transformation of the data in order to remove the trend effects can lead to short run rather than long run elasticities, thus underestimating the size of the coefficients. Thus, first differences of logs are likely to yield larger elasticities than logs of first differences. Thirdly, Mincer [18] has shown that cross-section estimates of income elasticities in transport studies which do not consider the opportunity costs of time in choosing the preferred mode over the competing mode, overestimate the size of the income elasticity, owing to the wage rate, which is assumed to determine the value of time saved, being positively correlated with the income of the passenger.[15] Fourthly, most studies do not include estimates of the impact of advertising on the elasticities, particularly on price elasticities, yet clearly the impact of a price concession can be made far more effective if promoted by an intensive advertising campaign.[16]

All these factors lend caution to our interpretation of the coefficients, particularly with respect to aggregate data results. One further check is to examine the revenue that airlines expect from their pricing policies. There is considerable evidence filed by the CAB in the USA, such as in 1969 when a roughly 5 per cent increase in fares was expected to increase revenue by 3.8 per cent.[17] Such a figure suggest prices which are inelastic, but of course this does not consider the (likely) changes in costs expected to arise, nor does it account for the (perhaps) implicit effects of income increases between the date of introduction, and the time during which the lagged response has worked itself out. However, most of these estimates seem to suggest price inelasticities.

Turning to individual routes, one would expect wider divergencies owing to the specific nature of many of the economic conditions. There is enough evidence to suggest that non-business traffic is more income and price elastic than business traffic, consequently the composition of journey purpose will determine the size of the coefficients. As we have pointed out in earlier sections, the estimated models contain a frequency term which we consider to be important, such that models not containing this variable are likely to have biased estimates. The individual domestic routes have price elasticities less than 1 on all except the London to Newcastle route, perhaps reflecting the business composition of this route. Income elasticities with the exception of the London/Newcastle route are greater than 1, (very high on the London/Manchester route) and of course higher than the price elasticities. Frequency variables, represented by the lagged endogenous variable were significant and of the right sign.

The individual international routes offer a wide range of elasticities (as summary Table 4.9 illustrates); high price elasticities are generally observed on the shorter European routes, where surface transport (largely sea transport) is an important competitor. The long haul routes again have high price elasticities, and on most routes income elasticities are greater than 1. One exception, surprisingly, was the London/New York route. The coefficients on this route changed considerably with the model applied, suggesting perhaps that averaged prices on this route are an inadequate method of dealing with the complex fare changes which have occurred over the last 10 years.

In interpreting the coefficients in Table 4.9 an important cautionary remark must be added. The table of results, Table 4.5, section 4.2.4 contained details of the Durban Watson statistic (denoted as $D.W.$ in the tables) and in many cases the size of this statistic suggested serial correlation existed. In the 'ordinary' least square estimating model, the presence

Table 4.9

Summary of the best estimates of air demand elasticities

Route	Elasticities			
	Price	Income	Time	Frequency
Domestic				
London/Manchester	−0.20	+ 4.07	−1.95	−0.26
London/Edinburgh	−0.15	+ 1.62	−0.70	−0.47
London/Glasgow	−0.32	+ 1.69	−3.19	−0.05
London/Newcastle	−1.83	+ 0.43	−0.12	−0.31
International				
London/Zurich	−3.1	1.17		−0.18
London/Frankfurt	−0.17	+ 1.08		−0.68
London/Paris	−0.25	+ 1.75		−0.23
London/Rome		+ 1.16		−0.25
London/Amsterdam	−1.37	+ 2.40		−0.26
London/New York	−1.13	+ 0.44		−2.87
London/Sydney	−7.29	+11.50		−0.79
London/Johannesburg	−1.27	4.12		−0.72
London/Nairobi	−1.05	2.3	−0.04	
London/Tel Aviv	−1.21	0.20	−2.75	
London/Beirut	−1.02	+ 3.0	−1.39	

Note: These elasticities summarise the resulting coefficients of the most acceptable models for the particular routes concerned.

of serial correlation leads to inefficient rather than biased estimates, i.e. the sign of the standard error (shown by the figures in brackets under the coefficients) is likely to be underestimated. Thus, although the regression coefficients may be unbiased, the bias (downwards) in the standard errors will distort the test of significance, causing them to appear significant when they are not. Further problems enter, however, when models with the autoregressive model are estimated, for it is highly likely that bias in the coefficients could enter owing to the error term not being independent of future values of the explanatory values. Griliches [21] has shown these biases can be quite considerable. However, the autoregressive models estimated in this study include exogenous variables as well as the autoregressive term, and as Malinvaud [22] has shown, this reduces the biases.

We shall therefore accept these coefficients, fully aware of the possible biases in the coefficients and deal with these problems at a later stage.[18]

4.5 Conclusions

The characteristics of routes are varied, such that models used to estimate meaningful elasticities need to be flexible in order to encompass varying growths and differing modal competition. The survey of models suggest that elasticity of substitution models are inappropriate, and instead what is needed are models which account for the trend in traffic growth and the effects of certain variables, such as frequency. Earlier estimates have dealt insufficiently with the latter, such that the estimates are open to question, owing to the importance of frequency as a determinant of passenger demand. Furthermore, in situations where surface competition is unrestrained, tests of simultaneity in the independent variables need to be made if significant results are to be obtained. The autoregressive model, which included the frequency variable, performed well, but there is reason to believe that bias in the estimates may exist. However, the varied models do yield good and significant estimates of income elasticities, which in the event of the difficulty of forecasting fare changes (which in any case may be endogenous and *determined by* future traffic growth) will be the primary coefficient used in forecasting future passenger demand.[19]

An examination of individual route elasticities shows that on the whole income elasticities exceed fare elasticities, although the former are subjected to changes over time. From a forecasting point of view this would suggest that airlines should be more concerned with predicting income (i.e. GNP) than with undue concern with fare levels. Certainly, the relative magnitude of the elasticities shows passenger demand to be most responsive to income changes.

The behaviour of the legislator in most countries has been to introduce strict operating controls, often in the form of price control. Although individual airline price elasticies are likely to be elastic, and therefore traffic is likely to shift between airlines if open fare competition[20] is allowed, there is no reason to suspect that such price wars would be any less disruptive than the present equipment wars which have directly followed from the prohibition of price competition. If these rigid controls are to be maintained the varied characteristics of the routes, and the range of price elasticities, suggest that rigid across-the-board changes are inappropriate[21] if the industry is to satisfy its financial objectives. A more flexible administrative policy is therefore required, particularly with the onset of more competitive surface transport.

132

4A.1 Passenger fares

Table 4A.1

Ordinary fares and maximum charges on British Railways
1951–68

Date of application	7 April 1951		May 1957	September 1958				
Date of authorisation	May 1952		August 1957	8 May 1959				
Date of introduction	1 May 1952	June 1955	September 1957	November 1959	June 1960	September 1961	June 1962	February 1965
Ordinary fare (pence per mile)	1.75	1.88	2.00	2.25	2.50	2.75	3.00	3.75
Maximum authorised	1.75*	2.00*	2.00	3.00	3.00	3.00	3.00	

* Maximum of 2d per mile authorised in 1952 to come into operation in 1953. In February 1966 ordinary passenger fares for journeys above 200 miles were raised. Mid week returns were reduced from 25 per cent to 20 per cent between May to October in 1966.

Table 4A.2

Rail 'across the board' changes related to
selected individual routes examined in the study

Date of fare change	Second class (pence per mile)	Second class fares on selected routes					
June 1955	1.88	1.88	1.88	1.87	1.88	1.88	1.88
September 1957	2.00	2.00	2.00	1.99	1.99	2.00	2.00
November 1959	2.25	2.22	2.22	2.26	2.26	2.25	2.11
June 1960	2.50	2.22	2.22	2.53	2.51	2.50	2.11
September 1961	2.75	2.46	2.46	2.74	2.75	2.75	2.36
March 1962	3.00	2.71	2.71	2.99	2.99	3.00	2.43
February 1965	3.75	2.96	2.95	3.25	3.24	3.26	2.49
January 1966		3.12	3.11	3.25	3.24	3.26	2.70
April 1967		3.20	3.19	3.25	3.24	3.26	2.85

Note: These figures relate fares (second class ordinary, adjusted for the paper) to the 'standard' across the board changes. Notice that between 1955 and 1962 the fares relate to maximum fares, after that date the railways were not constrained in their pricing policies.

Source: British Rail timetables

Table 4A.3

Fare applications and authorisations
on UK domestic air routes,
1953–70

Date of application	Nature of application	Commencement	Comments
1954	10% increase	1 April 1954	The increase excluded social air services in Scotland and the Channel Islands
September 1956	10% increase in fares	December 1956	The increase on the London to Belfast route was 6%. The aim was to bring London/Scottish fares into line with other major trunk routes. Channel fares went up by only 2½%
August 1957	Application to bring fares in line with international routes	April 1957	General fare increase authorised
December 1959	Cheaper domestic flights	April 1960	The routes were London/Belfast, Glasgow and Edinburgh. These had cheaper night flights but single tourist class fare was increased by 3½%
October 1960	Simplification of the fare structure	April 1961	The 10% discount on a return ticket was abolished & replaced by a fare double the single. However, the single

Date of application	Nature of application	Commencement	Comments
			fare was reduced by about 10 to 15%. Offpeak travel charges were half the then excursion fare. First class fares on the London to Manchester route up 25%
September 1961	A reduction to £3.3.0d for offpeak flights on the main routes	November 1961	British Railways appealed against the granting of this fare, claiming that this fare was below BEA's marginal costs. The hearing was on 21 February 1962. The Ministry of Transport upheld the ATLB decision to grant the application in July 1962.
December 1962	General fare increases of 5–20%	April 1963	These increases were put forward by BEA and opposed by British Eagle. The ATLB overruled British Eagle & sanctioned the increases in February 1963
August 1964	2½% increase		This application was refused by the ATLB

Date of application	Nature of application	Commencement	Comments
October 1965	6–7% increase on all domestic routes	April 1966	Approved by the ATLB
March 1966	Removal of the winter season differentials	–	The application was refused in July 1966. It would have meant increases of about 14 and 30% on those approved in January 1966
1967	Domestic fare increase from 10 to 15%	September 1967	This was applied for by BEA and opposed by Antair and a number of Scottish towns. British Eagle attempted to resist the increase but then withdrew. The increase was of the form 11 to 15% but with reduced fares for young people from 12–21 years of age
1970	Application for 10–11% rise in UK domestic routes	–	These were rejected in December 1970. The fare increase was not seen to be profitable 'if only because they have been quickly followed by further increases in costs. Moreover, fare increases may reduce the number of passengers carried; at best they slow down the growth rate.'

Table 4A.3 continued

Date of Application	Nature of application	Commencement	Comments
			The ATLB advised BEA to meet losses out of international profits 'notwithstanding the views we have often expressed about cross-subsidy'. The general economic conditions were also brought to bear in the decision. 'The inflationary spiral cannot be halted unless price increases granted only if they are inescapable. We believe the airlines must now try to meet cost increases by expanding turnover and increasing productivity.'

British Rail standard and maximum charges

Table 4A.1 gives details of the changes in actual standard charges made. The Transport Tribunal in 1952 reduced the full fares on ordinary fares from the level of 2.44d. per mile, which was operating at the time, to the level of 1.75d. per mile. The option of increasing this to 2d. per mile was also authorised. The railways adopted this maximum of 1.75d. per mile in 1953, raising it to 1.88d. per mile in June 1955, and to the limit of 2d. per mile in 1957.

The maximum limit was again raised in 1959, this time to 3d. per mile for second class ordinary fares, and, as the table shows, this maximum was reached in June, 1962. Beyond that date, the 1962 Act came into operation, and maximum charges were abolished.

UK domestic air

Details of fare applications and authorisations are given in Table 4A.3. Most of the fare changes refer to the main trunk routes, but not in all cases. The list does not include every fare application, but it includes the main ones.

4A.2 Calculations of per capita income for particular UK cities

The exercise was to obtain a time series of per capita income for the particular town pairs under examination. Before examining the data availability and the ensuing calculations, one conceptional difficulty should be mentioned. We refer to income *per capita*, which in the context of the model implies travel decisions are taken on an individual basis as distinct from a 'household decision'. Lansing's [27] studies indicate household decisions may be the major decision units, and we have the further complication that many inter-city travel decisions will be taken by business firms. These are aspects which we have tried to deal with in calculating the time series, but we have been handicapped in not having detailed data over time.

We were unable to obtain income data of particular towns over this period, nor were the available indicators of income suitable. Rateable value for instance, is unsuitable for use in time series studies owing to its uneven movement due to periodic revaluation.

Unweighted income per head of particular regions, 1953–66
(annual income in £s)

Region	1953	1954	1955	1956	1957	1958
Northern	175.17	191.3	207.0	227.2	238.3	254.6
East and						
West Riding	188.4	205.2	221.5	238.8	282.6	307.6
N. Midland	189.0	202.5	224.6	268.2	290.6	291.5
GLC	187.1	219.8	232.9	253.4	277.0	300.1
S. West	185.35	199.0	213.0	227.5	241.1	255.6
Wales	183.07	196.2	208.8	221.5	243.3	247.2
Midland	190.1	209.9	228.0	246.6	266.3	285.0
N. West	192.1	208.3	224.0	239.9	256.6	272.7
Scotland	175.1	189.3	203.0	217.5	230.4	244.8

We were compelled therefore, to construct our own income per capital data, and to survey the available regional data. A number of studies [28], [29], discuss in detail the available regional income data and its inadequacies. The basic material we have relied upon is the census of household income and expenditure, which has been published fairly regularly over the period, and is in fact the bases of our time series (see Table 4A.4). Our second important source is the Inland Revenues personal income surveys, for Administrative counties, which has been taken for the years 1954, 1959 and 1964 (see Table 4A.5). The Registrar General's Annual Census of Population has served as the source for our population measures.

The data available is on a regional basis, and in some cases there are regional inaccuracies to be accounted for here, but more of that below. We want income per head for particular cities and towns. The procedure adopted was as follows. The family expenditure survey gave the best time series of regional average family incomes. The Inland Revenue figures were able to provide us with average personal earned income per 'taxable unit' for particular counties, as well as for the regions. The assumption made was that the income per capital in the county in which the particular town was placed was equal to the income per capital of the particular town. The next step was to find from the Inland Revenue data, the income per capita of particular counties. This provided us with rates for the particular counties (and thus by our assumption, for the particular towns)

1959	1960	1961	1962	1963	1964	1965	1966
270.2	286.9	303.7	306.3	291.6	305.2	357.6	394.3
231.1	356.3	381.5	386.4	399.3	410.3	474.3	465.7
314.1	336.9	360.6	365.1	379.8	393.9	457.3	452.0
322.4	349.1	376.4	365.1	404.8	397.7	497.8	495.7
270.4	284.4	399.4	343.7	344.3	349.6	394.3	385.0
260.1	273.2	287.1	276.2	349.9	375.8	386.1	398.4
305.9	324.4	345.0	372.6	375.0	389.1	430.0	444.9
288.9	306.2	322.9	323.9	342.1	367.7	401.97	439.3
258.5	272.2	287.1	288.7	313.9	331.6	368.2	375.7

for three years. These weights were then averaged over the time series and used to weight the family survey income data.

The two main sources of information differed in a number of ways. The family survey data was of incomes for family units, while the Inland Revenue data was for 'tax units'. In order to correct for some of the discrepancy, data on family composition was used to adjust the family survey data (this information was available in the family expenditure surveys).

The figure used was that of the average number of wage earners per family unit. Over the period considered, regional boundaries changed, although some of these changes did not affect the study, because there were no town pairs located in these regions. The main boundary changes affecting our study were:

Old region	New region
East and West Riding	Yorkshire and Humberside
North Midland	East Midland
Midland	West Midland
London and South-East	
London County	Greater London Council
Greater London	
Remainder	Rest of South-East

Table 4A.5

Income per head of selected counties, 1953–66
(annual income in £s)

Region	1953	1954	1955	1956	1957	1958
W. Riding	184.6	201.1	223.7	288.4	302.4	337.8
Gloucestershire	237.2	254.7	285.7	318.5	352.0	388.5
Warwickshire	212.9	219.7	254.9	270.3	288.7	305.5
Lancashire	188.2	204.1	218.6	233.2	248.4	262.4
Cheshire	205.0	219.7	233.8	248.0	262.4	276.9
Glamorgan	223.3	239.7	252.6	268.0	283.5	299.1
Aberdeen	169.8	183.8	204.2	226.6	248.3	272.7
Caithness	154.1	166.6	191.2	218.4	245.6	276.1
Lanarkshire	199.6	215.8	233.4	252.4	169.5	288.8
Midlothian	185.6	200.6	219.2	239.2	258.0	279.1
Northumberland	308.3	336.7	349.8	362.1	372.2	380.8

In order to obtain a time series we made the following assumptions. We equated East and West Riding region with the new Yorkshire and Humberside region. As regards the Midlands, we took the mean of the new East and West Midlands regions to obtain a figure for the 'old Midlands' regions, while in the case of the old North Midlands region, the West Midland figures were used. The boundary changes in London and the South-East were also caused problems. In this case, the earlier figures for 'Greater London' were related to figures for the Greater London Council.

Details of these figures are given in table 4A.5.

Personal income on a county basis

This data was taken from the Inland Revenue's Personal Incomes Surveys which were taken for the years:

1954: 99th Report of the Inland Revenue
1959: 106th Report of the Board of Inland Revenue (Cmnd. 1906)
1964: 110th Report of the Board of Inland Revenue

The data used was that of personal earned income before tax. This was considered to be the most reliable of the sources, owing to the distortion

142

1959	1960	1961	1962	1963	1964	1965	1966
374.1	394.8	414.7	411.5	416.5	419.2	474.3	465.0
427.2	425.1	422.1	455.4	426.9	403.7	421.9	411.0
324.2	343.2	363.3	391.2	392.4	405.8	447.2	462.0
277.3	293.0	307.6	307.7	323.8	346.7	377.8	412.0
291.3	304.1	317.7	303.8	382.4	408.4	417.0	430.0
312.1	319.1	326.4	305.2	375.4	391.6	389.9	399.0
297.3	302.7	308.0	298.8	312.9	317.7	338.7	343.0
307.6	310.3	312.9	300.2	310.7	311.7	327.7	332.0
307.6	316.6	326.4	320.4	339.9	350.5	379.2	384.0
299.8	309.8	320.7	316.1	336.8	348.8	379.2	384.0
386.3	394.4	400.9	385.9	369.3		371.9	409.0

in the income from investment, which is recorded at the place of business and not the place of residence.

Household income and expenditure for particular regions: details of statistical sources

This data was taken from the various census reports on household income and expenditure.

A complete time series is not available, and the details contained in the reports varies. Below are details containing the contents of the various censuses used:

- 1954: *Report of an Enquiry into Household Expenditure in 1953–54.* In this report the expenditure of particular households is grouped according to standard regions and given in the form of income per household.
- 1959: *Family Expenditure Survey: Report for 1957–58.* Household income and expenditure for 1959 is grouped according to administrative regions.
- 1962: *Family Expenditure Survey: Report for 1962.* Expenditure by the regions for the years 1961 and 1962.

1963: *Family Expenditure Survey: Report for 1963*. Household income and expenditure for 3 years, 1961–1963, for the standard regions.

1964: *Family Expenditure Surveys: Report for 1964*. Household income and expenditure for 3 years, 1961–1963, for the standard reigons.

1965: *Family Expenditure Survey*. Income and expenditure given for the regions.

1966: *Family Expenditure: Report for 1966*. Household income and expenditure for 3 years, 1964–1966, for the standard regions.

Notes

[1] The solution of this differential is $y = \dfrac{L}{1 + b \exp(-at)}$. The logistic curve is one of the family of S curves which are popularly used to describe growth curves. Two of these are the Gompertz curve and the lognormal curve.

[2] See Brown, S. L. and Watkins, W. S. [3]. This study was a time series regression up to 1966.

See also Wright, T. P. [4] for an earlier study, in which it is suggested that the potential market for air passengers varies inversely with the cube of the fare (up to 30 per cent of the market). Here the threshold income appears to be a function of average fare level, and income to be distributed log normally.

[3] Let $\rho(t)$ be the continuous rate of growth from year t to $t + 1$
Therefore

$$X_{t+1} = X_t \, e^{\rho(t)}$$

Thus

$$\log_e X_{t+1} - \log_e X_t = \rho(t)$$

where X_t and X_{t+1} are successive annual observations.

[4] See Ellison, A. P. and Stafford, T. [11] for a description of this data on UK routes.

See also Long, W. [13], 'City characteristics and the demand for inter-urban air travel', *Land Economics* XLVI, May 1968.

[5] Roskill [16], p. 9.

[6] Fares were, of course, deflated by retail price indicies.

[7] Hibbs [17] *Transport for Passengers*. Hobart Paper 23, 1963.

[8] See the section on simultaneity and multi-collinearity in section 4.0 for a development of this point.

[9] Air fares for instance show considerable differences. For instance, in 1965, differences in standard charges were as follows:

Route	Air mileage	Pence per mile
London/Scotland	325-338	4.6
London/Manchester	152	8.8
Highlands and Islands	79 (average)	17.6

[10] The structural equations would have been:

$$\log DA = \log PA + \log Y$$
$$\log DR = \log PR + \log Y$$

[11] The results of the London to Glasgow were even more unacceptable.

[12] See the Report from the Select Committee on Nationalised Industries (Reports and Accounts: The Air Corporations, May 1959), especially the following, which is part of the section dealing with BEA:

Question 1095: 'What is the reason for this decline (in load factors)?'

Answer: 'It is the general recession that has afflicted the whole of the airline world over the past year.'

Question 2442: In answer to this question concerning the low load factor a reason given for the slow recovery of the load factor in 1958/59 was that it was due to the fog in November, December, January and part of February.

Question 2447, enquiring further about the fog explains: ' . . . We cancelled 1,500 services during the months of November, December, January and February, and we reckon that the fog cost us £250,000.'

[13] The administered fares, unresponsive to market equilibrium in the short run and the shifts in supply, suggest that single least squares regressions estimate the demand curve and not some hybrid demand and supply curve.

[14] The relationship between expenditure elasticities and price elasticities is as follows:

Given S = price elasticity of sales (expenditure)

$$S = \frac{dPQ}{dP} \frac{P}{PQ}$$

$$\frac{dPQ}{dP} = Q + \frac{dQ}{dP}\, P = Q \left(1 + \frac{dQ}{dP} \frac{P}{Q}\right)$$

$$\frac{dPQ}{dP} = Q\,(1 - E) \text{ where } E = \text{price elasticity} = -\frac{dQ}{dP} \frac{P}{Q}$$

$$\frac{dPQ}{dP} = \frac{P}{PQ} = Q\frac{P}{PQ}\,(1 - E)$$

So $S = (1 - E)$

and $E = S - 1$

[15] For details of this point and the form of the upward bias it gives to the income elasticity see Mincer [18].

[16] For instance the total advertising expenditure on selected consumer goods in the UK in 1969 was as follows: Motor cars £5,233,900; washing machines £1,199,800 and Travel Agent Services £3,086,600 (Source: *Econoímist* Intelligence Unit Special Report No. 7, November 1970).

US airlines in 1965 spent $120 million on advertising.

See Kraft, G. [19] for estimates of the impact of US airline advertising on demand estimates.

[17] See *Flight International* 1969, pp. 122 and 155. For an early attempt at measuring elasticities see Broster, E. J. [20].

[18] For a discussion and method of dealing with this problem see J. Johnson [23] and R. Gamey [24]. The latter study examines the problem of air forecasts with an autoregressive model. See the technical appendix 10A.1 for a discussion of the likely biases in autoregressive models'.

[19] In order to forecast the growth rate of passenger demand from the models developed, the expected growth in income should be multiplied by the income elasticity (say B) and added to the product of the expected price change and the price elasticity (A). Thus, if income is expected to grow at 1 per cent per annum and price to fall at 1 per cent per annum, the growth rate would be $A + B$ per cent.

[20] See A. P. Ellison [25] for an examination of the UK Civil Transport Aviation industry in the 1930's when airlines competed by means of fares and frequency.

[21] See Appendix 4A.2 for details of UK domestic fare changes from 1954–70.

References

1   A. E. Evans, 'Intercity travel and the London Midland Electrification', *JTE and P*, Vol. III, January 1969.

2   A. D. Bain, *Growth of Television Ownership in the UK*, Cambridge University Press, 1964.

3   S. L. Brown and W. S. Watkins, 'The demand for air travel: a regression study of time series and cross-sectional data in the US domestic market', *Highway Research Board*, no. 213, 1966.

4   T. P. Wright, 'Some economic factors in air transport', *Aeronautical Engineering Review*, April 1957 (pp. 45–51).

5   F. Fisher, *A Priori Information and Time Series Analysis*, N. Holland, 1962.

6   M. Nerlove and P. Balestre, 'Pooling cross section and time series data in the estimation of a dynamic model: the demand for natural gas', *Econometrica*, vol. 34, no. 3, 1966.

7   M. R. Straszheim, *The International Airline Industry*, Brookings Institute, 1969.

8   *Characteristics and forecasts of demand in Europe*, Aeroport de Paris, Société d'Études Techniques et Economiques (ISETECI), Paris 1968.

9   The Port of N.Y. Authority, *Forecast of U.S. Domestic Air Passenger Market 1955–75*, 1957.

10   H. Wold and L. Jureen, *Demand Analysis*, Wiley, 1953.

11   A. P. Ellison and T. Stafford, 'Intercity passenger transport estimates for the UK'. A paper given at the Econometrics Conference, Amsterdam, September 1968.

12   M. J. H. Mogridge, 'Predicting car ownership', *Journal of Transport Economics and Policy*, no. 1, 1967.

13   W. Long, 'City characteristics and the demand for inter-urban air travel', *Land Economics*, XLIV, May 1968.

14   National Income and Expenditure of the UK 1954–1969.

15   R. J. Nicholson, *Economic Statistics and Economic Problems*, Chapter 8 (McGraw-Hill 1969).

16   Commission on the Third London Airport, *The Roskill Report,* Papers and Proceedings, vol. VII, 1970.

17   J. Hibbs, 'Transport for Passengers', *Hobart Paper*, no. 23, 1963.

18   J. Mincer, 'Market Prices, Opportunity Costs and Income Effects' in *Measurement in Economics: Studies in Mathematical Economics and Econometrics in memory of Y. Grunfeld*, Stanford, 1963.

19   G. Kraft, 'The role of advertising costs in the airline industry' in *Transport Economics*, NBER, 1965.

20   E. J. Broster, 'Railway Passenger Receipts and Fares Policy', *Economic Journal*, 1937, pp. 451–64.

21   Z. Griliches, 'A note on serial correlation bias in estimates of distributed lags', *Econometrica*, vol. 29, no. 1, 1961.

22   E. Malinvaud, *Statistical Methods in Econometrics*, pp. 458–467.

23   J. Johnstone, *Econometric Methods*, McGraw-Hill, 1963.

24   R. Gamey, 'Long range forecasting of domestic and international boarding passengers at Canadian airports by multiple regression analysis, M.A. Thesis, University of British Columbia, 1969 (pp. 76–78).

25   A. P. Ellison, 'The Edwards Report on civil aviation in the 1970s', *Journal of the Royal Aeronautical Society*, June 1970.

26   H. S. Houthakker and L. D. Taylor, *Consumer Demand in the US, 1929 to 1970*, Cambridge, Mass., 1966.

27   J. B. Laing, *The Changing Travel Market*, The Institute for Social Research, Ann Arbor, Michigan, 1962.

28   M. J. Pullen, 'Unemployment and regional income per head', *The Manchester School of Economics and Social Studies*, vol. XXXIV, no. 11, January 1966.

29   B. E. Coats and E. Rawstron, 'Where will the budget bite?', *The Guardian*, 1 April 1967.

30   J. G. Moore and W. M. Wallace, 'Calling the turns', Boeing 1968.

5 Capital Stock Measurement

5.1 Introduction

The measurement of capital stock forms a major difficulty in applied economics. Enumeration is difficult, and there are problems of aggregating heterogeneous capital units of differing ages and technologies. The measures adopted, such as the use of monetary stock values depreciated at some constant rate, have often been statistically convenient but fundamentally unsatisfactory. Thus, convenience has resulted in concentration on the determinants of net investment and replacement investment in terms of the size of the capital stock. Interesting relationships, such as those between scrapping and ordering have often gone untested for want of detailed information.[1] This is fortunately not the case with the civil aviation industry. The comparative youth of the industry and the numerous 'aircraft spotting' groups make it possible to pursue in detail the life of an individual aircraft over time and across international boundaries. These sources[2] have provided information on date of entry, sales and scrapping of about practically every aircraft type ever produced. Such information allows us to consider the age, capacity and value of individual aircraft types in formulating capital stock measures. This is important, for as we shall see in Chapter 7, capital stock plays a central role in the purchasing behaviour of airlines.

5.2 Stock measures

Capital, of course, can be viewed in various ways.[3] The airline considering an addition to capital stock considers the productivity of the aircraft, the passenger-miles capacity, and in this production function sense, evaluates capital in physical terms. For tax and legal purposes, the airlines consider the monetary value of the aircraft, the value in the book. These values are likely to be determined from an historical cost basis in which annual depreciation is calculated on a straight line basis. A value figure will be written off each year until the scrap value is reached, at which point the asset ceases to exist in the accounting sense.[4] In the physical sense, of course, the asset may still be in operation. The use of the book value of capital as a basis for aggregating capital units is clearly unsatisfactory' for aggregate book values do not accurately account for the productivity of the asset.

Various value measures have been the more common measure of capital stock, according to data availability. Often, for convenience, constant proportionate rates of depreciation (declining balance) have been used in which replacement is seen to be proportionate to capital stock.[5] In this method economic and physical depreciation is accounted for but the problem is the choice of the depreciation rate. One method of measuring capital decay would be to observe aircraft rents over time. This could be obtained by observing the difference in the price of an aircraft over a period of 1 year, and then adding to this difference the opportunity cost of retaining resources in the aircraft over the year. Used prices, given an efficient second hand market, could yield the price differences, while the market rate of interest could provide the opportunity cost measure. Computational convenience has often led to the use of constant rates of depreciation, but as we shall see from an examination of the used aircraft market, used prices over time do not show a constant proportionate fall. Figure 5.1 shows the relationship between large and 'other'[6] used aircraft prices and their original prices. These prices are shown on a calendar basis, illustrating the variation of prices over time, and also the appreciation above the original values of certain aircraft in the years before 1956. This evidence,[7] refuting the assumption of invariance of the depreciation rate

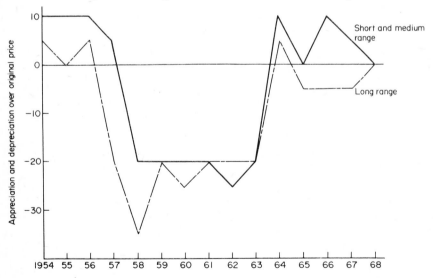

Fig. 5.1   Depreciation and appreciation rates 1954–68 of aircraft types of differing ranges

Table 5.1

ICAO member airlines aircraft passenger stock 1954—70

Year	(1) Number of passenger aircraft in ICAO fleets	(2) Number of new aircraft entering the stock	(3) Δ Stock	(4) Known scrapping and crashes	(5) Estimated scrapping (new entries - Δ stock)	Lay ups Net departures	Lay ups Net re-entry
1954	3,563	214	13	52	201	149	
1955	3,671	131	108	39	23		6
1956	4,021	345	350	46	5		41
1957	4,386	426	365	46	61	15	
1958	4,520	297	134	60	163		102
1959	4,817	355	297	90	58		32
1960	4,700	342	(117)	119	459	340	
1961	4,780	310	80	119	230	111	
1962	4,750	144	(30)	174	174	–	
1963	4,714	137	(36)	116	173	57	
1964	4,829	218	115	155	103		52
1965	4,957	307	128	112	179	67	
1966	5,122	442	165	153	277	124	
1967	5,420	493	298	160	195	35	
1968	5,851	760	431	127	329	102	
1969	6,278	623	427	61	196	135	
1970	6,470	350	192	70	158	30	

The scrapping figure for 1970 has been estimated, for the prime sources often only go up to the third quarter of 1970.
We have treated lay-ups and conversions together, as we have little information with respect to cargo conversions.

Sources: See Appendix 5.1 to this chapter.

with respect to time, is important, for Hall has shown that if this assumption does not hold, then a capital aggregate cannot be expressed as a stationary weighted sum of past purchases, as is done with the constant (declining balance) rate of depreciation method.

In view of the earlier discussion of airline behaviour, the more appropriate measure of airline stock would appear to be a measure of physical units. A number of problems have to be faced, however, if we are to use this measure. Firstly, capital is durable, it is productive over time but it is not indestructible. Technical performance tends to deteriorate over time. Secondly, some aircraft are more productive than others. We need therefore to consider the extent of the physical deterioration of capital and the heterogeneity of the stock. Simply to add units of aircraft over time would be to give the same weight to each aircraft, irrespective of their productive capacity or age. Dealing with productive capacity, we can obtain technical details of each aircraft type and then weight each aircraft according to their potential or average[8] productivity. Such a process transforms a stock of aircraft numbers into a stock of currently available services. Durability can be dealt with by weighting stock according to the life expectancy of the units. Thus, given the age of an aircraft, its future potential productive life can be obtained by weighting according to the life expectancy derived from survivor curve information. Such a calculation would yield a capacity measure of capital depreciated according to life expectancy.

A means of achieving such a measure is to use survivor or mortality tables of individual aircraft types. These have been calculated and are presented in the next section. The data sources from which these tables are calculated are also important in actually calculating the number of aircraft in the stock in any one year. One of the problems in calculating a capital stock figure is to distinguish between those aircraft which are registered, and those which are not registered but are still in existence and potentially airworthy. The stock figure sought must take account of both registered and non-registered aircraft, since this total number will influence the number of aircraft ordered, not merely the number recorded in the registers. This is particularly important in civil aviation, where licences are not renewed on some aircraft even though they are airworthy. Instead they are left in storage longer and brought back into use (or scrapped) at a later date. The most comprehensive register of world civil aviation fleets is that compiled by ICAO.[9] There are reasons to believe, however, that these registration figures underestimate, sometimes to a large degree, the actual existing stock of aircraft. This can be shown by calculating the number 'scrapped'. The figures for scrapping can be obtained by subtracting from the number of new aircraft delivered the figure representing the change in aircraft stock.[10]   Figures shown in Table 5.1 suggest that for some years the calculated scrapping figure is unacceptable; take for instance 1956, where the number is 5, an unacceptable figure, for scrapping is likely to be greater than this. Clearly, these ICAO stock measures fail to account for departures into storage and reentries. In order to obtain an accurate measure of stock we require information on departures from stock due to scrapping and crashes. Fortunately, this is possible with the detailed information provided by the aircraft life histories. Such wastage will be examined in this chapter, and temporary departures discussed in Chapter 9.

In view of the foregoing discussion, two measures of aircraft stock will be used: aircraft numbers and aircraft capacities. Both measures will be deflated[11] to take account of age and therefore life expectancy, resulting in four sets of stock measures. The deflated figure of aircraft life expectancy has been obtained from a cross-section of jet aircraft in 1969, and is shown in Table 5.4 of the next section.

Weighting by life expectancy information provides a means of describing the durability of particular aircraft, but it does not altogether account for the decline in economic performance resulting from technological change. An aircraft in the hands of an airline may be considered inferior to another available type, in which case its economic productivity will be incorrectly represented in the airline stock if measured in capacity units or numbers. This technical depreciation is unlikely to be accounted for in the life expectancy tables, for a well developed second hand market makes it possible for an airline to dispose of an aircraft by selling rather than scrapping. A means of dealing with this is to express technological change not by deflating the stock measures, but by including measurable aspects of the technological change in the variables determining airlines' desired stock. The models of airline ordering behaviour are dealt with in Chapter 7, and it is sufficient to note here that we shall use the price of aircraft as one of the variables affecting airlines' desired stock. Using the method developed by I. Adelman and Z. Griliches [5] we have calculated a price index of aircraft and then deflated it by the changes in aircraft characteristics which are seen to represent aspects of the technological change in aircraft.[12] Given our four measures of capital stock, our price adjusted indices are: price per tonne kilometre capacity and the average price paid per aircraft.

5.3   Aircraft wastage

Aircraft departures take place for a number of reasons. They may depart because of crashes, causing the aircraft to be written off, of they may be scrapped independently of accidents. Departures, however, may not be permanent. Cannibalisation is often performed, when the damaged aircraft is joined together with another to form a new registration. In other cases the aircraft may have its licence withdrawn, only to be renewed at a later date. For our purposes, 'wastage' will refer to departures due to scrapping or crashes. Fortunately, we have extensive life histories of all the jet aircraft, and practically all of the propeller aircraft ever built and operated,[13] which allows us to note the time of entry, the age and calendar date of departure resulting from crashes or scrapping, and the aircraft age and date of first sale. In this way we can calculate for any year the number of entries, the number departing, the non-renewed licences and the re-entries.

This information also allows us to calculate wastage rates in a number of differing ways. Comprehensive information on entries for any particular year permits us to calculate wastage rates over time. In particular, details of individual aircraft lifes allows us to calculate wastage rates for particular types. In this way comparisons between jet and propeller, short and long range aircraft can be made. Another measure of wastage rates can be obtained by comparing the number of aircraft aged, say, 5 years recorded in a particular year with the number surviving a further year, by which time they will be 6 years old. A large number of wastage rates can thus be calculated, over a series of years, for aircraft of differing ages.

The method by which the individual aircraft life histories have been presented in Table 5.2 (a to d), is to divide them up roughly into propeller and jet, and a further subdivision into long range and short range. This is partly for convenience of presentation, and it also allows us to compare the differences, if any, between the aircraft types. The information is presented in the form of survivor data, i.e. the percentage surviving a particular age. Departures, or wastage, in any one year refers to the difference between the survivor figures[14] between years t and $t + 1$.

The striking result of these survivor curves is the considerable difference in life histories. This is borne out more clearly in Figures 5.2 to 5.4, where some of these survivor tables are represented. Not all aircraft survivor tables have been shown, primarily because many types have so few mortalities to record. This is particularly the case with the jet aircraft, a factor which makes comparisons between jet and propeller aircraft somewhat difficult. Nevertheless, there is evidence for the 10 years or so during which jets

Table 5.2a

Percentage of aircraft surviving: piston engine and turboprop (long range)

Age	L1049	L1649	L749	L049	DC-4	DC-6	DC-6A	DC-6B	DC-7	DC-7B	DC-7C	Canadair C54	Bristol Britannia
1	100	100	98	91	98	94	100	99	100	100	99	100	99
2	99	100	96	86	95	94	98	99	99	98	95	97	99
3	98	100	95	86	93	94	95	99	99	97	94	97	99
4	96	97	94	85	92	93	90	99	99	97	93	97	98
5	92	93	93	84	89	92	87	98	97	97	92	95	97
6	89	93	92	83	87	92	83	98	94	96	90	95	97
7	85	90	91	80	87	92	78	98	85	92	90	91	97
8	80	86	91	77	86	91	77	96	83	90	89	89	96
9	74	67	90	75	84	90	75	96	77	76		89	96
10	67	51	88	75	83	90		94	65			89	96
11	59	34	86	74	81	90		92	63			86	96
12	49		83	74	80	90		91				84	96
13	42		81	74	78	89		90				84	94
14	38		76	62	76	89		90				67	93
15	38		75		75	86		89				65	92
16	35		69		74	85						47	
17	32		60		72	85						34	
18			47		70	84						30	
19			38		69							23	
20			37		68							21	
21			34		68								
22			33		67								
23					67								

Table 5.2b

Percentage of aircraft surviving:
piston engine (short range)

Age	DC-3	CV-240	CV-340/ 440	Martin 202-440	Vickers Viking	Curtis C-46
1	99.1	92	98	100	94	100
2	98.2	82	95	86	91	100
3	97.5	80	94	86	91	99
4	96.4	77	91	84	91	97
5	95.3	74	90	83	86	97
6	93.9	70	89	82	82	96
7	93.1	67	88	81	80	96
8	92.0	63	87	73	77	93
9	91.0	59	87	67	74	91
10	90.5	59	86	60	70	91
11	89.2	57	80	58	67	91
12	88.3	53	76	52	63	90
13	87.5	50	72	52	58	90
14	86.8	31	68	44	47	90
15	86.2	17	64	43	34	88
16	85.1				26	87
17	84.3				22	84
18	83.8				18	82
19	82.6				16	80
20	81.7				16	79
21	81.3				13	77
22	80.6				12	74
23	79.7				11	72
24	78.7					71
25	78.0					70
26	77.7					68
27	77.2					68
28	77.1					67
29	77.1					
30	77.0					

Table 5.2c

Percentage of aircraft surviving:
turbo jets

Age	Boeing 707	DC-8	Caravelle
1	98	98	98
2	98	98	96
3	97	98	96
4	97	97	96
5	96	97	96
6	96	96	96
7	96	96	95
8	96	96	95

Table 5.2d

Percentage of aircraft surviving:
turbo props

Age	Lockheed 1-Electra	V-700	V-800	Fokker F-27
1	97	94	93	98
2	96	92	92	98
3	96	92	92	97
4	96	90	92	97
5	96	89	91	97
6	96	87	91	97
7	96	86	90	96
8	95	85	89	
9	85	85		
10	84	85		
11	84			
12	80			
13	72			

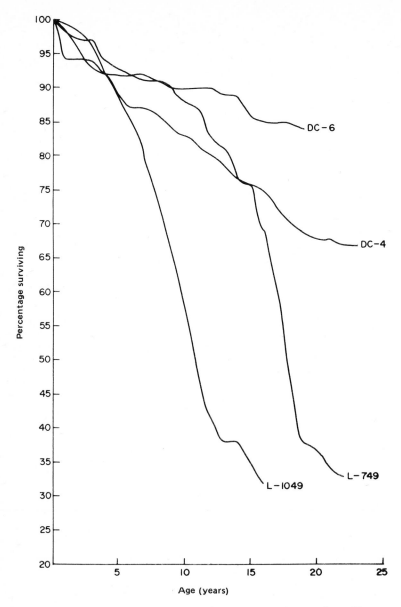

Fig. 5.2   Survivor curves, long range piston aircraft

have been operating to suggest from these survivor tables and curves that
the durability of the jet is higher than that of their propeller forerunners.
This is particular marked between long range jets and propellers. Take for
instance the life histories of the DC-4, DC-6 and L1649 and compare them
with the life histories so far of the Boeing 707s and the DC-8s. Only one

158

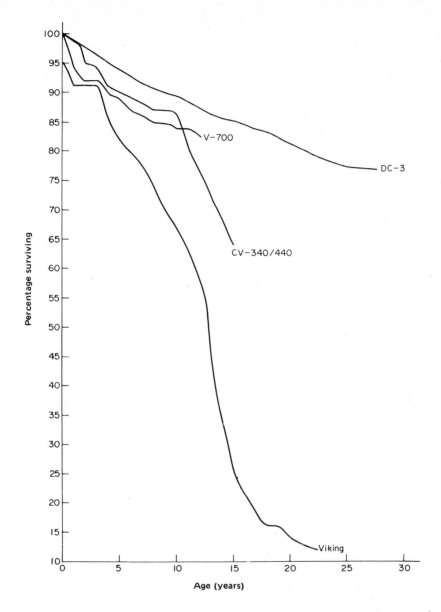

Fig. 5.3   Survivor curves, short range aircraft (prop. and turbo prop.)

long range propeller aircraft, the DC-6B, approaches the durability of the long range jets. This observation, however, does not altogether hold for short range propeller aircraft. The amazing DC-3 for instance has a history which shows remarkable durability,[15] resulting partly because of its excellent manufacture, but also because the aircraft manufacturers were unable

159

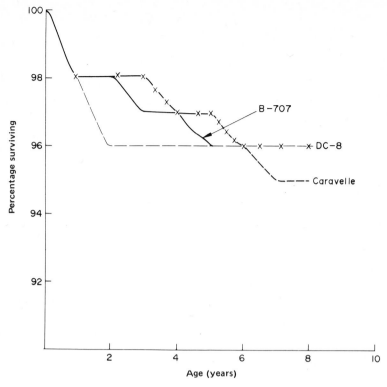

Fig. 5.4　Survivor curves, turbo jet

to produce a propeller model which could supersede the DC-3's performance.

An overall picture of the durability of propeller aircraft compared with other transport vehicles is shown in Figure 5.5, where two survivor curves are shown, one obtained by taking a weighted aggregate of long range propeller survivor and the other data taken from a 1969 cross-section. These are compared with survivor studies of auto and naval craft vehicles.[16] Propeller aircraft, according to these studies, falls between the car and the ship in its durability. Such comparisons, however, are likely to be influenced by economic conditions, for scrapping as distinct from departure due to a crash is not necessarily related to age. As we have seen above, the durability of the DC-3 is partly due to its superiority over later rivals and so the reluctance of airlines to scrap even when economic prospects deteriorate. This is brought out more clearly by examining Tables 5.3 and 5.4, where wastage rates annually from the mid fifties to late sixties have been calculated from jet and propeller stocks. Table 5.4 shows the jet stock, suggesting the loss across all age groups to be around

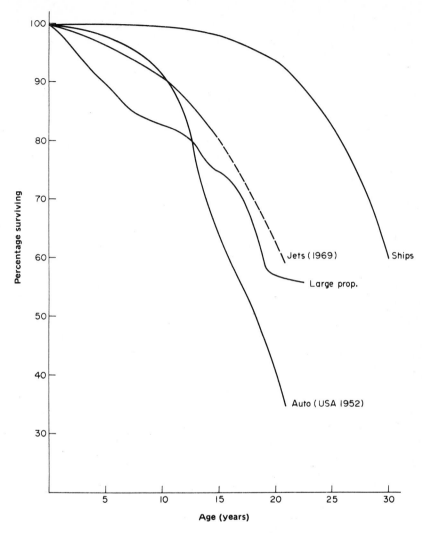

Fig. 5.5   Comparative survivor curves

1 per cent. In considering these figures, however, note should be taken of the small number of jets entering in the early years (1955–58) and consequently the instability in the departure percentages for the subsequent age groups. Comparisons with the propeller aircraft are perhaps surprising. Interestingly enough until the early 1960s the propeller aircraft appear to be just as durable as their jet counterparts, but around 1960 to 1962 we find heavy losses in a wide spread of age groups. As we will show below, the greater proportion of departures in these years is due to scrapping rather than crashes. The large disparities between aircraft types shown in

Table 5.3

Percentage of propeller aircraft stock surviving annually

Age / year	1	2	3	4	5	6	7	8	9	10	11	12	13	14	15	16	17	18	19	20	21	22	23
1944	100.0																						
1945	98.2	97.6																					
1946	97.6	97.0	100.0																				
1947	98.0	97.5	100.0	100.0																			
1948	89.8	98.0	96.8	96.8	92.9																		
1949	100.0	100.0	99.5	97.4	97.4	83.0																	
1950	92.9	98.3	87.7	100.0	100.0	99.3	91.8																
1951	100.0	100.0	100.0	97.8	97.8	93.2	98.6	98.8															
1952	100.0	100.0	100.0	100.0	100.0	93.2	98.3	99.3	97.7														
1953	100.0	100.0	100.0	100.0	100.0	92.4	97.3	100.0	97.9	89.6													
1954	100.0	97.3	98.8	100.0	96.5	94.6	94.6	97.3	99.7	98.5	98.7												
1955	97.4	97.6	99.1	100.0	99.0	100.0	94.5	90.3	92.0	98.6	98.2	83.1											
1956	100.0	97.4	99.2	100.0	96.5	90.5	100.0	100.0	100.0	98.5	97.8	97.8	92.1										
1957	99.3	99.2	100.0	100.0	99.0	100.0	94.5	94.2	95.9	99.1	98.2	100.0	98.5	98.3									
1958	100.0	100.0	100.0	100.0	99.2	100.0	97.4	100.0	100.0	100.0	99.1	96.8	97.7	97.7	98.6								
1959	—	96.8	100.0	99.4	96.0	100.0	100.0	94.2	95.9	93.6	75.4	96.8	88.7	90.6	100.0	96.4							
1960		—	89.6	96.6	95.3	87.5	100.0	92.7	97.3	100.0	100.0	95.5	58.9	65.9	97.1	98.4	87.2						
1961			—	96.4	97.8	97.2	87.3	93.6	94.1	95.8	89.5	90.0	100.0	56.5	69.4	84.0	98.4	97.9					
1962				—	71.2	95.6	97.2	81.8	94.8	79.1	97.1	93.0	82.5	97.5	76.9	80.0	98.2	98.4	100.0				
1963					—	85.7	51.8	95.4	55.5	81.9	100.0	100.0	93.9	97.4	60.0	70.0	100.0	100.0	99.2				
1964						—	93.8	95.2	36.0	100.0	86.8	100.0	93.9	93.7	93.5	84.2	69.0	100.0	100.0	100.0			
1965							—	14.2	79.2	86.1	55.5	89.0	93.9	93.7	100.0	86.2	75.0	50.0	72.8	100.0			
1966								—	60.0	91.6	97.8	40.0	95.0	98.1	100.0	83.0	83.0	87.5	49.0	92.3	97.6		
1967									—	—	97.4	97.7	30.0	98.7	96.7	90.0	72.0	85.7	100.0	78.0	58.3	99.2	
1968										—	96.0	96.9	97.3	28.2	83.0	90.0	83.3					97.6	99.1

Figures 5.2 to 5.4 are in fact largely due to the rate at which the individual aircraft have been scrapped. Crashes appear to be spread over an aircraft life for both jet and propeller aircraft, although it does appear that in the first year a higher than average number of departures due to crashes has taken place. The questions now are whether scrappings are determined by economic variables and whether departures from stock are an important determinant in the aircraft order cycle.

5.4 Departures and orders

Wastage, due to scrapping and crashes, leads to a loss in aircraft stock, and to a leftwards shift in the supply curve of aircraft services (assuming utilisation to be constant). However, the effect of such a departure is not exclusively confined to a leftwards shift in the supply curve, for it may induce new aircraft to be ordered. If such a direction of causation exists, wastage effects positive shifts in supply because of the stimulation it gives to replacement orders and thus future deliveries.

The structure of the industry is important in understanding the relationship between orders and wastage. Purchases of new aircraft are concentrated among a few airlines of the world, probably around 20.[17] These 'front rank' airlines are differentiated from the rest of the airlines in that they are almost exclusively purchasers of new aircraft, whereas the latter 'second rank' airlines choose between used and new aircraft. The front rank airlines therefore account for a large proportion of first purchases and they are the largest sellers of used aircraft. Table 5.5 shows the age of aircraft stock of these front airlines compared with the age of the total stock, showing clearly the rapid turnover of equipment. In order to explain the relationship between new orders and departures it follows that we need to consider departures from stock due to scrapping, crashes and sales. Sales are obviously important, for as Table 5.6 shows, the number 'surviving'[18] the first owner drops rapidly after around 5 years. Individually aircraft types differ, which again suggests economic and technical conditions in particular years are important in explaining these departure rates.

A possible explanation of the cycle in civil aircraft orders is that it is determined primarily by technological factors which define rigorously the structural strength and efficiency of the aircraft equipment. Thus, it is suggested that the technology of the aircraft defines the age at which the aircraft becomes susceptible to failure, and the rate at which operating costs increase with age. A number of assumptions can now be made which

Table 5.4

Percentage of jet aircraft stock surviving annually

Age year	0	1	2	3	4	5	6	7	8
1954		95.6							
1955		100.0	100.0						
1956		100.0	95.0	95.4					
1957		97.1	100.0	100.0	100.0				
1958		98.6	96.0	98.9	97.3	100.0			
1959		95.6	100.0	100.0	100.0	100.0	100.0		
1960		97.2	100.0	98.6	100.0	98.9	95.2	100.0	
1961		96.6	99.3	99.6	99.3	100.0	97.0	97.2	100.0
1962		98.3	98.6	99.0	98.4	99.2	97.9	100.0	100.0
1963		96.6	100.0	99.6	99.6	98.7	99.2	100.0	100.0
1964		99.6	99.3	99.5	97.9	99.0	99.6	98.5	97.9
1965		98.0	99.6	97.1	98.7	99.6	99.3	99.0	99.2
1966		97.9	99.4	100.0	98.5	98.7	99.6	100.0	100.0
1967		99.4	99.2	100.0	99.2	100.0	98.3	99.2	98.0
1968		99.1	99.7	99.4	98.8	99.2	97.7	98.7	99.2
1969		98.7	99.6	99.7	99.8	99.4	99.2	96.9	100.0
1970		99.3	99.2	99.6	99.8	99.8	100.0	98.8	97.2
Means		98.0	99.0	99.0	99.0	99.4	98.5	98.8	98.9

will allow us to use these points and to suggest a relationship between new orders and the age of the aircraft stock.

Firstly, we assume the market is one with no second hand market. Secondly, there is no technological change in the design and efficiency of the aircraft types. Thirdly, the market is stationary, so that new orders are merely replacement orders for existing equipment. The age of the equipment will then be the major determinant of the timing of replacement orders, the age distribution within the stock at any one time determining the magnitude of the order. If for any (exogenous) reason there has been a bunching of orders and deliveries in the past, this will result in similar bunching of scrapping and replacements after a period of time determined by the life of the equipment. Because we have suggested that the life of equipment is sharply defined, past fluctuations in deliveries will be reflected in order and delivery 'echoes' in the future.

In this simplified model, we have suggested that fluctuations in aircraft

9	10	11	12	13	14	15	16	17	18
100.0									
100.0	100.0	100.0							
98.8	100.0	100.0	100.0						
100.0	100.0	100.0	100.0	100.0					
100.0	100.0	100.0	100.0	100.0	100.0				
99.3	97.0	97.8	100.0	100.0	100.0	100.0			
99.0	98.1	96.2	92.3	97.7	100.0	100.0	100.0		
99.6	98.9	98.7	96.8	92.9	98.8	100.0	100.0	100.0	
99.1	98.9	99.3	98.3	97.5	98.7	97.6	100.0	100.0	100.0
98.9	99.1	99.0	97.9	97.0	99.3	98.8	100.0	100.0	100.0

orders are determined largely from the supply side in that they are due to sharply defined technological conditions. As economic efficiency declines with age, then the older aircraft will be replaced by similar but newer models when the average variable costs of the old aircraft exceed the total costs of the new aircraft. It is suggested that this will be concentrated around a narrow age range; in other words there will be a sharp rise in the average variable costs of the old aircraft around a given age. Furthermore, given the nature of the market in which there are no second hand buyers, the decision to replace will be accompanied by a decision to scrap. New orders, therefore, will be timed closely with the timing of scrapping.

If we remove some of the assumptions, it can easily be seen that the relationship between scrapping and replacement orders is not as close as is suggested in this simplified model. Once the assumption of zero growth is removed, demand as well as supply determines the cyclical behaviour of replacement orders. If the market experiences positive growth, orders will

Table 5.5

Age of aircraft stocks, 1953–68

Year ending	Front rank airlines	Age of total aircraft stock
1953	5.49	11.64
1954	5.66	11.96
1955	6.07	12.44
1956	5.78	11.11
1957	6.08	11.41
1958	6.10	12.21
1959	5.90	9.34
1960	6.16	9.26
1961	6.35	9.73
1962	6.65	10.75
1963	7.26	11.50
1964	7.19	11.54
1965	7.64	11.85
1966	7.17	11.04
1967	7.20	10.46
1968	6.30	9.34

consist of replacements and net additions to stock, the latter being determined by expectations of future growth in the market. We therefore have to explain both elements if we are to explain total orders. Unfortunately, we are not able to explain replacements of scrapped equipment wholly by means of life expectancy. This is simply because the age of scrapping, for a variety of aircraft types (see Table 5.7), is far from similar. Wastage rates appear to be economically, rather than rigidly determined by aircraft technology. We need, therefore, to examine the determinants of departures because of wastage, and then to see the relationship between orders and wastage rates.

It has been outlined above that the decision to scrap is one which is determined by market conditions as well as technical ones. Given that crashes appear to be randomly distributed over the age of the aircraft life (see the last section), an aircraft will be scrapped when its average variable costs exceeds the selling price prevailing in the market. Whether the scrapping induces a replacement order depends upon the relationship between the expected long term selling price (RL) and the total costs of the new aircraft

166

(*TC*). If *TC* = *RL*, then a replacement order will be advanced, but none will be ordered if *TC* > *RL*.

Scrapping is likely to be positively related to operating costs of older equipment, and negatively related to the selling price. The relationship of scrapping to new orders, however, is affected by the market segmentation between front rank purchasers of new aircraft and the second rank airlines who choose between new and second hand machines. In a market situation when rates have fallen, scrapping will tend to increase, yet such aircraft are likely to be in the hands of the second rank operators. These airlines, if they are to make a replacement for their lost equipment, have a choice between second hand or new equipment. The impact of the wastage rate on new orders will depend upon the division of the aircraft stock between the two classes of operators, and the relative movements of new and used aircraft prices. If a high proportion of the scrapped aircraft are in the hands of second rank operators and if the prices of used aircraft fall more (or rise less steeply) than new aircraft, this is likely to lead to a purchase of used aircraft instead of new aircraft. The relationship between orders and departures may be indirect if departures from first owners through wastage and sales stimulate new orders. It is more likely however that the relationship between orders and departures is in the other direction. Sales are likely to occur after new aircraft are delivered, when rates decrease because of the rightwards shift in the supply curve. It is more likely then that wastage is determined by deliveries, rather than being a major determinant of orders. We have shown in Table 5.8 the modal year of departure, and how it differs between the aircraft types. The evidence is that the assumption of a closely defined average life expectancy is not valid, but that there exists a strong relationship between scrapping and economic variables. Thus, although there is no relationship between age and departure, there may be a relationship between the calendar date and the scrapping rate between differing aircraft types. In an attempt to examine the possible relationship between departures and economic/technological conditions, we related the percentage departing for each type to the calendar year, to see if the rise in scrapping had any cause. There appeared to be close timing in the departures for individual types, such that we reexamined our data, recording the calendar date of departure due to scrapping. This information is shown in Table 5.8.

Table 5.9 shows that the distribution between ownership and scrapping has largely been performed by first owners. With the exception of 1964, first owner scrapping has exceeded second[19] owner scrapping. The age of scrapping is interesting, the arithmetic means suggest considerable variation in age between years, which is another piece of evidence refuting the

Table 5.6

Sales departures from first owner

AGE	MODEL L1649	Viscount 700	Canadair C-5	L-749	L1049	L049	Viscount 800
1	0	0		2	1	11	6
2	0	0		0	2	4	3
3	9	2		3	1	0	3
4	11	0		0	5	14	1
5	9	8		3	5	7	0
6	14	1		4	7	2	0
7	2	2		2	8	4	3
8	7	1	4	2	9	4	7
9	0	5	0	1	10	11	7
10		7	4	0	11	2	0
11		1	9	2	8	3	1
12		2	0	3	13	2	
13			2	4	3	1	
14			8	6	4	0	
15			2	3		12	
16			0			18	
17			0			0	
18			2				
19							
20							

suggestion that aircraft scrapping is rigidly determined by technological factors.[20] In order to relate these departures to economic variables, we have presented in Table 5.10 the number scrapped for the years 1954 to 66, and related them to the load factor and an index of used aircraft operating cost. The former is the weight load factor obtained from ICAO sources, and has been used as an indicator of market conditions. The international market in civil aviation, of which most of these aircraft are engaged in serving, is characterised by rigid fares.[21] Load factors, reflecting the demand and supply in the final market gives a more accurate representation of the airlines' future prospects than the average airline fare. A high load factor represents a buoyant market when demand approaches supply, while the reverse holds for the case of a low load factor. The used aircraft cost index has been obtained from the data contained in D. Sawyers and R. Millers (5) Appendix I. (The data refers to operating costs, less depreciation, of the aircraft types covered in the study.[22])

With these two variables, load factor and operating costs, we postulate that aircraft scrapping will be positively related to aircraft operating costs

| DC-6B | DC-7C | DC-7B | DC-7 | DC-6 | DC-6A | Fleets standardised to 100 | |
						All aircraft	Small aircraft
	1				6	3	4
	3		1		7	2	2
	5				20	2	3
1	3				10	4	2
2	1		20	1	8	5	6
4	5		16	2	7	4	1
12	8	29	16	2	3	5	2
8	13	14	4	1	5	5	4
7	1	14	21	0	3	7	7
5	1	12	9	0	3	6	5
10	1	6	5	7	3	4	1
4			2	2	6	6	2
3				6	3	4	2
7				6		4	1
7				7			
				3			
				5			
				3			
				4			

and negatively related to load factor.[23] In times of market growth, with load factor rising, even though used aircraft costs are rising, scrapping is likely to be delayed owing to the demand for equipment to provide the final demand for services.

A regression run on the data contained in Table 5.8 resulted as follows:

Scrapping regressions
The dependent variable: number scrapped

Constant	Load factor	Used aircraft operating costs	R^2	
370	−5.95		0.88	(5.1)
	(0.65)			
4.23	−6.61	+0.14	0.88	(5.2)
	(1.28)	(0.23)		

log linear

16	−8.3		0.84	(5.3)
	(1.06)			
19.5	−9.6	+0.59	0.85	(5.4)
	(2.1)	(0.87)		

Note: The load factor variable (proxy for price expectation) appears to be more significant than used aircraft operating costs.

It is suggested therefore that aircraft scrapping is a function of economic variables and not of technological determinants of aircraft operation. Secondly, the relationship between aircraft scrapping and new orders appears to be only a slight one. Table 5.9 shows that in most years the number of aircraft scrapped as a percentage of total aircraft orders is small. For those years in which there is a large percentage of orders, such as 1962, it can be shown that, in terms of capacity, the capacity scrapped is a small percentage of the total capacity ordered. This is brought out in Tables 5.11 and 5.12.

Table 5.7

Modal age of aircraft departures

Model	Modal age
L 1099	12
Canadair C-4	14
L 1649	11
V - 800	1
V - 700	1
L - 749	17
L 049	1
DC-4	12
DC-7C	2
DC-7B	9
DC-6A	4
DC-6	1
DC-6B	11
DC-7	7
Viking	15

Table 5.8

Departures: scrapping 1954–66

Date	Age at departure Scrapping age (mean)	Number scrapped		
		Total	First owner	Second owner
1954	5.5	20	16	4
1955	7.9	15	10	5
1956	4.5	21	18	3
1957	12.0	19	17	2
1958	16.2	34	28	6
1959	14.2	47	43	4
1960	8.0	41	33	8
1961	9.6	63	37	26
1962	9.4	94	61	33
1963	9.5	64	36	28
1964	10.7	66	32	34
1965	11.9	55	37	18
1966	11.3	58	34	24

Table 5.9

Deliveries, orders and departures

Table: date	Sales from first owner	Total wastage	Number of aircraft ordered	Wastage as a percentage of orders	Number of aircraft delivered
1954	30	20	85	23	140
1955	18	15	359	4	106
1956	41	21	300	7	290
1957	24	19	143	13	280
1958	16	34	143	17	300
1959	62	47	180	26	216
1960	74	41	260	15	197
1961	112	63	256	24	247
1962	169	82	163	50	164
1963	98	64	254	25	102
1964	134	66	375	17	213
1965	132	55	872	6	277
1966	85	58	832	6	351

Table 5.10

Wastage, load factor and used
aircraft costs

Date	Wastage due to scrapping	Load factor	Used aircraft cost
1954	20	59.0	100
1955	15	59.0	99
1956	21	59.3	103
1957	19	57.4	105
1958	34	56.3	96
1959	47	57.0	101
1960	41	55.2	109
1961	63	51.6	119
1962	94	50.8	132
1963	64	50.5	128
1964	66	51.1	140
1965	55	51.7	151
1966	58	52.8	140

Table 5.11

Relationship between the size of aircraft scrapped
and the size of aircraft ordered in 1962

Capacity (Average production capacity) million tonne km per annum	Numbers:	
	Scrapped	Ordered
0 - 5	73	49
6 - 9	4	27
10 - 15	2	12
16 - 20	3	75

In 1956, the year of the jet ordering boom, the relationship between
the aircraft stock and the new orders was such that the new orders were for
much larger aircraft than the existing stock. In 1962, the capacity scrapped was likewise much smaller than the size of aircraft ordered. Thus, even
if all aircraft which were scrapped stimulated a new order, these orders as
a percentage of total orders were small, even in those years when scrapping
has been heaviest.[24]

Table 5.12

Size distribution of ICAO fleet in 1956

Size (Average production capacity) million tonne km per annum	In use in 1956	On order at end of 1956
Under 1,000	1596	—
1,000 – 2,000	1078	—
2,000 – 3,000	735	210
3,000 – 4,000	396	—
4,000 – 8,000	—	168
8,000 – 10,000	—	30
10,000 and above	—	248

Scrapping is, therefore, not technologically determined, nor is it the main cause of cycles in ordering. If scrapping is the main cause of the industry's cycle, it would coincide with peak ordering; clearly this is not the case, for scrapping and orders are not causally linked. It is suggested that the direction of causation is as follows: order – deliveries – low load factors – high scrapping.[25]

Notes

[1] An interesting exception to this is a study of the tankship market by Zannetos [1].

[2] See the end of this chapter for statistical sources.

[3] For an interesting discussion of the many implications of capital stock measures see Z. Griliches [2]. This section of the chapter draws heavily from the points made in the article. See also P. Redfern [3].

[4] See Table 4 Chapter 8 for details of the accounting practices of the major US airlines.

[5] Given that a_{54} is the aircraft stock in 1954, and that d represents the depreciation rate. Then assuming a constant rate of depreciation, replacement stock in 1954 is calculated as follows:

$$a_{54} = (1-d)^{10} a_{44} + (1-d)^9 a_{45} + \ldots + (1-d)a_{53} + a_{54}$$
$$a_{55} = (1-d) a_{54} + a_{55}$$
$$a_{56} = (1-d) a_{55} + a_{56}, \text{ etc.}$$

[6] See Figure 6.3. Chapter 6.

[7] Figure 5.1 has used information supplied by BAC Weybridge. In recognition of the different markets for long and short range aircraft, we have divided aircraft up according to whether their potential output (as measured by ICAO data) exceeded 6 million tonne km per annum.

[8] See ICAO measures for the calculation of these average figures. These estimates are used in the study. To quote ICAO's definition of average productive capacity: 'It is the product of the average block speed and available payload for each type. The block speed figure is obtained by reducing the mean cruise speed by 15% to allow for the time spent in climb and descent and in other delays in the air such as diversions and stacking. The available payload figure is obtained by reducing the maximum payload by 20% in order to allow for varying configurations and conditions of operation.' See ICAO Circular 89-AT/15, July 1968, p. 39.

[9] See the end of this chapter for details on the ICAO stock measures.

[10] Aircraft stock = Deliveries of new aircraft − Aircraft scrapped.

Aircraft scrapped = Deliveries of new aircraft − Aircraft stock

[11] The survivor curve used in the deflation, taken from Table 5.4 of this chapter, was as follows:

Age	1	2	3	4	5	6	7	8	9	10
Percentage surviving	98.7	98.3	98.0	97.8	97.2	96.4	93.3	93.3	93.9	91.8

11	12	13	14	15
90.5	87.3	80.2	79.0	79.0

[12] The real price index was obtained by deflating the observed price index by a quality change index. The quality adjustments were obtained by taking cross-sections at various years which provided weights of the quality variables. The quality dimensions which appeared to be the most important were speed (S) and seating capacity (C). Two of the cross-sections used were as follows:

1955   Price = 2.3 + 0.2 (C) + 0.030 (S)

1966   Price = −2.6 + 0.54 (C) + 0.004 (S)

These weights were used in a chain index in which changes in the observable quality dimensions were used to deflate the price index. For details of construction see I. Adelman and Z. Griliches [5] and for data sources see the end of this chapter.

[13] See the end of this chapter.

[14] The basic approach is that developed by insurance firms for purposes of calculating human life expectancy. Let l_0 be the initial number of

aircraft built. Let l_x be the number of aircraft still existing x years after delivery, when l_0 is 'standardised' to 100, l_x corresponds to the survivor table of the life. $d_x = l_x - l_{x+1}$ where d_x is the number of aircraft departing at the age of l_{x+1}. $q_x = \dfrac{d_x}{l_x}$ is the departure probability of an aircraft leaving at the age x from its owner due to a crash or scrapping.

[15] See for instance Miller and Sawyer [6] p. 104. 'A large part of its amazing performance during the war was due to the exceptional durability of the DC-3. It was designed and first produced 30 years ago — at a time when much less was known about many aspects of aeronautical engineering. As a consequence the DC-3 was, in a sense, over designed in many respects, and more so than in recent airliners. At many points in the aircraft, materials were used which were stronger than would have been necessary, or methods were applied which would have been adequate for larger, more advanced air planes.'

[16] Sources of the auto survivor curve taken from Boulding [7] and that of ships from Parkinson [8].

[17] For details of the concentration of ownership see Table 6.1, Chapter 6.

[18] The survivor tables have been calculated from the same sources as those including only crashes and scrapping. For details see the statistical sources listed at the end of this chapter.

[19] Second owner here refers to owners other than first owners. Hence, the airline scrapping could in fact be the third, fourth or fifth owner, etc.

[20] If this were so, one would expect the ages at which aircraft are scrapped to be similar.

[21] For the relationship between load factors and fares see Chapter 3, section 5.

[22] For details of the data used see statistical sources listed at the end of this chapter.

[23] If scrapping necessitates replacement, then during a slump scrapping is likely to be delayed. Of course, scrapping is encouraged if it can be undertaken without replacement. We suggest that the latter condition generally prevails.

[24] In the heaviest year of scrapping, the percentage scrapped was only 3.9 per cent of the total stock.

[25] The relationship between sales, orders and deliveries is developed and estimated in Chapter 7.

References

1 Z.S. Zannetos, *The Theory of Oil Tankship Rates*, MIT Press, 1966.
2 Z. Griliches, 'Capital stock in investment functions: some problems of concept and measurement', *Measurement in Economics: Studies in Memory of Y. Grunfeld*, Stanford, 1963.
3 P. Redfern, 'Net investment in fixed assets in the U.K. 1938–53', *J. Royal Statistical Soc. Vol. 118*, 1933 Series A.
4 R. Hall, 'Technological change and capital from the point of view of the aviation industry', *Review of Economic Studies*, Jan. 1968.
5 Irma Adelman and Z. Griliches, 'On an index of quality change', *American Statistical Association Journal*, September 1961 (pp. 535–48).
6 R. Miller and D. Sawyer, *The Technical Development of Modern Aviation*, Routledge & Kegan Paul, London, 1968.
7 K. Boulding, 'An application of population analysis to the automobile population of the US', *Kyklos*, vol. VIII, 1953.
8 J. R. Parkinson, 'Ship wastage rates', *Journal of the Royal Statistical Society*, vol. 120. Series A, 1957 (pp. 71–84).

Statistical sources

1 *Aircraft stock*

The two major sources of annual figures are various *ICAO Statistical publications* (in particular circulars 89–AT/15, 73–AT/10, 76–AT/11 and 77–AT/12) These give figures at the year's end, whereas Esso's *Inventories of Airline Fleets* takes mid year estimates. Other major sources are Jane's *All the World's Aircraft* and various annual publications in *Flight International*.

Individual data on pre jet aircraft were obtained from various *Air Britain* monographs and *A.A.S. International* publications. The former provided life histories of the DC-4, DC-6, DC-7 and the Lockheed Constellation Series. The latter provided details on the DC-3, Convair Catalina and the Viking. Other sources of propeller aircraft were P. Brooks, *The Modern Airliner* (London, Pitman 1961), K. Munson, *Civil Airliners since 1946* (Blandford Press, 1967), P. W. Brooks, *The World's Airliners* (London, Putnam 1961) and the other historical studies in the Putnam series. The turboprop and turbojet aircraft details were obtained from G. Swanborough's *World Airline Registrations* (Ian Allan 1970). These sources provided information on the date of entry, sale, scrapping, etc.

176

2   Aircraft orders

This was obtained from the major UK aircraft producers BAC and Hawker Siddeley. Further supplementary information was obtained from Boeing and from *Flying Review International* which provided monthly inventories of orders and deliveries, and Esso's *Inventories of Airline Fleets.*

3   Aircraft prices

The new aircraft price index was obtained from various sources. These were *Aviation Studies International Ltd*, *Flight*, *Lloyds Civil Aircraft Register* and *Aviation Week*. Direct correspondence with producers also provided information. A comparative source was provided by Appendix II of R. Miller and D. Sawyer's *The Technological Development of the Modern Airliner* (Routledge & Kegan Paul, 1968).

Used aircraft prices were obtained from diverse sources. These were: *Aircraft-Exchange*, Wold and Associates, *Aviation Studies, Flight, Aviation Week* and *Lloyd's Civil Aircraft Register. Aircraft Exchange Services* provided the bulk of the information from 1961, and thanks to BAC, we were able to obtain monthly information on the behaviour of prices from this source.

4   Used aircraft operating costs

This information was obtained from R. Miller and D. Sawyer (*op cit*), Appendix I. In this appendix details were provided of operating costs of aircraft on USA routes. These costs were taken, after removing the depreciation item.

5   Labour cost index

This index, used to deflate the aircraft input price was obtained by taking the annual earnings provided by *F.A.A. Statistical Handbook of Aviation* of pilots, co-pilots and other flight personnel, and dividing by the number of workers in the categories.

6 The World Demand for Civil Aircraft

6.1 Introduction

In the last few years, civil air transport production, for so long a small portion of the aerospace industry, has been rapidly increasing its share of the industry's turnover. The turndown in the Vietnam war and the cutback in the space programme has left the industry vulnerable to the vagaries of the civil market. It is a market characterised by spectacular technological achievements − from Super Connies to the Supersonic Concordes in two decades. Fluctuations in orders have been sharp, lead times long[1] and profits slim. A question of some importance to the industry concerns the causes of these order fluctuations.

We have a number of reasons for attempting to answer this question, to discover the relationships between market structure, technological change and order fluctuations; to evaluate these relationships, to produce forecasts and to offer some suggestions as to the likely effects of altering aspects of the market structure. Here, we shall concentrate on the first task by outlining the structure of the industry, and then suggesting and testing alternative explanations of order behaviour.

The industry is characterised by high concentrations among aircraft producers and buyers. Table 6.1, for instance, shows the proportion of aircraft bought first hand by particular aircraft companies. With the exception of a few short range aircraft (e.g. the HP Herald, the Fokker F-27), purchases have been concentrated among a few airlines, usually the larger US trunk carriers and a few European and Commonwealth operators. Barely twenty airline companies in the world have been consistently first hand purchasers of aircraft. Production is even more concentrated, Boeing having provided 49 per cent of the jet aircraft produced, Douglas 29 per cent, 6 per cent by other USA manufacturers, while the rest of the world has provided the remaining 16 per cent.[2]

The buyer concentration, particularly among the larger jets, reflects the small number of airlines competing on routes where fares are rigidly controlled and product differentiation an important competitive weapon.[3] Aircraft purchases in such a market structure are important decisions in

Table 6.1: Buyer concentration of aircraft

Aircraft type	Number of buyers of first hand aircraft	Percentage of total number purchased by the largest airline buyer	Number of airlines accounting for over 50 per cent of purchases	
			No.	Names
Viscount 700 and 800	48	16	4	Air Canadian, BEA, United, Capitol
Vanguard	2	23	2	BEA, Air Canada
Electra	13	23	3	Eastern, American, KLM
Comet IV	8	41	2	BOAC, Aerolineas
Trident	8	80	1	BEA
VC 10	4	80	1	BOAC
Boeing 707	30	21	3	Pan Am American, TWA
Boeing 727	30	26	3	American, United, Eastern
DC-8	23	28	3	United, Delta, Eastern
DC-9	26	16	4	Air Canada, TWA, Delta, Eastern
BAC I-II	20	33	2	BEA, American
Boeing 720	16	19	3	United, American, NW
Convair 880	4	44	2	TWA, Delta
HS 748	13	20	2	Aerolineas Argentinas, Varig
HP Herald	21	25	9	
Fokker F-27	23	10	12	
FH 227	5	31	2	Ozark, Mohawk
Convair 990	7	98	2	American
Canadair C-54	2	50	2	Air Canada, BOAC
DC-4	8	33	2	Pan Am, American
Lockheed Connies	6	58	1	Pan Am
Caravelle	23	8	10	Pan Am
DC-7C	13	20	4	Pan Am BOAC, KLM, SAS

the battle over market expansion. Inability to have attractive new equipment when competitors are already operating them could mean losing a large share of the market. Decisions to purchase new aircraft types are therefore likely to be similar to price decisions in an oligopolistic market, such that when the price leader reduces price, the rival firms quickly follow. The two major postwar equipment decisions, the jet purchases in 1955 and the jumbo jets of 1966, have in fact been characterised by very rapid airline response. The jet purchases in 1953, set off by Pan Am in ordering twenty B707's on 13 October 1955, were so rapid that before the end of the year all the major world airlines had ordered their jet fleets.[4] The response to the Pan Am decision to order twenty five B747's on 13 April 1966 was a little slower, non-American airlines JAL and Lufthansa being next in line. Nevertheless, the reponse was rapid and the capacity ordered within the second quarter was enormous.

Both ordering peaks were sufficiently high to cause concern. Over ordering, it was claimed,[5] was due to the oligopolistic nature of the market. Airlines competing for market shares ordered all at once, for to do otherwise in a price regulated market would have meant competing with rivals who had differentiated their product. The speed of response once a rival had ordered was too rapid[6] to allow an airline to consider the aggregate behaviour of the industry. The individual airline ordered along with its rivals, all receiving their aircraft within a short space of each other. Order bunching was reflected in delivery bunching. It was usually at the point of delivery that criticisms of the industry structure were made, yet clearly overcapacity entering the stock may reflect not excess capacity ordered, but over-estimates of demand at the time of ordering.

This *ex post* reasoning is often confused, mistaking over-optimistic forecast for over-ordering. The result is the same, though the difference lies in the explanation given for the cause. Ruling out incorrect demand forecasts, excess capacity when delivery takes place has been explained by the oligopolistic structure. Take for instance Caves [2] commenting on the jet ordering in 1955:

> Market share aspirations are highly rivalrous, and this would be even more apparent if the availability of finance did not restrain the smaller carriers so significantly. As the volume goes to press (1961), the impression grows that the trunks orders for jet aircraft have totalled more than enough to supply the probable demand, indicating a weak recognition of oligopolistic interdependence in planning aircraft investment.

The year 1961 was the biggest trough the industry had fallen into since the war, yet in the same year, Foldes [4] presented a different interpretation. 'Experts say that there will be excessive capacity, and the airlines are far from being over confident, yet they are driven to buy jets in order to complete, I should be inclined, on the whole, to attribute these recent bursts of investment to necessity rather than folly.'

The confusion in the argument has been caused by relating economic conditions at the time of delivery instead of at the time when the orders took place. The two peaks in ordering, in the third quarter of 1955 and the second quarter of 1966, took place during periods of general economic optimism. During 1955, the US economy grew by 5 per cent (GNP *per capita* in real terms), the then highest postwar growth year, while 1966 was also a period of high growth (6 per cent). In the third quarter of 1955, traffic on US routes was up by 15 per cent on the equivalent period in 1954. In 1966, revenue passenger miles were estimated to be 26 per cent up on the previous year, and along with increased traffic the airlines showed increased earnings. For the first 9 months the airline industry's revenues were $4.2 billion, up 14.2 per cent for the comparable period of 1965, while net earnings were up by 11.3 per cent. The prospects of the industry were reflected in an all time high for the airline shares, yet 4 years later when the orders materialised in deliveries, share prices had dropped by 75 per cent. By 1970 capacity had outstripped growth, resulting in load factor drops from 58·5 in 1966 to 50·0 in 1970.

The ordering peaks have in fact been in line with the US economy high points, while the troughs have also coincided. This is to be expected in an industry selling a product with a high income elasticity and a large proportion of business purpose traffic. This close relationship with the national trade cycle and the long lead times in the industry suggest demand forecasting has been largely at fault for the excess capacity in 1961 and 1970, rather than any oligopolisticly induced over-ordering.[7]

The point of interest, however, concerns the timing and the magnitude of the ordering process. The capacity ordered may or may not be excessive with respect to actual demand achieved. From the point of view of forecasting, we wish to discover whether the orders and ordering peaks can be explained, and therefore predicted, by economic models of firm behaviour.

The problem in achieving this has been mentioned earlier. It is the effect of the industry's structure on the ordering process. Orders are likely to be affected by changes in demand, aircraft prices, rates of interest, etc. and also by the industry's oligopolistic structure. The timing of a large ordering spree may be due to the availability of a new aircraft, the extent and duration of the orders by the intense equipment rivalry of a few large airlines. In such a market structure, the timing of orders may be explained, if representative measures of technological change, income, prices, etc. are obtained and correctly specified in an acceptable model of firm behaviour. The extent of the ordering spree is unlikely to be adequately explained. It is likely to be determined by equipment rivalry and inter-company prestige, factors which are non-quantifiable but which follow from price restricted competition. In such a situation, discussion can only centre on the adequacy of the most acceptable model in explaining orders, and the likely effects on order peaking of removing industry controls, such as non-price competition.

Such an exercise requires comprehensive data. This was obtained from diffuse sources. The prime sources were the leading aerospace producers: Hawker Siddeley, BAC, McDonnell Douglas, Boeing and Lockheed. Cross-checks were made by using order details published in *Interavia, Flight International, Airline Management* and the now defunct *Flying Review International*. The monthly figures which these sources revealed were aggregated into quarterly totals, providing a continuous time series from 1954 to 1969. The explanatory variables used in the models were financial variables, capital stock, aircraft price and a measure of technological change.

Representative financial variables as such are difficult to calculate, owing to the heavy government subsidies enjoyed by many airlines and the changing structure of finance which the industry has gone through since the early 1950s. We concluded that profit variables would be of little use owing to the heavy government subsidies given to many airlines, details of which are difficult to obtain. Instead we relied on the rate of interest as a financial variable which both expressed a financial constraint and represented an important variable in the financing arrangements of the new, expensive jets. The problem was the choice of an appropriate rate. Owing to the predominance of the US market, and the fact that many foreign airlines have recently raised money there, we chose the rate prevailing in this market.

Two measures of aircraft stock were used; aircraft numbers and aircraft weighted by their respective capacities.[8] Both measures were deflated by information on aircraft life expectancy, details of which are to be found in Ellison and Stafford [7].[9] Of the two measures, the deflated aircraft capacity measure of stock was found to offer the most acceptable explanation. Hence, the model estimates using capital stock as a variable refer to this measure.

The new aircraft price index was also compiled from varied sources. These were Aviation Studies International Limited, *Flight*, Lloyds Civil

Aircraft Register and *Aviation Week*. Direct correspondence with aero-space producers provided a check, and a comparative source was found in R. Miller and D. Sawyer [8], appendix II. The index was deflated by taking a labour cost index, taken from the annual earnings provided by the FAA *Statistical Handbook of Aviation* of pilots, co-pilots and other flight personnel, and divided by the number of workers in the categories.

Technological change was handled by considering new aircraft prices and then deflating by changes in aircraft characteristics which were seen to represent aspects of the technological change in aircraft. The method of calculation was the same as used by I. Adelman and Z. Griliches [9], who calculated a similar measure of technological change in motor cars. The real price index was obtained by deflating the observed price index by a quality change index. The quality adjustments were obtained by taking cross-sections at various years which provided weights of the quality variables. The quality dimensions which appeared to be most important were speed and seating capacity.[10] The weights obtained from these cross-sections were then used in a chain index in which changes in the observable quality dimensions were used to deflate the price index. Technological change, therefore, was represented by a quality deflated price index of new aircraft.

The data used in the models is displayed in Table 6.2, with the exception of the dependent variable, aircraft orders. A number of the aerospace manufacturers allowed their data to be used, on condition it was not publically displayed. An idea of the magnitude of the orders, however, can be obtained from Figures 6.2 to 6.8.

6.2   Order models

Aircraft are durable factor inputs whose services are inputs into the production of aircraft flights. The demand for such an input is derived demand for the service produced by the factor inputs. It is also determined by the production function of the airline and the supply conditions of other factor inputs. It is the stock of the aircraft which enters the production function and so the demand for aircraft is the demand for a stock of aircraft and not the annual purchases of new aircraft. Thus, the annual demand for new aircraft, aircraft investment, is derived from the demand for aircraft stock.

Explanations of investment have often started with a stock demand model, causally linked to economic variables by means of time lags. Often these time lags encompass a series of decisions starting with the change in

Table 6.2

World figures

Date		Price index of aircraft PA	Price index - quality change PQ	Financial* variable FV	Date		Price index of aircraft PA	Price index - quality change PQ	Financial* variable FV
1955	1	101	102	3.09	1963	1	163	163	4.35
	2	101	97	3.14		2	168	168	4.35
	3	102	99	3.18		3	170	170	4.40
	4	102	98	3.19		4	175	175	4.45
1956	1	104	100	3.29	1964	1	175	174	4.48
	2	105	101	3.45		2	175	174	4.50
	3	106	95	3.62		3	176	175	4.48
	4	108	99	3.89		4	176	175	4.49
1957	1	110	101	3.84	1965	1	177	169	4.47
	2	112	103	3.86		2	178	170	4.50
	3	114	105	4.19		3	178	170	4.59
	4	119	110	4.21		4	179	171	4.71
1958	1	121	119	3.79	1966	1	180	172	4.92
	2	123	120	3.78		2	181	170	5.12
	3	125	123	3.67		3	182	171	5.40
	4	127	125	4.20		4	183	172	5.48
1959	1	132	131	4.23	1967	1	183	172	5.23
	2	137	136	4.44		2	183	172	5.43
	3	142	141	4.61		3	183	172	5.78
	4	147	146	4.73		4	182	171	6.19
1960	1	149	148	4.70	1968	1	183	172	6.81
	2	150	159	4.59		2	183	173	7.03
	3	152	151	4.47		3	185	175	7.27
	4	153	144	4.47		4	187	177	7.60
1961	1	153	144	4.40	1969	1	187	177	6.81
	2	153	144	4.41		2	188	178	7.03
	3	153	144	4.42		3	189	179	7.27
	4	153	144	4.55		4	152	182	7.68
1962	1	155	145	4.54					
	2	158	149	4.45					
	3	159	150	4.48					
	4	160	156	4.39					

*Moody's yield on AA shares

economic variables, the formulation of new plans, the appropriation of new funds, the ordering of the new investment and the actual delivery. All these decisions are likely to involve time lags, such that the assumptions often used in models with deliveries as the dependent variables are invalid.[11] We shall concentrate here on the variables determining the decisions to order an aircraft and the time lag involved in this decision.

Deliveries at t are, of course, orders $t-n$ periods ago, assuming a given delivery time and non-cancellation of orders. Similarly, stock is approximately the integral of former orders. It is reasonable therefore to conceive of a 'stock' at the ordering stage, an inventory stock, that after the production lag becomes the actual delivered stock figure. The desired stock is a future desired stock and is likely to enter airline (investment) order determination. However, formulation of an order model from the usual stock adjustment model is subject to certain difficulties.

Let us take the simplest model, for example:

$$K_{t+1} - K_t = \gamma(K_{t+1}^* - K_t)$$

where K is the actual model, K^* is the desired stock and γ is the coefficient of adjustment. This offers a behavioural explanation of aircraft orders.

While accepting the behaviouristic assumption that airline investment is derived from the demand for aircraft stock, it is not certain how the airlines perceive their future desired stock. One problem is the delivery time and its variation. Airlines may not accurately predict this delivery time. More important is the competitive framework within which orders are made. Rather than responding with a lag to the determinants of desired stock, the response may be rapid and orders heavy, due to the oligopolistic interdependence of the investment decisions. For inputs subjected to such market conditions the adjustment path to equilibrium has special significance. In the usual adjustment model, such as the one above, coefficient γ embodies the order lag and the order delivery lag, and as such is not apportioned any behaviouristic significance. In the case of the aircraft market, however, the path of adjustment towards the equilibrium can provide information as to the impact of market structure. Indeed, the ordering cycle in the industry has been a highly fluctuating one, such that there is a need to formulate an adjustment path which can account for this, and at the same time to have a credible behaviouristic interpretation.

The models developed and estimated show that the form of the model can have important effects on the adjustment path. The pertinent questions these models have to answer are what determines (a) the timing and (b) the magnitude of order placing in the aircraft market. It is easy to identify the peaks roughly with the adoption of a new type of aircraft, i.e. a technological change, to which one then asks, can such peaks be predicted?

Section, 6.2.1, sets out and tests various forms of the stock adjustment model, while the last model concentrates on airlines' investment and its determinants, divorcing investment from desired stock on the grounds that the airlines buy in a market of such interdependence that notions of

186

future desired stock are of little importance. Such considerations are swamped in the competitive interdependence of airlines buying equipment in order to expand to maintain their share of the market. The model is simply an explanation of order behaviour.

6.2.1 *Introductory concepts of aircraft ordering*

It is recognised that fleet planning is directed towards 'equalising expected traffic and proposed fleet capacity'. Let us suppose that in the past an order policy has been succesfully pursued in order to arrive at a constant load factor. This assumes that orders are placed in each time period proportional to the divergence between present stock and a notional demand. The point is that airlines are assumed to have an equilibrium load factor [12] in mind, so that when demand increases and pushes up the load factor [13] beyond the equilibrium, aircraft orders are stepped up.

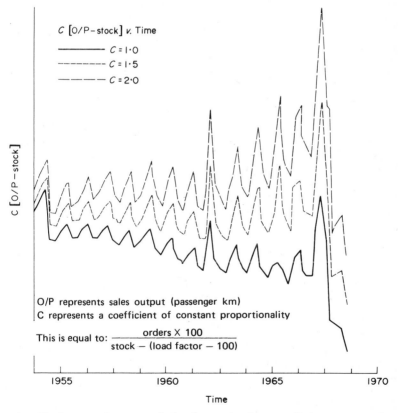

Fig. 6.1   Various estimates of the hypothesis: equalising expected traffic and proposed fleet capacity

The curves of Figure 6.1 illustrate such a divergence and exhibit the peaking effect found in the order data, with rather more seasonal characteristics and an extra peak in 1961. The airlines would surely take account of production time and be more concerned with a divergence in forecasted demand and stock, rather than current demand and stock, and hence the curves of Figure 6.1 would be smoothed for the purposes of such a simple order model. Apart from the peaking, such an observation is not sufficiently helpful in explaining the order data in a conclusive way, and thus we seek a further explanation.

It is clear that each of the ordering peaks is linked with the adoption of a new aircraft type such as the jet, the jumbo, etc. Such forms of technological change stimulates growth in sales of aircraft, derived from the expected increased sales of seats to a novelty conscious travelling public. The ordering pattern is linked with the stock pattern, since the latter is approximately the integral of the former. Thus, a stock growth model will incorporate the ordering process, and if suitably formulated, will do so in an explicit manner.

If it becomes practical to conceive of a 'stock' at the ordering stage, i.e. an inventory stock, this may be equated to the cumulative order total. If cancelled orders can be neglected, and a simple order-delivery lag in production assumed to be T quarters, then the 'ordered stock', W, becomes equal to normal stock, K, after a time delay, T.

$$K_t = W_{t-T}$$

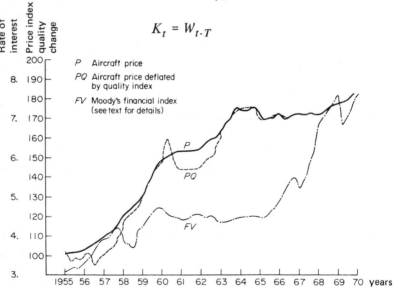

Fig. 6.2   Independent variables used in the aircraft order models plotted over time

It is clear that ordering takes place in times of economic optimism, so that financial indices may yield a clue to the ordering pattern and, again, technological and economic aspects of aircraft available over the time scale studied will play a part in the ordering process. A plot of three proposed explanatory indices is given in Figure 6.2.

The adoption of a new aircraft type, such as the jet, can be considered to follow a time path somewhat similar to that of a number of other durable commodities such as television sets, cars and computers. The path of this adoption can be described in terms of capital stock in the following way.

The natural growth of any new product, y, will eventually tend to zero, as the market is saturated, unless the saturation or equilibrium level is altered. Even with a fixed equilibrium level, however, as appears with a new but unalterable product, the growth depends positively on the existing level, because of the increased contact between potential buyers and the product, as the latter becomes accepted. These two characteristics, equilibrium (saturation) and contact growth, may be built into a simple model according to:

$$\frac{dy}{dt} = \alpha \, y(y^* - y) \qquad\qquad (6.1a)$$

$$\frac{dy}{dt} = \alpha \, y(\log y^* - \log y) \qquad\qquad (6.1b)$$

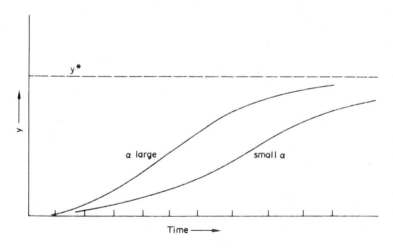

Fig. 6.3   Gompertz characteristic

189

where y^* is the equilibrium level or, more directly, using the differences equation equivalent:

$$\log y_t - \log y_{t-1} = \alpha(y^* - y_{t-1}) \qquad (6.2a)$$

$$\log y_t - \log y_{t-1} = \alpha(\log y^* - \log y_{t-1}) \qquad (6.2b)$$

The response to either (6.2a), (6.2b) to fixed y^*, and with initial value of zero, is of the form of Figure 6.3. It is clear that other models could be devised to give such a response shape in particular distributed lag models might be employed. However, because of the usefulness of the Gompertz and logistic curve, as discussed in [12], this initial investigation employs equations (6.2a) and (6.2b).

6.3 Capital stock adjustment model

The above use of an adjustment model is conveniently associated with the capital stock adjustment model. Thus, an overall study of the growth of stock might be based primarily on the equation,

$$\frac{d(\log K)}{dt} = \alpha(\log K^* - \log K) \qquad (6.3)$$

without reference to the ordering process. Although it is clear that an incremental capital stock adjustment model is equivalent to an order adjustment model, with the attendant practical complications of a distributed lag, it is clear that a more sluggish system, for example one with a greater mean time lag, must produce a slow response to a technological or market demand change, which is characterised by a small value of the fixed parameter α. This is merely equivalent to expanding the time scale, and it becomes evident that two entirely different order-delivery processes may through this macro (or aggregating) study yield nearly equal values of α, because the effect of the difference weighting factors β in the expression:

$$D_t = \Sigma_i^t \beta_i O_{t-1} \qquad (6.4)$$

where O represents aircraft orders. To reflect fully the order-delivery process, and hence perhaps to arrive at the ordering policy, a stock adjustment model incorporating distributed lags shall ideally be employed.

190

However, it may be hoped that some insight may be gained using the following simplified model.

If we express equation (6.3) in delivery terms, and assume a simple order-delivery lag of ℓ, then

$$\frac{d \log \Sigma^t D_i}{dt} = \alpha (\log K_t^* - \log K_t) \qquad (6.5a)$$

$$\frac{d \log \Sigma^{t-\ell} O_i}{dt} = \alpha (\log K_t^* - \log K_t) \qquad (6.5b)$$

or transforming, to include orders at the present time,

$$\frac{d \log \Sigma^t O_i}{dt} = \alpha (\log \hat{K}_{t+\ell}^* - \log \hat{K}_{t+\ell}) \qquad (6.5c)$$

Both terms on the right hand side are future estimates, designated by ^, the simple, assumed known, order-delivery lag precisely determining the stock ℓ time periods ahead. (This, of course, is in error if the lead time is incorrectly assessed.) The difference equation that may be used to replace the left hand side describes the dynamics of the ordering process.

To obtain $\hat{K}_{t+\ell}^*$, we assume, for example, that future desired stock estimates are related to future aircraft prices and future passenger output x, z by

$$\hat{K}_{t+\ell}^* = a \, \hat{x}_{t+\ell}^b + c \log \hat{z}_{t+\ell}^c \qquad (6.6)$$

or

$$\log \hat{K}_{t+\ell}^* = \text{constant} + b \log \hat{x}_{t+\ell} + c \log \hat{z}_{t+\ell}$$

Thus, given estimates of x, z at a time ℓ periods into the future a regression may be made that checks the order policy hypothesis at the current time, once again under the assumption that this kind of model is an acceptable description, and also with an assumed smoothing method. The left hand side of equation (6.5c) is expressed as either:

$$\log K_{t+\ell} - \log K_{t+\ell-1} \qquad (6.7)$$

or

$$\log \Sigma^t O_i - \log \Sigma^{t-1} O_i$$

This expression, representing the logarithm of the growth rate of the cumulative order total, is the means by which the delivered stock equation

Table 6.3

Growth rate in cumulative orders

$$\frac{\sum^{t_0}_i}{\sum^{t}\overline{o}_i^1} = V_t = \frac{W_t}{W_{t-1}}$$

		V				V
1955	1	—		1963	1	1.032
	2	1.382			2	1.031
	3	1.331			3	1.035
	4	1.833			4	1.050
1956	1	1.116		1964	1	1.070
	2	1.055			2	1.043
	3	1.080			3	1.082
	4	1.095			4	1.062
1957	1	1.034		1965	1	1.099
	2	1.036			2	1.113
	3	1.096			3	1.127
	4	1.014			4	1.072
1958	1	1.017		1966	1	1.125
	2	1.024			2	1.169
	3	1.098			3	1.101
	4	1.021			4	1.078
1959	1	1.025		1967	1	1.050
	2	1.014			2	1.036
	3	1.079			3	1.058
	4	1.051			4	1.065
1960	1	1.076		1968	1	1.204
	2	1.068			2	1.046
	3	1.046			3	1.015
	4	1.109			4	1.020
1961	1	1.062		1969	1	1.019
	2	1.089			2	1.012
	3	1.012			3	1.005
	4	1.074			4	1.003
1962	1	1.022				
	2	1.039				
	3	1.022				
	4	1.046				

$$\log \left(\frac{K_{t+\ell}}{K_{t+\ell-1}}\right) = \alpha \left[\log \hat{K}^*_{t+\ell} - \log \hat{K}_{t+\ell-1}\right]$$

is transformed into an ordering policy model.

The attached Table 6.3 gives the growth rate in the cumulative stock at the order stage, at a given time t. Any orders made at time t, if account is taken of the production time of aircraft, will make eventual contributions to the delivered stock, after a certain time interval. Since data of delivered stock, passengers, financial variables, etc. only exist in useful form from 1955, it is only possible to obtain three year forecasts from 1958, four year forecasts from 1959, etc. It is therefore not possible to make use of all of the data of ordered stock, W.

Taking equation (6.7), where ˆ indicates a forecast figure and assuming a simple lumped lag of ℓ periods, then putting the left hand side in terms of current orders O_t (that will have eventual effect at time $t+\ell$), we obtain the growth rate (V) equation:

$$\log V_t = \left[\log \hat{K}^*_{t+\ell} - \log \hat{K}_{t+\ell-1}\right] \tag{6.8}$$

Replacing $K^*_{t+\ell}$ by the unspecified variables $\log \hat{FV}_{t+\ell}$, $\log \hat{PA}_{t+\ell}$, $\log \hat{PQ}_{t+\ell}$, we regress the known $\log V_t$ against the logs of the forecast quantities stock, sales, price index of aircraft, price index deflated for quality. Quarterly data for the period 1955–1969 is used (as shown in Figure 6.2).

Table 6.4

Estimates of the ordering policy model

Dependent variable log W	Independent variables				Four year model			
Constant	log R	log K	log PA	log FV	log PQ	R^2	DW
−0.69	+0.25	−0.4	0.42			0.35	1.8
0.048	+0.19	−0.16		−0.11		0.34	1.7
0.11		−0.02		−0.067		0.13	1.3
0.03		−0.06			+0.04	0.09	1.2

Dependent variable log W	Independent variables				Three year model			
Constant	log K	log V_t	log PA	log FV	log PQ	R^2	DW
−0.06	0.21	−0.17		−0.14		0.34	1.67
−0.002	0.21	−0.2				0.27	1.53

Regressions based upon this model appear in Table 6.4, where surprisingly low R^2 values are obtained for 8, 12 and 16 quarters. Brown's method [14] is used for the forecast variables that influence $\hat{K}^*$, the forecast desired stock. The sign of the $\hat{K}$ coefficient is correct since a rise in forecast actual (delivered) stock should lead to a diminution in ordering. Figure 6.4 shows the observed and predicted growth rate in 'ordered stock', i.e. cumulative orders, where a roughly consistent pattern is obtained, despite the low R^2 value. (See also Figure 6.5.)

6.3.1 *Linear capital stock adjustment models*

The logarithmic forms chosen allow easy manipulation of a series of hypo-

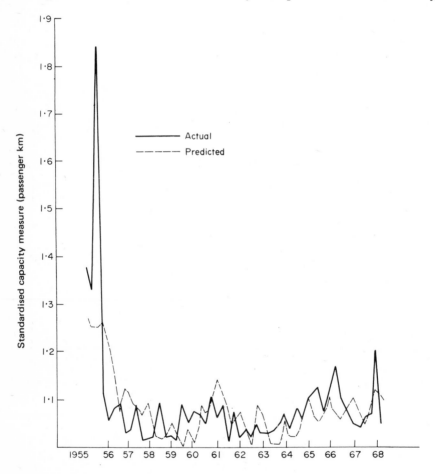

Fig. 6.4 Growth rate V of ordered stock W. Four-year forecast model $R^2 = 0.35$ $D.W. = 1.8$

194

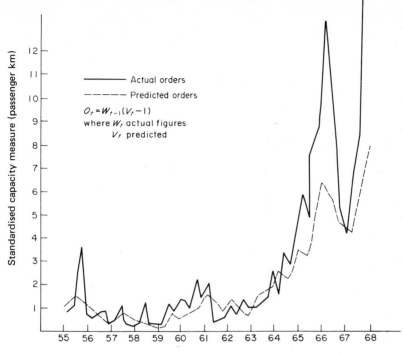

Fig. 6.5   Four-year log model

thetical relationships for y^*. Clearly, however, the response of linear systems might have some applicability, for example:

$$y_t - y_{t-1} = k(y^* - y_t) \qquad \text{First order linear model}$$

$$a\,y_t + b\,y_{t-1} + c\,y_{t-2} = y^* \qquad \text{Second order model}$$

The second of these equations may be derived from a diffusive system to ensure one point of inflection and no overshoot by fixing a, b, c at a given ratio.

The cumulative orders W_t may again be employed as a 'future stock', and the dynamics derived in W_t should offer a policy in O_t. The cumulative order curve W predicted from the linear models are found to strongly agree with the observed W values.

Typical results are:

$$W_t = 24.4 + 1.2W_{t-1} - 3.98FV_{t+8} \qquad\qquad R^2 = 0.99 \;\; D.W. = 1.7$$

$$W_t = 6.7 + 1.45W_{t-1} - 0.39_{t-2} - 1.4FV_{t+8} \qquad R^2 = 0.99 \;\; D.W. = 2.1$$

195

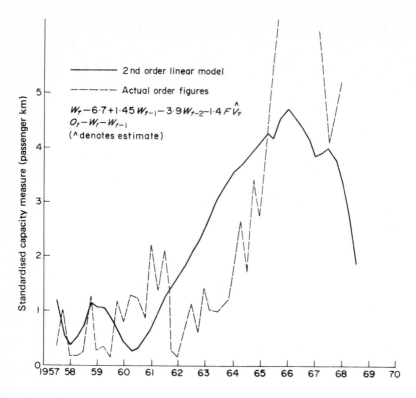

Fig. 6.6   Linear capital stock model: estimated orders compared with actual orders 1957–69

but it is evident that the first order model is unstable, that is, as soon as the ordering policy $O_t = W_t - W_{t-1}$ is inserted, the ordering magnitudes become unstable. The second order model, on the other hand, is stable and the results of model compared with actual figures appear in Figure 6.6, where a certain degree of peak following exists. Essentially, however, it is realised that the ordering pattern will not be explained fully by any such linear model, except with regard to mean trends. The extremes of the ordering pattern can hardly be due to a smooth function of reasonably constant variables. Either (a) a non-linear ordering policy exists of such a type that the structure suddenly changes (dependent on variables already present) or (b) the exogenous variable y^* suddenly attains dramatic heights, i.e. an additional y^* appears, or (c) the aggregation process has masked individual ordering policies that would point towards these critical peaks.

A more sophisticated treatment of the order-delivery model, which leads to a more viable ordering policy, and also possibly (since this de-

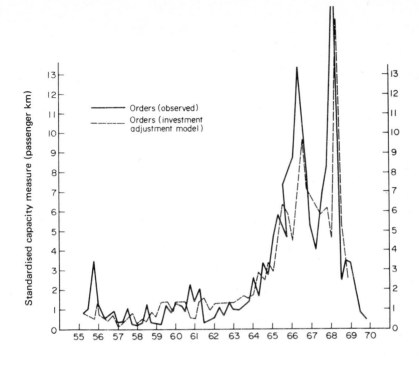

Fig. 6.7   Linear capital stock model: estimated orders compared with actual orders 1955–69

pends on the degree of sophistication) a more descriptive model, recognises the distributed nature of production processes. Assuming:

$$D_t = \Sigma^t \, O_i \, \beta_{t-1}$$

then   where D represents deliveries

$$K_t = \Sigma^t \, D_i \qquad\qquad (6.9)$$

so that O_i has an effect on many future values of K. Equally, K_t depends on all the O_i made previously or better, on K_{t-n} plus $O_{t-1}, O_{t-2}, \ldots, O_{t-n}$ where n is the lag order. Order policy at time t is linked with an eventual error citerion of $\Sigma_i [K_i^* - K_i]^2$, where the summation limits extend over the distributed lag. This can be posed as a dynamic programming problem given that the current ordering policy aims to keep the stock as near to a desired level as possible. A characteristic of the regressions of Table 6.4 is the low values of R^2 which, in conjunction with a log model, imply doubtful

197

predictive accuracy. This is borne out by Figure 6.7, where the features of interest are to be found in that the predictions are in no way related to the ordering peaks, and therefore a new approach has to be sought. It is felt desirable, however, to maintain the idea of an equilibrium towards which the dynamics act, except that the basic equilibrium is an equilibrium level of the rate of ordering.

Since a new aircraft can set off a wave of orders, a technological change is viewed as a permanent excitation that affects the equilibrium level K^*. However, if the technological change willy-nilly sets off an ordering response, with no reference to the future effect of this ordering on stock levels, then this represents a highly fashion-conscious (or service competitive) system. This will now be investigated and compared with the more measured and leisurely form of policy based on future desired and projected stock.

6.4 Investment adjustment model

Remembering that the dynamics of ordering follow equations (6.2a) or (6.2b), we imply that there are constraints that prevent an order immediately being made equal to a desired (equilibrium) order level.

Instead of the previous capital stock adjustment model, we now propose that movements in aircraft price index, total registered aircraft stock, output sales, etc., have a direct effect on orders placed. These variables define a desired level of ordering, to which the aggregate industry adjusts. If this desired level presists, then the ordering pattern becomes constant so that major peaks in the ordering pattern must be due to strong variations in the desired order rate. No explicit account of future trends is taken, and the absence of a forecasting method and therefore smoothing, allows small sudden variations in the explanatory variables to produce sudden order rate changes. No assumptions of a pure production lag are necessary since ordering is carried out, on this model, without reference to the eventual delivered stock.

Equation (6.3) then is written:

$$\frac{d\,[\log O_t]}{dt} = [\log O_t^* - \log O_{t-1}]$$

or

$$\log O_t - \log O_{t-1} = [\log O_t^* - \log O_{t-1}] \qquad (6.10)$$

Table 6.5

Estimates of investment adjustment model

Dependent variables		Constant	$\log O_{t-1}$	$\log(FV)_t$	$\log(P)_t$	$\log(PQ)_t$	$\log(K)_t$	RSQ	DW
(a)	$\log O_t$	−0.34	+0.69	+1.08				0.64	2.17
(b)	$\log O_t$	−2.9	+0.64	−0.027		+1.56		0.67	2.2
(c)	$\log O_t$	−3.5	+0.63	−0.28	−1.9			0.62	2.2
(d)	$\log O_t$	+0.94	+0.53	−1.15		+0.86	−1.5	0.69	2.06

Table 6.6

Estimates of investment adjustment model with additional sales variable

Dependent variable		Constant	$L\,O_{t-1}$	$L(FV)_t$	$L(P)_t$	$L(OQ)_t$	$L(K)_t$	$L(O/P)_t$	RSQ	DW
(a)	$\log O_t$		+0.56	−0.24		+0.22			0.68	2.2
(b)	$\log \bar{O}_t$	−0.72	+0.54	−0.64			−0.42	0.75	0.70	2.2
(c)	$\log O_t$	+0.88	+0.51		−1.1		−0.59	0.86	0.69	2.1

The oligopolistic system in a qualitative competitive environment, then, according to this model is based on a level of investment set by external, current factors. The test of this assumption is based upon regressions of $\log O_t$ against $\log O_{t-1}$, $\log (FV)$, $\log (PA)$, etc. Typical results are given in Tables 6.5 and 6.6 where Table 6.6 incorporates the additional variable of output sales $(D_t)t$. These results may be put into the Gompertz form of equation (6.2a) by, for example, the following manipulations. Taking the regression (a) of Table 6.5.

$$\log O_t = -0.34 + 0.69 \log O_{t-1} + 1.08 \log (FV)_t$$
$$= -0.34 + (1 - 0.31) \log O_{t-1} + 1.08 \log (FV)_t$$

Identifying α of equation (6.2b) with 0.31 we obtain:

$$\log O_t - \log O_{t-1} = 0.31 \left(-\frac{0.34}{0.31} - \log O_{t-1} + \frac{1.08}{0.31} \log (FV)_t\right)$$

so that $\log y^*$ is identified with $-1 + 3 \log FV$.

Neglecting for the moment the constant, it is possible to identify the possible forms of O^*, and from the signs of the coefficients, the validity of the model. Thus, we find the following values:

$$O^* = \delta (FV)^{1.08/0.31}$$

$$O^* = \delta (FV)^{-0.027/0.36}$$

$$O^* = \delta (FV)^{-0.028/0.37}$$

$$O^* = \delta (FV)^{-1.2/0.47}$$

where δ is a general constant of proportionality. The first result is ruled out according to this method. The relatively low values of R^2 place some doubt upon this hypothesis, but it is for the present, accepted.

Result (c), of Table 6.5, yields a predicted O_t' that in comparison with the capital adjustment model, bears a startlingly good approximation to the actual order pattern. However, the equilibrium value O^*, given by:

$$\log O^* = -\frac{0.72}{0.46} - \frac{0.64}{0.46} \log FV - \frac{0.42}{0.46} \log K + \frac{0.75}{0.46} \log (D_t)_t \quad (6.11)$$

is less satisfactory, although the coefficients of FV, K, $(D_t)_t$ are of the correct sign.

(d) of Table 6.5 yields:

$$\log O^* = \frac{0.94}{0.47} - \frac{1.15}{0.47} \log FV - \frac{0.87}{0.47} \log PQ + \frac{1.5}{0.47} \log K$$

or
$$O^* = 2\, FV^{-2.2}\, PQ^{-1.9}\, K^{3.1} \qquad\qquad (6.12)$$

The equilibrium level rises as the financial variable FV falls, as the quality deflated price index falls and as the stock, which reflects the passenger growth, rises. In the cases where both stock and output appear in the regressions (c) and (d) of Table 6.6, the coefficients are of opposite sign. This is expected to be normally the case, since while a passenger growth is likely to necessitate more aircraft, a rise in the aircraft stock is an indicator that if anything the order rate should fall off.

Of great interest is that the R^2 figures for each model appear much the same. Also if (c) of Table 6.6, for example, yields peaking at much the same points as the actual order data, then calculation of O^* should indicate the special conditions of FV, etc. that causes this ordering rush to take place. As both ordering peaks have taken place in times of economic optimism, to what degree then does a quality change in a new aircraft

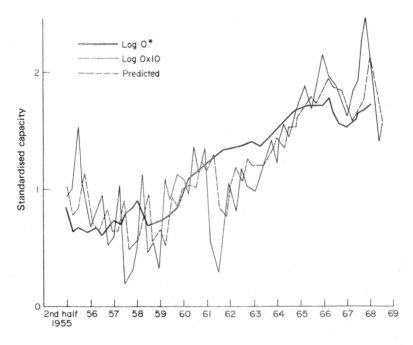

Fig. 6.8   Investment adjustment model: estimated orders compared with actual orders 1955–69

suddenly tip the scales? How do we incorporate 'newness' as a quality in the present model?

We can show that at critical times, due to a combination of correct conditions, the market goes off bang. The question is, does it do so every time these conditions are the same, or is this ordering sensitivity made insensitive after a buying peak from a newness point of view, i.e. that a novel aircraft is more novel the longer the time between its appearance and the last big market surge?

Referring to Figure 6.8, it is seen that O^* does not reflect the down-swing in orders that occurred in 1961 although the general trend of orders is similar to that of O^*. In 1955 and 1967, orders are seen to be predicted in timing if not magnitude by the 'equilibrium order level' O^*. The particular conditions of 1960 might be explained by a full expenditure commitment by the airlines, together with a slight pessimism with respect to O^* and the future expected O^*. Thus, as the slope log O^* flattens, the net impact is that the order rate drops, although when the slope change in O^* is seen not to preclude a general collapse, the ordering level rises again. The individual variations in actual orders may be assumed to reflect the slope changes in O^*, or log O^*.

Overall the concept of an equilibrium level yields a possible method of predicting a future order pattern. The general state of the airlines is one of optimism, buying when the market conditions are good, but with a 'new-ness factor' that effectively leads to times of pessimism when the signs of a good time to place orders are effectively ignored. Taking this period to be 8 years, then one might expect that if we can forecast the determinants of O^* for a period ahead, and succesfully include a meaningful measure of technical advance in an aircraft (such as quality deflated aircraft price,) then any time 8 years after 1965 will see a buying spree, the moment the first sharp rise in O^* is encountered.

The determination of where the rush initiates on this rise may be posed in stochastic terms as exemplified by a random (noisy signal) activating a threshold system. The random system in fact consists of the exact point of decision for the major airline managements to purchase. Unfortunately the random signal is impossible to forecast in any one particular case and can only be expressed over a large number of cases. Each of the other airlines follow suit and place orders rapidly, but at differing speed responses. The aggregate response, however, is given by the model taken from Table 6.5, equation (d):

$$\log O_t = 0.94 + 0.53 \log O_{t-1} - 1.15 \log FV - 0.868 \log (PQ) - 1.5 \log K \quad (6.1$$
$$ (0.2) \qquad\qquad (0.5) \qquad\qquad (0.4) \qquad\qquad (0.6)$$

202

The figures in brackets refer to standard errors and as can be seen, most of the variables are significant. There is no reason why these variables cannot be forecast into the future, and this model used as a forecast of civil aircraft orders.[15] There are, of course, many difficulties; the problem of interpreting monetary changes in the future is perhaps a more difficult task than forecasting technical changes.[16] At least the likely forecasters, the civil aircraft producers, do have a measure of control over the technical developments embodied in aircraft design.

6.5 Conclusions

Let us see how we have arrived at our present position. Although the aircraft seat is a perishable commodity, the aircraft providing the seat is durable, with a certain life span, and can thus be regarded as equivalent in some respects to computers, televisions, etc. However, unlike most durable commodities, where a saturation of ownership can be realistically considered to exist, there is no such foreseeable limit to the demand for air travel and to the purchase and ownership of aircraft. Nevertheless, the concept of an equilibrium level is convenient to employ and hence the technique of a saturation-type market reponse to innovation is carried over to this problem.

When this idea is further extended to include the idea of an equilibrium level of ordering, then the idea of instant action based on current market conditions arises, rather than action based upon forecast expected market conditions. A list or a description of such an ordering mechanism is found in Almon [15], where appropriations are influenced not so much by output, but by orders. Since expected variables are always smoothed versions of their origins, the investment adjustment model we propose inherently embodies more fluctuation than a capital stock adjustment model.

O^*, the equilibrium order rate indicates the peaking points, while the results of the regression compare reasonably with the actual order figures. It also appears, from equation (6.12), that the order peaks occur less than three quarters after the critical conditions O^* have taken a sharpish rise.

The investment adjustment model in fact offers the most convincing explanation [17] of aircraft orders. It suggests technological change sets off a desired order rate independently of expected future stock levels. Such tested relationships, plus the rapid speed of response, indicates that industry is subject to intense service competition, which in turn is due to the oligopolistic structure of the airline industry. It does not follow, however, that the structure is the cause of aircraft over-ordering. Whether the actual ordering rate exceeds demand is, of course, partly determined by the uncontrollable behaviour of demand. The problems of excess capacity over the last 20 years appear primarily to be due to the coincidence of the timing of major aircraft deliveries with serious economic depressions.

Considerable technological change, along with concentrated aircraft purchases do appear, however, to have been the cause of the considerable fluctuations in aircraft orders. This raises two points. Forecasts of future orders will have to consider not just the forecast of technological change, but the airline structure. For instance, will the growth of charter traffic lead to a widening of the first hand order market? This appears to be happening, and so reducing the order instability that this narrow market base has caused. Secondly, the aerospace industry's increasing dependence on civil sales forces consideration of these policy priorities to the management of the airline industry. If they view stability of sales as being a desirable object, then perhaps we shall see their increasing interest in the debates concerning the removal of price competition and the diminution of service rivalry.

6A.1 Appendix

A. Phillips' fundamental aim in his work *A Study of the Aircraft Industry* (Heath Lexington Books, 1971) was to establish the exogenous nature of technological change with respect to the civil aerospace industry of the US. His thesis, in summary, was that the exogenous technological change, developed in independent research establishments and military projects, effected and shaped the structure of the US civil aerospace industry.

Various approaches were used to establish the thesis including case histories and intensive detailed statistical analysis. From our point of view, however, Chapter IV contains the most interesting analysis. Using time series data taken from US trunk operators' records, he tested a three stage recursive model, in which a passenger demand, supply and aircraft demand model were formulated. The accepted model forms and results are contained in Table 6A.1.

Of particular interest is the third equation concerning the demand for aircraft. The dependent variables are aircraft deliveries, and not orders, and so differ from our estimates. Nevertheless, Phillips uses this variable and a measure of technological change to explain aircraft orders. The fit was poor . . .

. . . the fact that so small a portion of total variance in annual additions to the fleets can be statistically explained within the context of
a recursive market model indictates that aircraft demand arises from
sources other than those covered by the statistical model. And this
model is one which emphasises variables based on rather conventional economic reasoning.

If equation 4.11 (–in table I it is the last equation) or another
similarly specified variant of it had explained a large proportion of
the variance in the demand for aircraft, the weight of the evidence
therefore could not have been interpreted on being against the acceptance of the main hypothesis of this book. If the demand for
aircraft can be explained by passenger demand and by variables representing rational and controllable change in variables describing the
state of technology, then technology would itself appear as an endogenous aspect of the market process.

However, Phillips does recognise the practical difficulty of formulating
a meaningful measure of technological change, for he states on page 71:
'Successful major types of new aircraft appear discontinuously over
time . . . . No single variable captures the effects of technology on the
demand for aircraft.'

A number of comments on this study and the conclusions drawn:

1   Although the market studied is the major proportion of the world
market, the data is aggregated into annual estimates. As we have seen,
fluctuations are sharp, and occur within quarters. Furthermore, an analysis
of order fluctuations needs to consider production lags for, as we have
seen, these vary considerably over the period studied.

2   On a methodological point, the statement on page 69 suggests that a
model explaining aircraft demand implies that technology is an endogenous aspect of the market process. This does not follow. Surely proof is
not shown by failure in this case; all it shows is the inability of the few
models tested to explain aircraft demand. The form, model and data used
may be inappropriate, technological change is difficult to translate into a
form which has meaning to the airlines, but as we have seen in the models
tested in this study some measures provided a reasonable explanation.

However, a model explaining past demands is unlikely to be an accurate
predictor of future purchases. But then this is a failure of many models,
with or without technological variables.

Table 6A.1

Estimates of **Phillips'** aircraft demand model

Model	Variables	
	Dependent	Independent
Demand 1947–65		
$R^2 = 0.763$ $D.W. = 2.50$	$\dfrac{PM_t}{PM_{t-1}} =$	$1.114 - 1.372\,\dfrac{P_t}{P_{t-1}} + 0.848\,\dfrac{Y_t}{Y_{t-1}} + 0.610\,\dfrac{Y_{t-1}}{Y_{t-2}} - 0.019\,F_{t-1} - 0.016\,VA$
		$\qquad\qquad\;\;(0.308)\qquad\quad(0.372)\qquad\quad(0.336)\qquad\qquad(0.009)$
Supply 1947–65		
$R^2 = 0.691$ $D.W. = 2.59$	$\dfrac{SM_t}{SM_{t-1}} =$	$0.445 + 0.647\,\dfrac{PM_t^*}{P_{t-1}} + 0.028\,(U'_{t-1}) + 0.061\,(U'_{t-2}) - 0.003\,(t)$
		$\qquad\qquad\;(0.127)\qquad\quad(0.019)\qquad\quad(0.018)\qquad\quad(0.001)$
Demand for Aircraft 1947–65		
$R^2 = 0.491$	$\dfrac{NP_t \cdot}{S_{t-1}} =$	$-0.515 + 0.418\left(\dfrac{SM_t^*}{SM_{t-1}}\right) + 0.054\left(\dfrac{SM_{t-1}}{SM_{t-2}}\right) + 0.019\,(MA_t) + 0.017\,(NLR_t)$
		$\qquad\qquad\;\;(0.164)\qquad\qquad\quad(0.041)\qquad\qquad\;\;(0.061)\,(NNLR_t)$
		$\qquad\qquad\qquad\qquad\qquad\qquad\qquad\qquad\qquad\qquad\qquad(0.018)$

Variables

PM_t = **passenger miles of trunk line air transportation** demanded during time period t.

P_t = price per passenger mile during time period t.

Y_t = income during time period t.

q_{it} = qualitive aspects of air transportation relative to time period t (for example speed, safety, etc.) $(i = 1, \ldots, m)$.

SM_t = seat miles of trunk line air transportation supplied during time period t.

π_t = anticipated rate of return in supplying SM_t.

NA_t = number of new aircraft added to fleet during time period t.

t_{jt} = technical characteristics of new aircraft in existing fleets (e.g. speed, passenger capacity) $(j = 1, \ldots, n)$.

F_t = number of fatal accidents during time t.

NP_t = a dummy variable representing the introduction of a significantly new long haul aircraft.

U_t = load factor at time t.

U_t' = is an approximation of the ideal utilisation rate.

$PM*E$ = the 'planned' passenger miles.

SM_t^* = the 'planned' seat miles.

$NNLR_t$ = the sum for non long range planes.

NLR_t = the sum of the percentages of the first 12 months of deliveries of long range planes in a given year.

Notes

[1]   See A. P. Ellison and E. M. Stafford [1]

[2]   See ICAO Bulletin May 1971, p. 39.

See Caves [2] p. 306 where he points out that the early jets had a stimulative effect on demand of between 5 to 10 per cent.

[4]   See United Airlines 'Chronology of domestic carrier initial jet orders' exhibit No. U-5. New York to San Francisco non-stop, Case Docket no. 9214.

[5]   See D. A. Saunders 'The airlines' flight from reality', *Fortune* p. 217, L111, February 1956. A similar view, expressed with respect to the US Market, is found in A.J. Gellman [3].

[6]   See for instance the following quoted in 'Jet transport orders set airline future': *Aviation Week*, 1 October 1956: 'Most Airline Executives would have preferred to wait longer to make their decisions but in the airline industry, when one orders, all must order to avoid being left behind in the race for a faster, more novel product to sell.' Caves [2] p. 317—18 suggests over-ordering is due also to impulsive management, and to competition for route awards. In the latter case, airlines have been know to buy equipment in the hope that this will influence a licensing decision in their favour. Failure to win naturally results in a lost gamble, and excess capacity.

[7]   The arguments concerning market concentration and investment variation are in fact still in contention. At one side of the argument is Duesenbury [5] p. 113—33 who suggests that non-price competition places service reliability to the forefront of competition. During peak demand the firm with capacity reserves is likely to retain the patronage of customers, a factor which motivates oligopolists to expand their market shares by means of extending productive capacity. During expansion, it is likely that investment will be considerable but sharply curtained when growth declines. On the other hand Richardson [6] p. 67—70 and 128—36, suggests markets characterised by price fixing and mergers create information sources which helps to produce the correct amount of investment to meet the required demand.

[8]   The capacity measure uses ICAO data. To quote from their statistical circular 89—AT/15, July 1968, the definition of average production capacity is given as 'the product of the average block speed figure and the available payload for each type. The block speed figure is obtained by reducing the mean cruise speed by 15% to allow for time spent in climb and descent and in other delays in the air such as diversions and stacking. The available payload figure is obtained by reducing the maximum pay-

load by 20 in order to allow for varying configurations and conditions of operation.'

9 This reference [7] also gives details of the stock figures used, the various conceptual problems in measuring aircraft stock, and the methods and details of calculating aircraft mortality figures.

10 Two of the cross-section estimates used in the quality deflation were:

1955 Price = 2.3 + 0.2(c) + 0.030(s)
1966 Price = -2.6 + 0.54(c) + 0.004(s)

where s = speed and c = seating capacity.

11 See [10].

12 See [11].

13 Load factor refers to the number of seats which are actually sold as a proportion of seats which are available. Expressed in percentage terms it measures the deviation between demand and supply at the fixed fare level.

14 See Brown [13] and also P.J. Harrison [14].

15 The orders above in capacity units are now distinguished from aircraft order numbers by a dash, O'_t will thus replace O in equation (6.13), for example, when we are considering aircraft numbers at the same time as capacity (see Chapter 9).

16 A more difficult problem, however, is predicting the response of the airlines to the technology embodied in the new aircraft.

17 A similar approach was tried by Phillips [15] Chapter 4. His model, however, related annual aircraft deliveries to such variables as technological change and the supply of aircraft devices. Using a three stage estimating model on US trunk data 1947–65, he obtained poor fits. See the Appendix to this chapter.

References

1 A.P. Ellison and E.M. Stafford, 'The order delivery lag in the worlds' civil aircraft industry', *Applied Economics,* 1973, 5, pp. 19-34.

2 R.E. Caves, *Air transport and its regulators*, Harvard Univ. Press, Cambridge Mass., 1962.

3 A.G. Gellman, 'The effect of regulation on aircraft choice', unpublished Ph.D. Dissertation, MIT 1968.

4 L. Foldes, 'Domestic air transport policy', *Economica*, May and August 1961.

5 J. Duesenbury, *Business Cycles and Economic Growth*, MacGraw-Hill, 1958.

6   G.B. Richardson, *Information and Investment*, O.U.P. 1960.

7   A.P. Ellison and E.M. Stafford, 'How many aircraft are there?', *Shell Aviation News*, April 1972.

8   R. Miller and D.S. Sawyer, *The Technological Development of the Modern Airliner*, Routledge & Kegan Paul 1968.

9   Irma Adelman and Z. Griliches, 'On an index of quality change', *American Statistical Association Journal*, September 1961.

10   Z. Griliches, 'Distributed lags—a survey', *Econometrica*, vol. 35, no. 1, January 1967.

11   R. Nivet, 'Methods of selecting the most suitable aircraft for a particular pattern of operations planning fleet procurement', *Oxford R.A.S. Course*, April 1958.

12   G. Chow, 'Technological change and the demand for computers', *American Economic Review*, pp. 1117–30, 1970.

13   R.G. Brown, *Smoothing, Forecasting and Prediction of Discrete Time Series*, Prentice Hall 1963.

14   P.J. Harrison, 'Short-term sales forecasting', *Applied Statistics*, vol. 14, 1965.

15   S. Almon, 'Lags between investment decisions and their causes', *Review of Econnimics and Statistics* vol. 50, 1968.

16   A. Phillips, *Technology and Market Structures: A Study of the Aircraft Industry*, Heath Lexington Books, 1971.

7 The Order - Delivery Lag in the World Civil Aviation Industry

7.1 Introduction[1]

It is now two decades since the orders were placed for the first commercially operative turboprop aircraft. Over this period the advent of subsonic, supersonic and wide bodied jets have transformed both the airline and aerospace industries. The airline industry has grown to dominate large sections of the economically advanced nations' international and inter-city transport networks, while civil aircraft sales have now risen to a substantial share of the world aerospace industry's turnover. Fluctuations in the final passenger market have considerable repercussions on the aerospace industry, which in turn can have considerable effects on national economies. In order to understand the relationship between passenger and aerospace market fluctuations, an examination of the past behaviour of the order delivery lag is essential.

The delivery time of a new aircraft is important in a number of ways. The time elapsing between the commitment to a firm order and the delivery is important in influencing the airlines' notional lead time. The lead time is important in determining the airlines' forecasting horizon, while departures between expected lead times and actual delivery times result in unplanned supply and instabilities. Not surprisingly, rivalry among aircraft producers on delivery dates is intense.

This study examines the order-delivery lags of civil aircraft between 1954 and the end of 1970, a period in which the jet aircraft came to dominate the civil aviation industry. The (quarterly) data[2] consists of all civil aircraft orders and deliveries made during this period, covering the whole of the world with the exception of the Communist block countries. The study is therefore rather distinct from estimates of the same process in other industries, the estimates relating to an international, as opposed to a national industry, and the dependent variables being represented by physical units (aircraft) rather than the more usual monetary measures of output. Nevertheless, an examination of similar studies was considered useful, partly in order to place the order-delivery lag structure of the aviation industry in perspective, and secondly as an introduction to the techniques used in the study. The following section 7.2, therefore, briefly surveys some of the more important lag structures and their estimates in the UK and US economies, serving as a prelude to the model formulation and estimates of the following sections, 7.3 and 7.4.

7.2   Distributed lag studies of engineering processes

We will find that the lag between orders and deliveries may be considered as the summed effect of

(a)   the time taken between the receipt of an order and the start of production, and
(b)   the actual production time.

Peaks and troughs in orders are often helpful in determining the relative importance of these lags. For instance, the lowest backlog in orders is likely to occur when the delivery is at its lowest so that at this point (b) becomes the major determinant of the lag.

As with most industries the lag is distributed, such that an order placed at any time is completed only over a number of delivery periods at later times. Conversely aircraft deliveries in any period are the partial effects arising from a series of orders placed in the past.

Most studies have been conducted in the USA using appropriations and expenditure in monetary terms, rather than the physical order-delivery terms which we will employ. The latter description avoids the time profile associated with payments, and refers to a specific commodity. In comparison, the studies upon whose techniques we draw are concerned often with product mix covering many classifications. However, in one respect at least there is a common characteristic, namely that production is largely to order, and hence deliveries are a function of past net orders.

In setting the dynamics of the aviation industry in a clear relationship to other engineering industries, we are highlighting the problems that face those making decisions in the airline industry. There is not only an interest in techniques of obtaining a 'correct' distributed lag structure, but also great significance in different forms of structure in the different industries.

Popkin [1] in a fundamental study of machinery and equipment[3] obtained quantitative information initially by examining related peaks and troughs in order-shipment data. Although the fluctuations in this data

212

reveal a distributed lag nature, a simple lumped lead time, if estimated at different points in the cycle, reflects the changes in business activity, productivity and the relative contributions of the times (a) and (b) above, to the ratio of unfilled orders to new orders. This ratio is low, since business activity is low. Thus, the actual work time (b) dominates over the time taken between receipt of an order and start upon it.

At troughs, then, some measure of the actual work time may be obtained, while the extent to which unfilled orders act as a buffer, so that increase backlogs lengthen the time before work on incoming orders can be started may be roughly assessed. It becomes probable that a time varying lag is needed to describe the system. Popkin [1] chooses a two quarter model to describe an engineering area characterised by lead times varying from 4 to 7 months, using weighting coefficients modified by a backlog. Hence,

$$D_t = \alpha_1\, O_{t-1} + \alpha_2\, O_{t-2}$$, where D refers to deliveries and O to orders

and where
$$\alpha_1\,(t) = \beta_0 + \beta_1\,(U_t/D_t)$$

$$\alpha_2\,(t) = 1 - \alpha_1\,(t)$$

$$U_t = \sum_{j=1}^{t} O_j - \sum_{j=1}^{t} D_j$$, where U refers to the order back log

His monthly data is aggregated to give quarterly figures by experiment, and upon subsequent adjustment of deflation method,[4] satisfactory peak and trough coincidence between real and modelled process is obtained, together with R^2 of 0.94 and DW of 1.965.

Almon [2] introduced a fixed lag method which expressed a largely undefined lagged structure as a polynomial expansion of a chosen set of functions. This enables a multi-lag system to be defined by a few expansion coefficients, and model regressions to be formulated without attendant problems of serial correlation.

This elegant method upon which the current technique is based has been employed for manufacturing industries of all kinds, and adjusted for seasonal variation and such capacity constraints as strikes or cancellation of orders, by the use of additive explanatory variables in the regressions. However, it seems more reasonable to propose a variable distributed lag, since this is clearly a process by which backlogs influence delivery time, and an extremely simple model (Popkin [3]) yields better R^2 and DW figures for the same data than Almon [2].

Studies based upon the variable distributed lag have leaned upon a linearised modification of the weighting coefficients. Tinsley [4] formu-

213

lates a general influence of a modifying variable Z on the weighting coefficients, w, as:

$$y_t = \Sigma_{i=0}^{i=N} \ w_t \ (i) \ X_{t-i} \tag{7.1}$$

where N is the length of the lag, and where

$$w_{t-i} \ (i) = f \ (Z_{t-i}) \tag{7.2}$$

If the function f of the modifying variable is linear in Z, e.g. via

$$w_t \ (1) = C_1 + v_1 \ Z_t \tag{7.3}$$

then the expression in equation (7.1) is concerned with variables X and also XZ. If the modifying influence is non-linear, then linearisation has to be effected in order to use this method. It should be pointed out that the use of the lagged variables themselves (Maw Lin Lee [5]) results in poor estimates and, as an indication of serial correlation, low DW statistics. [6]

Following Tinsley, further work by Nobay [7], see Table 7.2, Trivedi [8], and Bispham [9] in the UK, using monetary appropriations and expenditure data, has confirmed a technique to a point where the role of explanatory variables can be fully argued; in particular the validity of insertion of constants, the additive nature of seasonals, and the determination of suitable indices of capacity utilisation for the industry in question.

When we specifically examine such studies with attention to aircraft manufacture it is seen that few results pertinent to our problem exist. Early studies in aircraft order-deliveries yield a mean industry time of about three quarters during the Second World War and the Korean War (Table

Table 7.1

Lead times in US manufacturing industry:
Mayer and Sonnenblum [10]

	Quarters
Mean lead time	3.1
Mean lead time	3.0
Aircraft	3.0
Aircraft engines and parts	3.0
Aircraft parts	1.0

214

Table 7.2

Lead time in UK manufacturing industries:
Nobay [7]

(All figures in quarters)

Category	Queueing (first come, first served)	Production	Total
Metal	2.11	1.23	3.34
Industrial engines	8.50	0.74	9.24
Engineers' small tools	0.70	0.75	1.45

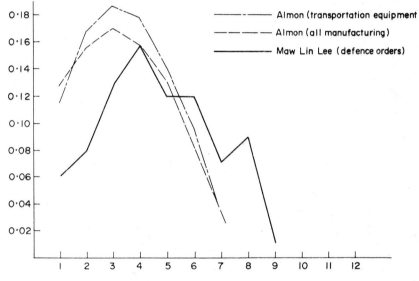

Fig. 7.1   Comparison of three distributed lags

7.1). This compares with the mean manufacturing industry lead time of 3.1 quarters, and while outside the period studied gives some idea of lags during wartime conditions applied when aircraft units were smaller and production runs long. The work of Mayer and Sonnenblum [10] may be further compared with the distributed lag study carried out on defence products (Maw Lin Lee [5]). Different product mixes including aircraft, communications equipment and aircraft parts were derived from Bureau of Census data. An average result is compared with estimates from other studies in Figure 7.1.

215

Despite the numerical nature of Lee's work [5], the conclusion merely states that 'the statistical estimates of the parameters of inventory and shipment on lagged orders indicate that the impact of defence procurement on economic activity is spread over a period of approximately two years to two years and six months'. His use of up to 30 lagged variables in the regressions, and consequent low DW's underlines this hesitance, and the brave assumption that least squares estimation on the lagged variables might be employed 'because of the wide variations in the successive values of new orders' seems to be largely untenable.

To summarise results obtained from the engineering industry over a large number of distributed lag studies: an average figure for the US manufacturing production lag is four quarters, while for the UK industry an average figure is 3.6 quarters. The US defence production lag extends over about eight quarters. In most cases a smooth single humped form of the distribution exists, with no evidence of any double hump.

To what extent are the above studies of use? A quick answer from consideration of order/delivery data is 'not very much'. The mean lead time of aircraft production is so much greater than aggregated machinery data that no characteristic can be expected to be common. However, the techniques and the a priori arguments for variables that modify the distributed lag structure are adapted easily to the aircraft production process.

Monetary units have been employed in all the work above, so that deflation methods ideally should be only applied ex post, i.e. after the distributed structure has become known. In the case of the airline industry the use of physical units greatly eases this problem.

It should be noted that in an aggregate market description, the distributed lag envelope will not enclose all possibilities, and that upon formulating a structure of maximum lag, N, the isolated case of an order—shipment delay of $N + 2$, say, periods is not ruled out. The distributed structure is an average one. Implicit in such formulations as above, and also to those to be applied to the airline production, is of course the assumption of non-stochastic lag coefficients. In other words the coefficients may be allowed to change with time, but in a deterministic way,[5] while the standard deviations of these coefficients are calculated on a least squares assumption of additive white noise. If, however, the coefficients are random, particularly non-Gaussian, then the estimation procedure includes effects of heteroskedasticity, and becomes accordingly complicated. The non-random nature of the lagged distribution coefficients is assumed here. The experience of the (civil) aerospace industries may be very different, of course.

An investigation now follows into the possible distributed lag structure.

216

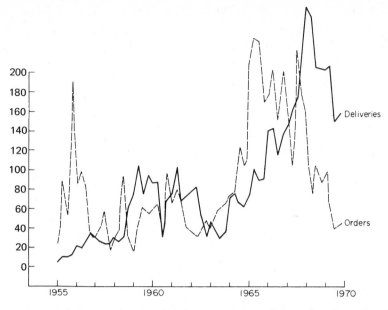

Fig. 7.2   Orders and deliveries (aircraft numbers)

This description is necessarily technical in nature, yet being based upon well understood economic variables leads to model characteristics that represent the production of aircraft with some validity.

7.3   Exploratory model fitting

While the peaking in the order data appears to be reflected in the delivery data (Figure 7.2), the effect does not suggest a single production lag. Modelling the order-delivery production process by a linear time delay τ, so that an order made at t is delivered at time $t + \tau$, it is found that in the best case only 50 per cent of the error can be explained away (Table 7.3). However, such an exercise is useful in that a mean time lag of twelve quarters appears to apply, which influences the form of distributed lag assumed in later investigations. To further yield general information on the spread of the distribution, a linear distributed lag model is then tried according to different trial distributions. These functions, A,B,C,D in Figure 7.3a, extend over 15 quarters of ordinates w_i, such that a new order measure $\overline{O}_t$ is produced by weighting the order data O_t. Thus:

$$\overline{O}_t = w_1 \, O_{t-1} + w_2 \, O_{t-2} + \ldots + w_{15} \, O_{t-15}$$

217

Table 7.3

Single production lag estimates

τ quarters	Constant	Coefficient	R^2	D.W.
0	52.15 (14.3)	0.39 (0.13)	0.128	0.21
4	34.1 (12.4)	0.64 (0.11)	0.373	0.58
8	39.4 (12.0)	0.64 (0.11)	0.411	0.78
12	41.9 (11.1)	0.73 (0.11)	0.504	0.68
16	73.4 (14.7)	0.49 (0.15)	0.183	0.32

Table 7.4

Exploratory weighting functions

Weighting functions	Constant	Coefficient	R^2	D.W.
A	8.8 (9.3)	0.12 (0.01)	0.76	0.71
B	11.2 (9.8)	0.13 (0.013)	0.69	0.53
C	9.15 (8.2)	0.16 (0.011)	0.81	0.84
D	5.45 (8.6)	0.16 (0.011)	0.80	0.87

The new variables $\bar{O}_t$ are regressed against deliveries D_t. These weighting functions are not normalised, except to the extent that the maximum ordinate is unity. D exhibits the character of a double hill of a type met in some processes (Evans [11]) while ABC are chosen to emphasise different regions of the lagged distribution range. The results are given in Table 7.4. Figure 7.3b yields the predicted model deliveries compared with the actual data. It is noted that a much smoother curve is obtained by using the model: it is expected in any case that a distributed lag process tends to smooth the input data.

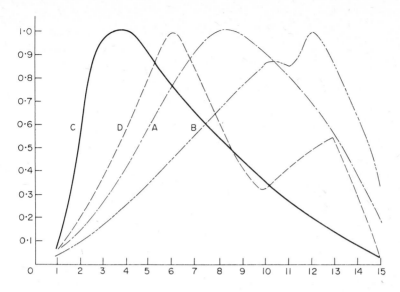

Fig. 7.3a　Exploratory forms of weighting coefficients

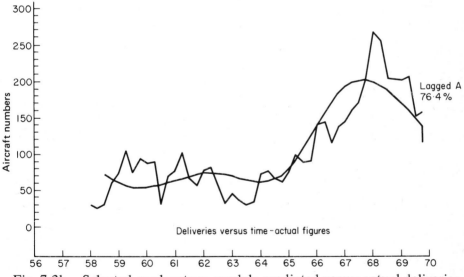

Fig. 7.3b　Selected exploratory model: predicted versus actual deliveries

The studies above tend to point to curve D as a possible lag structure. However, the precise evaluation of the weighting coefficients is now more conveniently carried out by the Almon method. It is further possible to allow for a changing distribution pattern, i.e. a set of weighting coefficients that alter with exogenous explanatory variables. Such an influence acting upon the distribution structure must be linear or, if non-linear, must be considered in a linearised form. This systematic method (Almon [2], Tinsley [4]) of obtaining the correct weighting structure is not quite automatic, since a statement is required of the maximum lag expected in the process, and also of the order of the polynomial description of the lag profile.

Taking a single constant, a response modifying variable Z of time integers with 1954 as a base, and again examining the quarterly order/delivery data, we obtain:

Length of lag	Order of polynomial	R^2
16	4	0.88
14	4	0.87
12	4	0.82

The predicted values appear in Figure 7.5 and the distribution coefficients in Figures 7.4a, and 7.4b.

Forming a measure of backlog at current time t as Z_t via

$$Z_t = \frac{\Sigma^t O_i - \Sigma^t D_i}{D_t}$$

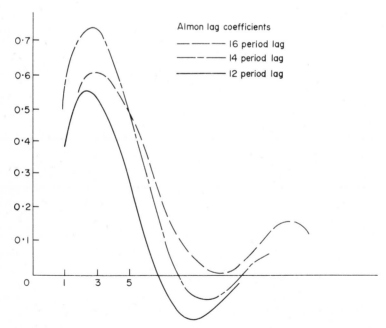

Fig. 7.4a   Tinsley's (time as modifier) unrestricted coefficients

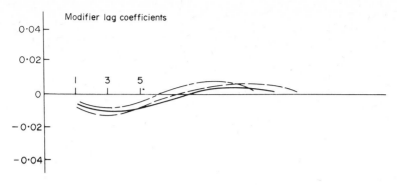

Fig. 7.4b   Modifier lag coefficients

the regressions yield Figure 7.6:

Length of lag	Order of polynomial	R^2	$D.W.$
16	4	0.89	1.6
14	4	0.85	1.19
12	4	0.80	0.85

The distribution coefficients are given in Figure 7.4b. The model results (also in Figure 7.5) show that the time modifier, a variable roughly associated with a hypothetical productivity trend, has much the same effect as the backlog modifier, where this latter variable affects the time before receiving the order and the commencement of work upon it.

The above completes the exploratory measures taken to model the distributed lag.

7.4   Accurate distributed model derivation

The Tinsley results quoted above do not restrict the coefficients in any way; however, in the order-delivery situation certain constraints become apparent.

Firstly, the weighting coefficients are necessarily positive; secondly, the sum of these coefficients, under the assumption that all orders are eventually delivered, becomes unity. In the technique employed here, the weighting coefficients are each split up into a constant value plus a time varying, modified quantity.

Thus, $w^t(i)$ the ith weight at time t is written as

$$w^t(i) = c_i + v_i z_t$$

221

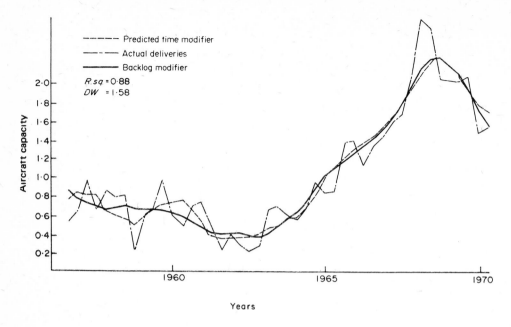

Fig. 7.5   Tinsley's 16 length distribution, fourth order

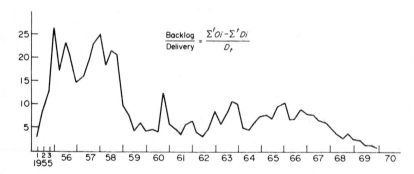

Fig. 7.6   Order backlog/delivery

where the constraints apply, in the case of an n-lag process,

$$\Sigma_0^n \, c_i = 1 \qquad\qquad \Sigma_0^n \, v_i = 0 \qquad\qquad \text{(7.4a and b)}$$

The extent to which the data naturally satisfies these constraints or, alternatively, the extent to which the problem has to be distorted in order to satisfy them is easily seen when both restricted and unrestricted cases are calculated. It has also been argued that the bias, and thus confidence in the coefficients eventually is naturally affected by the constraint situation, so that a decision has to be made that is a compromise at the present state of the art.

Summarising the additive seasonal results, we obtain the results as shown in Table 7.5.

The variation of R^2 between restricted and unrestricted sets of results is found to be roughly related to the sums $\sum_i N_{cj}$ and $\sum_i N_{\nu i}$ in the unrestricted cases. The 'backlog' variable represents the ratio of unfilled orders to the current delivery rate, and is thus associated with the weighting time (a). The time parameter is a rough measure of capacity utilisation, in the absence of further measures.

One objection to the results of Table 7.5 is the fact that the seasonal variables enter into the equation as additive regressors, whereas their influence should be multiplicative action on the order data, i.e. they should ideally be treated as modifiers of the weighting coefficients, see Table 7.6.

Table 7.5

Tinsley's distributed lag model
(additive seasons)

Dependent variable	Regressors	Unrestricted R^2	D.W.	Restricted R^2	D.W.
1 Deliveries	Constant seasonals $S_1 S_2 S_3$ order, modifiers Z, T (two modifiers)	0.94	1.65	0.89	1.05
2 Deliveries	Constant orders modifiers Z, T (i.e. no seasonals)	0.89	1.90	0.86	1.44
3 Deliveries	Constant seasonals $S_1 S_2 S_3$ orders, modifier Z (one modifier)	0.91	1.44	0.855	0.91
4 Deliveries	Constant seasonals $S_1 S_2 S_3$ orders, modifier T (one modifier)	0.92	1.25	0.85	0.77
5 Deliveries	Orders seasonals $S_1 S_2 S_3$ modifier Z (non-constant)	0.90	1.06	0.89	0.91

Table 7.6

Tinsley's (multiplicative seasonal) model

	Unrestricted		Restricted	
	RSQ	*D.W.*	*RSQ*	*D.W.*
Constant orders Modifiers Z, S_1 S_2 S_3	0.92	1.74	0.84	1.52
Orders Modifiers Z, S_1 S_2 S_3 (i.e. no constant)	0.93	1.68	0.85	1.61
Constant orders Modifiers T, S_1 S_2 S_3	0.94	1.89	0.87	1.52
Orders Modifiers T, S_1 S_2 S_3	0.93	1.71	0.88	1.52

The results above are typically of the form

$$D_t = C_o + a_1 S_{1_t} + b_2 S_{2_t} + c_3 S_{3_t} + \Sigma_i(c_i + v_i Z_{t-i})O_{t-i}$$

$$D_t = C_o + \Sigma_i[c_i + \alpha_i S_{1_{t-i}} + \beta_i S_{2_{t-i}} + \delta_i S_{3_{t-i}}] O_{t-i} + v_i Z_{t-i}$$

where C_o is a constant and where lag coefficients c, v, a, β, γ have been obtained using a standard programme (see [9]). It is less easy to detect non-positivity of the overall distributed lag in the same type of formulation, since the individual contributions to the total distributed lag at any period in the time series may themselves contain negative distributed lag coefficients.

The first formulation is preferred, since over a 16 quarter lag, the seasonals should not contribute any but a local time varying behaviour. The time modifier as a measure of productivity is regarded both from other studies and from the results above as inferior to the backlog modifier as a sole weighting distribution modifier.

Sixty data points are used, 16 of which are lost with the choice of a 16 lag distribution, so that the regression ultimately predicts the last 45 points. It should be noted that the order figures are scaled for numerical figures in a manner different from that required to explain the occurrence of the order figures (see Chapter 6).

How do we determine the correct model from several yielding good R^2 and acceptable DW figures? The assumption of non-cancellations of orders is tested by comparing the sums of lag coefficients in the unrestricted and in the restricted case. Thus, we have the results summarised in Table 7.7.

In Table 7.7 non-cancellation of order data requires the order O coefficient sum to be unity, while the sum of coefficients of all other modifiers should be zero. At first sight results (7.5c) and (7.5e) appear the best, but for each the restricted problem yields low DW statistics of 0.91. Additionally, this assumption markedly modifies the R^2 in the two cases.

It is also found that the seasonal coefficients are large so that seasonal modifying effects appear to be predominant in the distributed response of deliveries to orders; more important, for example, than the backlog modifier. The results of Table 7.6 are for this reason rejected when ap-

Table 7.7

Sum of lag coefficients:
unrestricted case

Additive seasonals: Table 7.5			Multiplicative seasonals: Table 7.6		
(7.5a)	O	5.99	(7.6a)	O	−1.27
	Z	0.101		Z	0.04
	T	−7.57		S_1	2.61
				S_2	1.94
(7.5b)	O	6.17		S_3	6.52
	Z	−0.675			
	T	−7.39			
(7.5c)	O	1.27	(7.6b)	O	−3.92
	Z	0.019		Z	0.22
				S_1	11.92
				S_2	2.19
				S_3	5.97
(7.5d)	O	4.02	(7.6c)	O	−5.28
	T	−4.23		T	−4.16
				S_1	18.73
				S_2	6.68
				S_3	11.64
(7.5e)	O	1.14	(7.6d)	O	−4.35
	Z	−0.02		T	0.58
				S_1	9.92
				S_2	0.35
				S_3	10.35

Table 7.8

Selected distributed lag model

	Almon coefficients	Modifier coefficients		Almon coefficients (no modifiers) Restricted results	
		Z	T	$R^2 = 0.70$	$D.W. = 0.6$
t-1	0.275	−0.095	−0.480	0.017	
t-2	0.374	−0.128	−0.617	0.032	
t-3	0.353	−0.118	−0.522	0.045	
t-4	0.257	−0.082	−0.290	0.056	
t-5	0.125	−0.032	0.0	0.065	
t-6	−0.011	0.020	0.280	0.073	
t-7	−0.126	0.065	0.505	0.079	
t-8	−0.204	0.097	0.640	0.083	
t-9	−0.234	0.112	0.666	0.086	
t-10	−0.214	0.109	0.584	0.087	
t-11	−0.149	0.089	0.403	0.085	
t-12	−0.05	0.057	0.157	0.081	
t-13	0.06	0.017	−0.115	0.074	
t-14	0.159	−0.021	−0.349	0.063	
t-15	0.211	−0.046	−0.471	0.047	
t-16	0.174	−0.045	−0.390	0.027	

plied to an aggregate worldwide process, and a choice is to be made between the models (7.5 a, b, c, d, e).

Table 7.5b yields the best result and incorporates a time modifier, as well as a backlog modifier. The coefficients become as shown in Figure 7.8, and the regression yields

$$D_t = 0.09 + 0.37\,A_1\,(O) + 0.35\,A_2\,(O) + 0.26\,A_3\,(O)$$
$$-0.13\,A_1\,(OZ) -0.12\,A_2\,(OZ) -0.08\,A_3\,(OZ)$$
$$-0.62\,A_1\,(OT) -0.52\,A_2\,(OT) -0.29\,A_3\,(OT)$$

where a fourth order polynomial requires three Almon variables, A_1, A_2, A_3 for the main dependant variable O, and the product variables (OZ) and (OT).

The total modifying distribution has been plotted over the period 16 quarters before 1970 and also for the same period before 1965 (not shown). This showed at the current time a smooth form of the overall function with a single hump of peak at about eight quarters. This is completely different from the distribution of fixed lag coefficients under modifier conditions, where a double hump appears. The separate modifier

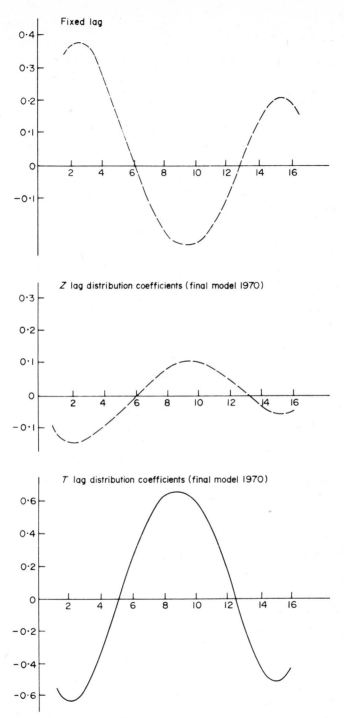

Fig. 7.7   Tinsley's modifier weighting coefficients

227

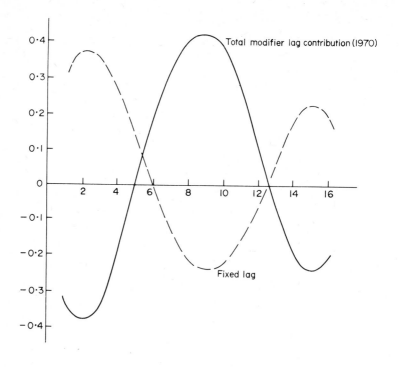

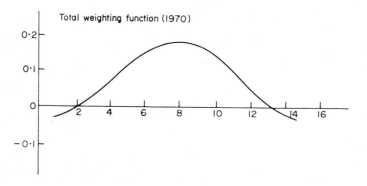

Fig. 7.8   Total weighting function of selected distribution

lag coefficients, which multiplied by the modifying variable form the time variable contribution to the overall distributed lag, are also given, see Figures 7.7 and 7.8.

Both Z and T lag coefficient distributions start ($i=1$) with a negative hump, followed by a positive hump ($i \simeq 9$). If the modifier is rising upwards with time (T, of course, is one of the modifiers as well) the leading portion is exaggerated and the negative hump stressed compared with the case of a constant modifier. Conversely, as the modifier data falls with time, for instance, if the backlog begins to fall, the most forward modifier coefficients have then less effect, and the positive part of the modifier distribution becomes predominant. The deliveries then rise, which is to be expected, in conditions of falling backlog. Equally, considering the total distributed lag, the effect of both modifier distributions is to shift the emphasis from the most recent data. When, however, the modifying variables decrease in value, and the leading negative part of the modifying structure has less effect, the total distribution is emphasised towards this leading portion, the deliveries at that time are largely derived from the more recent orders, and thus the delay in aircraft production has improved.

7.5 Conclusions

The estimates show that there is no one single fixed production lag; the most acceptable explanatory model had in fact time and order backlogs as two modifying variables. Such variability is not surprising when one considers the substantial variation in the product mix over the period considered — from the Viscount 700 to the Boeing Jumbo. Despite the problem of comparisons with other studies, it does appear that the order delivery lag is considerably longer in civil aviation than in other manufacturing processes. This has both inter- and intra-industry implications.

A longer lead time in one industry could be the source of its relatively larger instability, owing to the extra burden placed on forecasts with a longer time horizon. Here may lie one of the sources of the airline industry's instability, rather than the more often quoted argument that airlines tend to 'over-purchase' because of their failure to recognise their ologopolistic interdependence. For particular aerospace producers, the inability to meet such long delivery times can spell commercial extinction. As Elstub [12] pointed out, the longer than planned for delivery dates has been one of the major reasons for the poor performance of the UK civil aircraft industry.[6]

We shall explore the relationship between the order-delivery lag and the industry's instability in Chapter 9.

Notes

[1] This chapter is a modified version of the authors' published paper [13].

[2] See the statistical source used at the end of Chapter 5 for details concerning the data.

[3] Manufacturers' shipments, inventories and orders. Bureau of Census classification 'machinery and equipment' includes machinery, electrical machinery (excluding household, communications components) shipbuilding, railroads.

[4] Popkin [1] makes the point that even when order and deliveries are deflated by, for instance, the BSL wholesale price index, there arises an error due to the choice of an incorrect deflating time index. The deflating method presupposes the lag structure.

[5] This point was mentioned by Professor John Wise.

[6] See also A.P. Ellison and E.M. Stafford [14] for an analysis of the problems concerning the UK civil aircraft industry.

References

1 J. Popkin, 'Relationship between new orders and shipments', *Survey of Current Business*, March 1965 (pp. 24–32).

2 S. Almon, 'Distribution lag between capital appropriation and expenditure', *Econometrica*, Vol. 33, no. 1, January 1965 (pp. 178–96).

3 J. Popkin, 'Comment on the paper by Almon above', *Econometrica,* vol. 34, July 1966 (pp. 719–23).

4 P.A. Tinsley, 'An application of variable weight distributed lags', *American Statistical Association Journal*, December 1967, pp. 1277–89.

5 Maw Lin Lee, 'Impact pattern and duration of new orders', *Econometrica* vol. 33, no. 1, January 1965 (pp. 153–64).

6 Z. Griliches, 'A note on serial correlation bias in estimates of distributed lags', *Econometrica*, vol. 29, January 1961, pp. 65–73.

7 A.R. Nobay, 'Forecasting manufacturing investment – some preliminary results', *National Institute of Economic Review*, May 1970.

8 P.K. Trivedi, 'The relation between the order delivery lag and the rate of capacity utilisation in the engineering industry in the United Kingdom, 1958–67', *Economica*, February 1970 (pp. 54–67).

9   J.A. Bispham, 'The use of engineering orders for forecasting', *National Institute of Economics Review*, August 1969 (pp. 38–53).

10   I.T. Mayer and A. Sonnenblum, 'Lead times for fixed investment', *Review of Economic Statistics*, August 1955 (pp. 300–4).

11   M. Evans, *Macro-economic Activity: Fixed Business Investment*, Harper and Row, 1969.

12   Elstub Report, para 116, 117, section 111, 'The time scale of aircraf production', Ministry of Technology, HMSO, 1969.

13   A.P. Ellison and E.M. Stafford, 'The order delivery lag in the world' civil aircraft industry', *Journal of Applied Economics*, April 1973.

14   A.P. Ellison and E.M. Stafford, 'Concorde cuckoo', *New Society*, 8 June 1972.

8 Innovation and the Used Aircraft Market

8.1 The adoption of the jet

The aviation industry is popularly regarded as being in the vanguard of technological change. The advocates of increased government support to the industry broadcast the technical externalities, the 'fall out benefits' of expenditures on aircraft development. The growth of civil aviation with its increased noise and environmentally destructive airports has sharpened the debate over externalities yet surprisingly this is an area which has been relatively little explored.[1] This, however, is only one aspect involving technological development and the innovating process. Another aspect is the link between scientific knowledge and the application of this knowledge to aeronautical problems via the process of innovation. More precisely there is interest in the adoption of innovations by the aircraft manufacturers and the airlines' acceptance of new ideas when embodied in new aircraft types. The former has been extensively examined by Miller and Sawyer [4] in which they show rather surprisingly the slow adoption of many scientific and technical developments by the aircraft industry.[2] The introduction of new techniques by the airlines, the spread of the techniques and the role of the airline structure in the process of innovation has been relatively neglected. While the spread and speed of innovation are interesting in themselves these factors are also important in shaping the market in used equipment, for the speed of adoption of the latest aircraft will be affected by the airlines' ability to dispose of their existing fleets.

Chapter 4 examined the background to aircraft ownership and, as Table 4.1 in that chapter showed, new aircraft types particularly of the longer range aircraft were concentrated among a few aircraft companies. Furthermore, many of these airlines have been instrumental in the development of particular aircraft types although it has been suggested[3] that such collaboration has not always been successful. The introduction of innovation in the form of new aircraft types has been concentrated among the largest firms in the industry, a characteristic which has been observed elsewhere in the transportation sector.[4]

Table 8.1

Spread of the jet engine

Year	1955	1956	1957	1958	1959	1960	1961	1962	1963	1964	1965	1966
(a) World market												
Capacity (thousand million tonne km)												
Turboprop*	2	4	7	10.8	19.6	19	18	18	16	16	15	12
Turbojets				0.2	7.4	33	54	63	68	71	75	80
Total jets	2	4	7	11	28	52	72	81	84	87	90	92
Piston	98	96	93	89	72	48	28	19	16	13	10	8
Numbers†												
Turboprop		4	4	4	9	14	16	17	18	18	19	20
Turbojets				0.02	2	8	12	15	17	21	25	32
Total jets		4	4	4.2	11	22	28	32	35	39	44	62
Piston	96	96	96	95.8	89	78	72	68	65	61	56	48
(b) USA market												
Capacity (thousand million tonne km)												
Turboprop				3.9	13.6	11.0	11.7	10.4	10.0	9.5	8.7	6.9
Total jets				1.1	20.6	45.8	61.6	70.5	72.6	76.7	81.5	87.7
Piston				94.9	65.8	43.2	26.7	14.1	17.4	13.8	9.8	5.3
(c) USA market (international)												
Capacity												
Turboprop				5.7	0.7	0.1	0.1	0.1	0.5	0.2	0.1	0.5
Total jet				94.3	28.2	66.5	85.4	92.1	94.1	95.3	96.3	99.2
Piston					71.1	33.4	14.5	7.8	5.4	4.4	3.6	0.4

Sources:

The data on the world market is taken from ICAO Circular 73-AT/10 June 1965 Table 20. The USA data is taken from the CAB *Handbook of Statistics*. The international market refers to the capacity provided by USA international carriers.

Notes:

* Turboprops consist of the following aircraft types: Bristol, Brittania, Vanguard, Electra, Viscount 700 and 800, Convair 540, NAMCO YS-11, Hawker Siddeley 748, Handley Page Herald, Fokker and Fairchild F27 and Nord 262.

† The later percentages of the ICAO stock accounted for by different aircraft types were:

Numbers	1967	1968	1969
Turbojets	35.7	43.2	48.3
Turboprops	21.1	20.4	21.0
Total jets	56.8	63.6	69.3
Piston	43.2	36.4	30.7

Although there are relatively few first hand owners of aircraft such airlines still only constitute a small proportion of the total market as the concentration ratios contained in Chapter 1 showed.[5] In one sense this last statement is misleading in that the industry is really a constitution of many segmented sectors divided by international boundaries and buttressed by extensive controls and restrictions. As Chapter 1 has pointed out, the industry consists of spatially segmented markets in which equipment competition plays an important role. Such a market structure, as Schumpeter [6] and later Galbraith [7] have pointed out is likely to stimulate innovations. One would expect therefore a relatively swift spread of new techniques among airline companies.

The spread of the turbine engine affords a good example of an innovation embodied in various identifiable aircraft types. This engine type was developed in the UK and Germany in the latter part of the thirties, was used in military aircraft during and after the Second World War and was first introduced into commercial aviation when the de Havilland Aircraft Company produced Comet I in 1951. This aircraft unfortunately proved to have structural weaknesses and it was left to the Vickers Viscount to become eventually the first viable and highly successful turboprop powered civil aircraft. Although the medium range airlines were the first able to use the jets, it was the turbofan airlines for long haul routes which completed the jet revolution.

The spread of the jet engine can be measured in a number of ways. One method favoured in a number of studies[6] is to enumerate the number of firms adopting the new technique and to express the number as a percentage of the whole. The problem with this measure is that it does not consider the technological mix of the firm nor the extent to which the innovation is utilised. The assumption that the firm purchasing the new machine makes exclusive use of it is clearly an unwarranted assertion. A more useful measure is the capacity provided by the new innovation expressed as a percentage. It would be desirable to have two variables: the number of firms adopting the new technique and the capacity provided by the new technique. Detail of this kind is not easily available but capacity provided according to engine type has been collected. This is shown for the whole industry (i.e. ICAO members) in Table 8.1a where the percentages are compared with the numbers of jets expressed as a percentage of the total numbers. The difference between the two is considerable; the percentage of aircraft numbers clearly under-estimates the greater productivity of the jet aircraft. The USA data shows a higher rate of jet adoption than the ICAO states as a whole and the slow adoption and limited use of turbojets in this market.

Table 8.2

Comparative rates of diffusion
(USA Industry)

Percentage of the industry introducing the innovation	Number of years for the diffusion of the innovation					
	Aerospace*	Rail†	Brewing†	Coal†	Air transport	
					World‡	USA
25	4.5	3.6	2.5	2.0	5	3
50	6.0	11.6	4.6	4.3	6	5
75	7.0	18.3	4.8	7.6	7	8

* Source: H. O. Stekler, 'Technical progress in the aerospace industry', *Journal of Ind. Econ.*, July 1967, table II, p. 236.

† Source: E. Mansfield, 'Technical change and the rate of imitation', *Econometrica*, October 1962.

‡ Taken from Table 8.1.

Using Table 8.1 we can see that after less than a decade over 90 per cent of transport capacity is provided by jet engines. If we consider turbofan engines alone the period of 8 years has seen over 80 per cent of the transport capacity carried in aircraft powered by such engines. Compared with the speed of innovation in other industries this is a fast rate of adoption. Although the measures of innovation adoption are based on company figures, Table 8.2 gives some idea of the comparative speed with which the jet engine has been adopted.

The rate of adoption according to Table 8.2 is similar in speed to that of the coal industry, but considerably larger than in brewing. Compared with rail its speed of adoption is much quicker, for Mansfield [5] has shown that it took 15 years for the diesel locomotive and 25 years for the four wheel truck before all the railway companies in the US had made complete adoption.

The spread of the jet has been rapid and it has been aided by its superior productivity over earlier piston engines. The ownership of new aircraft, including the jet, has been concentrated among a few airlines but in percentage capacity terms these airlines constitute a small proportion of the market. Yet the proportion of flying by jet is high. This has come about because we are now in the second generation jet age, in which jets are available on most routes. The result has been that the latest jets have

Table 8.3

Number of owners of
various piston engine aircraft types
which were in operation for the years
1958, 1959, 1961 and 1962

Aircraft type	1958	1959	1961	1962
Canadair CL-44	3	4	5	9
CV-240	22	19	17	17
CV-340	20	21	19	22
CV-440	21	22	27	24
CV-Catalina	24	28	33	23
Curtis 46	82	91	104	97
DC-3, C-47	205	236	256	245
DC-4, 54	150	116	111	97
DC-6	19	23	24	26
DC-6A	11	23	26	27
DC-6B	33	29	40	60
DC-7, 7B and 7C	24	24	27	18
Martin 202	6	6	9	11
Bristol 170	16	20	18	19
Heron	35	26	39	33
Viking	24	22	21	–

Source: *Flight International*

been purchased by the front rank airlines, the older jets having found their way to smaller airlines. As Table 8.3 shows, the concentration of ownership spreads considerably after the first owner parts with an ageing fleet. The used aircraft market has played a central role in the re-equipment process and thus the spread of innovation. It has done this by allowing the front rank airlines to purchase the latest jets and to unload their older aircraft jets on to a wide second hand market.

The relationship between orders and sales has been mentioned in Chapter 5 where use was made of data contained in Table 8.10. This table also displays data relating deliveries and sales of large aircraft types. An estimate, (equation 8.1), using an unlagged form was performed on this data suggesting that sales were positively linked with deliveries. We shall see below how this relationship between deliveries and first owner sales helps to build up a used aircraft model:

$$S = 12.0 + 1.8\,D \qquad R^2 = 0.69 \qquad (8.1)$$
$$(0.7) \qquad DW = 1.3$$

where S = aircraft sales and D = aircraft deliveries.

8.2 The consequences of the jet for the airlines

Any examination of the effects of the innovation in civil aviation involves the governments and aircraft producers as well as the differing forms of airlines. It is the latter we shall examine in this section.[7]

Replacement of one aircraft for another in a competitive market will take place where the discounted present value of the costs of the new plane are less than with the older plane. Given fixed prices, revenues will be greater when replacement takes place than before, particularly if the plane is more attractive to customers than the older planes.[8]

The crucial question in examining the income effects between airlines of the kind of technological change just outlined is the pricing policy that will be pursued. Rigidity of fares and the minimal differentiation of fares between age and efficiency of aircraft have meant that airlines have gone headlong together in their purchases of the latest model, not wishing to be 'beaten to it' by their rivals who in the short run might enjoy the operation of equipment at the same price but with more passenger appeal.[9] Implicit in such purchasing behaviour, therefore, is the expectation of fares in the short run remaining undifferentiated and thus giving the latest model the advantage. Whether the new purchase results in increased revenue, of course, depends upon the relative actual running costs as opposed to the expected running costs. In the case of the propeller/jet transition in the late fifties and early sixties, what happened was that there was heavy buying of large jets by the front rank airlines and the selling of propeller planes to smaller operators, while fares on jets were subjected to a surcharge (lasting for four years on the North Atlantic route) even though in marginal cost terms the jets were cheaper than their propeller competitors.[10] What is interesting in this situation is the reason for such a pricing structure and the outcome.[11]

The airlines with older equipment using the unanimous voting rule were clearly able to safeguard their positions by pushing up the price of jet travel such as to dissuade passengers who were unwilling to pay an extra amount by gaining a reduction of travel time in travelling by jet.

The effect of the surcharge on profits, however, depended upon the time/price trade off of passengers. The time savings would have appeared to be sufficiently large for the majority of travellers to substitute the

239

faster but more expensive jets for the slower but cheaper (by 10 per cent) propeller aircraft. An examination of the large operators' profits suggests revenues declined and substantial losses were incurred owing to the high written down costs of propeller aircraft. Such losses could be attributed to two factors. One, the inability of the airline to foresee the effects of the introduction of technologically (and economically) superior equipment and secondly to a downturn in demand occuring as the jets were entering the market. Both appear to have been important.

Inability to allow for technological advance in the depreciation of existing equipment is a fault in the risk taking procedure of the airlines. In allowing for depreciation the airlines have a number of indicators with which to write off their capital, namely the price of equivalent aircraft in the second hand market and secondly the airlines' own estimates of the likely consequences of the introduction into airline service of the orders known to exist. In both cases present prices of aircraft assets will reflect the net present value of the services provided by the aircraft, the future value of services having been discounted. If the existing planes are expected to be inferior and to earn less this will be reflected in the price of the resale market. As we have seen in Chapter 5, Figure 5.1, despite the high level of orders for new jets in 1956 and 1959, the second hand prices of aircraft held up. In view of the precipitous slump in prices later this only suggests inaccurate forecasting of the consequence of jet travel. The depreciation policy pursued by the USA airlines as Miller and Sawyer [4] showed[12] varied considerably between aircraft type, but what is even more interesting is the depreciation on the larger propeller aircraft which were being replaced by the jets. Of relevance, therefore, is the depreciation policy pursued on the L1099 and the L1049, the former entering service just prior to the jets. In the case of the L1049, the data in [4] shows that the amount written down between 1956 and 1957 was reduced despite the high orders for jets building up in those years and only in 1958 when the first jets were operating did the depreciation allowance rise. The heaviest writing-off came in 1960, 1961 and 1963. The L1049, however, had been operating for over 10 years when jets were introduced but again the heaviest writing-off occurred in 1958 and not in 1956 or 1957.

Some losses, therefore, could be due to faulty evaluation of existing assets by the airlines who were perhaps misled by the second hand market. The second hand market could also have been discounting favourably future benefits from charter and other non-scheduled services provided by second hand propeller aircraft.

Mistakes were to be expected, for over-optimistic forecasts of propeller

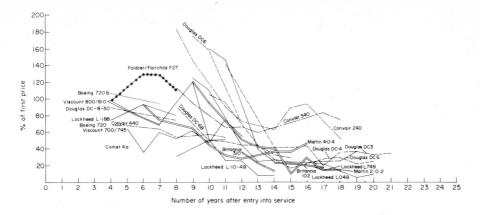

Fig. 8.1 Aircraft resale values. Source: BAC Statistics Division

sales were nurtured during the 1950s, when the shortage of passenger aircraft, particularly short range aircraft, meant many used prices exceeded purchase prices (see Figure 8.1). BEA for instance made over £900,000 during the 1950s on its sale of used propeller stock. The jet equipment programme saw an end to such a buoyant market, for although there was a growing market, the bunching of jet deliveries meant capacity far in excess of normal was created for a number of years (1961 and 1962). The problem of the long haul carriers was further aggravated by the arrival of the DC-7Cs at the same time as the first Boeing 707s and DC-8s. The DC-7C's prices dropped precipitously, far below their value in airline books. Many airlines lost heavily, among them BOAC, who in 1964 revealed to the Select Committee on Nationalised Industries an accumulated loss of £80.1 million (1957–1964), of which £31.7 million was accounted for by additional depreciation on the DC-7C, Britannia 102/312 and the Comet IV. In the case of the DC-7C the used market went down rapidly and it is difficult to see how the accountants could have foreseen the large drops in values that did occur. In other instances drops in value could have been realised if more foresight had been given to the market, and particularly to the purchasing and disposal policies of other airlines. This would have allowed write-offs to be spread over a larger number of years instead of concentrations in particular years.

The low priced aircraft would appear to be a gain to the second rank operators who purchased them, thus reducing considerably their capital costs. An examination of Table 8.4 a and b for the USA domestic market shows quite clearly the lower percentage of total operating cost accounted for by the depreciation of flight equipment in the local service carrier accounts. The table also shows a rise from a low of 7 per cent to a high of

241

11 per cent in 1961 for the Big Four, the larger USA carriers and the largest purchasers.

Technological change in the form of the jet suggests it favoured the small operator as opposed to the airlines that introduced the jets. This contributed to lower non-scheduled fares and to the pricing problems of the scheduled carriers.

8.3   The used aircraft market

The used aircraft market has grown in importance for the manufacturers and for the airlines.[13] This is partly due to the growing size of the aircraft stock, to the rate of technological advance and to the financial arrangements which airlines enter into with aircraft makers. Trading-in of used aircraft is one way airlines have financed new purchases and indeed the sale of used aircraft is an important source of finance for airline companies. Consequently, predicting used aircraft prices is of interest to both. In section 8.4 an attempt has been made to formulate an estimable model using available data which has been largely described in Chapter 5.

8.3.1   *Conceptual problems*

The centre of interest is the building of a model which will allow us to identify the demand and supply curves of used aircraft and from which we can derive elasticities. What we actually mean by an aircraft is important. We need to distinguish aircraft according to age and sizes. We shall see that there are crucial distinctions when we come to formulate estimable demand relationships.

Once an aircraft has been built its supply is fixed. The stock of aircraft of a particular type and age is given and will vary only when subjected to two influences:

1   If it is scrapped or crashes.
2   If it is converted and so moves into another market.

At a given (low) price the supply of this stock will be infinitely elastic, for holders of the stock of aircraft will scrap at a given low rate. Upwards of this price the stock will be infinitely inelastic although perhaps shifting from year to year because of crashes and conversions. For most types the magnitude of both these events can be considered slight. Let us, therefore, consider the determination of second hand prices for a particular aircraft of a particular vintage. We shall assume there is no scrapping or crashes. The stock will, therefore, be invariant from year to year. Secondly, the

242

Table 8.4

Depreciation and operating expenses: US airlines

(a)	*Depreciation charges as a percentage of operating expenses*								
Date:	1957	1958	1959	1960	1961	1962	1963	1964	1965	1966
Operator group										
Big Four	9	7	8	9	11	10	10	8	8	8
Local service	3	3	4	3	4	4	4	4	4	5
Other trunks	8	9	8	9	10	10	10	9	9	9

(b)	*Operating profit or loss by US airline groups (US $'000)*								
Date:	1957	1958	1959	1960	1961	1962	1963	1964	1965
Operator group									
Big Four	30,372	72,344	81,620	27,101	−23,732	9,586	37,825	161,753	223,796
Local service	760	1,658	635	2,172	9,359	13,374	11,939	16,966	24,091
Other trunk	28,457	21,131	11,722	22,581	23,616	7,449	12,616	65,342	71,409

Source: CAB *Handbook of Statistics.*

price variations will be assumed to be above the scrapping price; therefore, we have a fixed supply of aircraft. At a particular price we can distinguish two demands. The demands from airlines wishing to purchase a second hand aircraft, and the reserve demand of first hand owners, i.e. those wishing to 'hold on' at the particular price. In consequence, we have movements in demand and so are unlikely to identify the supply and not the demand curve. This means we are unlikely to identify the demand for aircraft of a *particular type* and of a given age. Even if there is scrapping and conversions the movements in supply are likely to be small compared with the movements in demand. However, if we consider a model which attempts to estimate the demand for aircraft of *a given age across aircraft types* we can overcome this problem. The term 'aircraft type' in this sense does not refer to, say, a Boeing 707 but to long haul aircraft types which, of course, include Boeing 707, VC-10s, DC-8s, etc.

The production of aircraft within this broad category has varied over time and consequently the supply of two year old, three, four and five year old aircraft has varied over time.[14] By considering similar commodities[15] (x year old long haul aircraft) we are able to identify the demand and the supply schedule.

8.3.2   Model

If we wish to develop a model explaining the determination of used aircraft prices we need to discover the behaviour of aircraft owners with respect to the departure from their stocks, for the date of scrapping or destruction clearly determines the number of a given age of aircraft surviving for some chosen period.

In examining detailed histories of aircraft types in Chapter 5 we discovered that scrapping was economically determined and that the sales of new aircraft from first hand owners were related to the delivery of new aircraft. We shall, therefore, treat the sales of used aircraft as a function of the delivery of new aircraft and the delivery of new aircraft as exogenous.[16] The varying deliveries and sales of aircraft over time allow us to identify the demand elasticities for (used) aircraft of particular ages.

More formally, given

q_{ij} =   number of j year old aircraft sold
p_{ij} =   price of j year old aircraft sold
z_i =   price of new aircraft

In an equilibrating market the structural equal would have been:

$$q_{ij} = bp_{ij} + \lambda z_i \qquad (8.2)$$

244

However, we have suggested that q_{ij} is predetermined. Equilibrium takes place by means of price adjustments. The demand curve should, therefore, be written as:

$$p_{ij} = \pi_1 q_{ij} + \pi_2 z_i \qquad (8.3)$$

with $\pi_1 = 1/b$ and $\pi_2 = -\lambda/b$

Since all the variables on the right of equation (8.3) are predetermined the reduced form parameters can be estimated by least squares regression. These price flexibility coefficients are then transformable into price elasticities, if required, as shown above.

8.3.3 *Estimation*

We have stated that estimates can be made of aircraft of age 1, 2, 3 years, etc. The practical problem of estimating is one of deciding which aircraft to include. The sales data [17] on aircraft types is largely confined to medium and long haul aircraft. The aircraft for which this detail is scanty consists largely of short haul pre-jet types: Convair 220 and 440, the Martin series, DC-3, Viking, Avro Tudor, Ambassador and the Boeing 377. We have dates, number delivered and crashes and scrapping, but sales data is thin. We could, however, estimate the expected sales of aircraft types for which we have no sales data and then apply these sales estimates to the information on prices. The latter exercise has been performed but with only varying success owing to data limitations.[18] Instead of attempting both estimates we shall concentrate on long haul aircraft types for which our information is sound.

The data on sales has been discussed in the last section and the details of sources are contained in Chapter 5. The price data up to 1961 comes from diverse sources as can be seen by examining the list of statistical sources in Chapter 5. Beyond 1961, however, aircraft exchange services information was available on a monthly basis. A characteristic of the market as shown by Figure 8.1 has been the high price of used aircraft in the early and mid-fifties when some prices exceeded the new aircraft prices. However, the demand estimates contain a new aircraft price index[19] and all price indices were deflated.

The regression results are shown in Table 8.5 where linear and log linear forms are presented. Using the criteria of best fit and significant coefficients, the results show that neither form is exclusively the best estimate relationship. The evidence is that own price elasticities are less than 1 but caution should be displayed owing to the presence of autocorrelation (as shown by the low Durbin Watson statistics).

Table 8.5: Estimates of the used aircraft model (the dependent variable consists of used aircraft prices)

Age (years)	LINEAR			LOG LINEAR			Equation number
	Constant	New aircraft price	Number of used aircraft	Constant	New aircraft price	Number of used aircraft	
5	890		−5.9 (2.7)	3.31		−0.43 (0.133)	
	R^2 = 0.67 D.W. = 0.67			R^2 = 0.53 D.W. = 1.20			
	2206	−8.39 (2.9)	−6.1 (2.0)	5.66	−1.08 (0.78)	−0.4 (0.12)	8.2
	R^2 = 0.67 D.W. = 1.13			R^2 = 0.62 D.W. = 1.30			
6	906		−8.9 (5.3)	303		−2.7 (0.20)	
	R^2 = 0.17 D.W. = 0.71			R^2 = 0.11 D.W. = 0.88			
	2139	−8.7 (310)	−7.8 (4.3)	7.9	−2.34 (0.84)	−0.17 (0.17)	8.3
	R^2 = 0.50 D.W. = 1.18			R^2 = 0.47 D.W. = 1.44			
9	532		−2.7 (1.18)	2.93		−0.27 (0.09)	
	R^2 = 0.30 D.W. = 1.65			R^2 = 0.43 D.W. = 1.87			
	1003	−3.94	−0.16 (1.07)	5.45	−1.29 (0.77)	−0.08 (0.089)	8.4
	R^2 = 0.71 D.W. = 2.26			R^2 = 0.71 D.W. = 2.59			

Note: The equation numbers refer to the general model developed in Chapter 2.

The results square with earlier studies in which inelastic price elasticities were estimated.[20] From a practical viewpoint, an airline contemplating selling a number of its fleet is likely to be interested in the effects of the sale on prices and so the price flexibility coefficients will be of direct interest to its forecasts. These results in fact are utilised in section 8.4 where the effects of selling off jet fleets on the used aircraft market are examined.

8.3.4 *Other studies of the used aircraft market*

We shall examine two studies here, both of which were undertaken at the time of the replacement of propeller by jet engines.

The earlier study [15] was undertaken on behalf of the United States Air Force in 1957. This study is interesting because unlike study [14] it examines the problem of forecasting by considering macro-variables in the market such as the orders placed by the airlines and the effect on capacity of the introduction of these aircraft into service. A global and regional breakdown is obtained of the expected demand and supply of aircraft services. By considering existing fleets and the expected operating costs of the jet fleets, the study estimates the requirements of used piston engine fleets. A further point of interest is the estimates of price elasticity obtained from a CAB questionnaire conducted in twenty two countries.[21] This concluded that the price elasticity over a large range was constant at around −0.3.

The later study by S.P. Sobotka and C. Schnabel [14] is an abbreviated form of research conducted at Northwestern Transportation Centre, in which an attempt was made to predict the prices of actual aircraft types. This approach differed from the 'naive' model above in that it employed a differential rent concept, i.e. the price paid for a used aircraft would be the discounted present value of the surplus accruing to an aircraft type. The surplus reflects the difference in operating costs between the given aircraft and its nearest substitute on routes they are expected to operate most efficiently. The point to note here is that the revenue earned per passenger mile was assumed to be independent of the type of aircraft. In other words, the value of aircraft relative to each other was determined by their operating cost performance. Although these conditions were subjected to alteration in the study, the inability to forecast accurately the differing pricing structures for jet and propeller aircraft which were introduced has perhaps accounted for some of the differences between actual second hand prices and those forecast by the Northwestern study.

8.4   The second hand market and depreciation in the early 1970s

The situation in the used aircraft market is interesting, poised as it is to handle deliveries of first generation jets from airlines re-equipping with long and medium range large jets. In order to provide some general frame-work, we have attempted to forecast the likely number of used aircraft entering on to the market with the first deliveries of the large jet orders. With this information, along with up to date details of individual airline accounting methods, we shall form some idea of the likely developments in the early 1970s, and to see whether the problems of a decade ago are to be repeated. Prediction of individual aircraft type prices is not attempted; instead the general direction is indicated, and thus a possible guide to depreciation rates is provided.

The price of used aircraft is, of course, like the price of any other commodity, determined by demand and supply. The problem with predicting used aircraft sales is that one has to consider the fallibility of airline forecasts of demand. Planned sales are the resultant of matching planned net capacity with predicted demand, unplanned sales the difference between net capacity and actual demand. Sales allow an airline to keep its capacity in line with demand, to stay in equilibrium. One of the problems with the disposal of aircraft is that deliveries are often bunched together, resulting from the intense qualitative competition in the industry which force all airlines to purchase at the same time. Uneven delivery leads to uneven disposal, leading to large fluctuations in used prices. It is clearly unrealistic to expect demand to compensate for the excess supply and to maintain prices within a small range. The large fluctuations in used prices have, in fact, been largely determined by big shifts in supply.

What of the plans of the re-equipping airlines? Their purchasing plans can only be seen in the context of their overall market strategy. Table 8.6 shows the aircraft stock of the top five carriers, converted into capacity figures, and related to their achieved growth since the orders were made. The jet buying of the mid-sixties shows up in the orders of all five, but some were quicker than others. Heading the list is Pan Am, who by the early 1970s have the major proportion of their capacity in operation. TWA, at the other end, have yet to feel the full effects of their orders. The latter have, in fact, embarked upon an aggressive expansionist policy, launched in 1966 when they filed an application to the CAB to expand in the Pacific and so join up Los Angeles with their Hong Kong network. The winning of the latter route in late 1968 along with domestic expansion showed TWA to be bidding for a considerably larger share of the US carrier's market. Of the non-American carriers, BOAC, Lufthansa and JAL

Table 8.6

Leading US airline aircraft capacities*
(tonne km '000's)

Airline		1966	1967	1968	1969	1970	Up to mid 1971
United	Stock	1720	2171	2648	2685	2973	
	Orders	600	659	1331	1236	1236	
	Deliveries		455	593	102	288	
	Departures		4	116	75	−	22
	Percentage annual growth in demand	+9	+39	14	4	(−1)	
Pan Am	Stock	1119	1443	1574	1723	2330	
	Orders	768	1024	960	736	416	
	Deliveries		324	164	248	640	32
	Departures			33	99	33	128
	Percentage annual growth in demand	34	13	10	3	13	
American	Stock	125⁵	1521	1803	1950	2014	
	Orders	712	592	1160	952	952	
	Deliveries		288	400	232	64	352
	Departures		22	118	85	−	43
	Percentage annual growth in demand	28	8	15	4	11	
TWA	Stock	1701	1052	1279	1320	1657	
	Orders	245	773	1316	1128	674	
	Deliveries		279	234	192	337	224
	Departures						
	Percentage annual growth in demand	7	19	8	13	11	
Eastern	Stock	894	1172	1611	1991	1861	
	Orders	404	335	939	683	683	
	Deliveries		278	439	380	95	344
	Departures					225	56
	Percentage annual growth in demand	(−1)	41	10	12	10	

* The stocks have been converted into capacity figures by using ICAO figures for individual aircraft average annual productivity.

have all launched considerable expansion plans covering the next 4 years.

The timing of orders is important for an airline, for if these are out of phase with economic conditions, excess capacity can develop in any one year, even though for the overall long run airline plan (of say 5 years), the capacity ordered may be no more nor no less sufficient to satisfy customer demands. Although Table 8.6 suggests enormous capacity orders in relation to stock, if viewed over the next 5 years or so, and in conjunction with expected stock unloadings, it can be seen that the airlines have not over-ordered. Certainly, excess capacity can be disastrous, and even in a large airline one high capacity jet too many can mean the difference between profits and losses, for as BOAC stated in their 1967/68 report: 'During 1964–68 capacity was tight. We could have made use of an extra aircraft. But as a matter of deliberate policy we kept ourselves short of one aircraft and this is largely responsible for our financial success.'

Table 8.7 shows that even allowing for no aircraft retirements, airlines will be adding to stock capacities which in the past they have been able to absorb. United will have the bulk of its capacity delivered in 1972, adding

Table 8.7

Changes in future aircraft capacities
of US carriers

(a) Percentage growth in capacity if no retirements			
Airline	1971	1972	1973
United	10	27	5
PAA	2	13	2
American	17	20	3
TWA	12	3	10
Eastern	18	2	16

(b) Percentage growth in capacity if projected* retirements take place			
Airline	1971	1972	1973
United	8	18	—
PAA	—	—	—
American	8	18	3
TWA	8	1	6
Eastern	7	—	—

* See Table 8.4 for details.

some 27 per cent to its capacity, yet in 1967 it achieved a growth in demand far in excess of this figure. If examined in the context of declared aircraft unloadings, certainly most of the big five appear to be keeping their capacity in line with demand. Pan Am for one appear to be hoping that the excess capacity they have in 1970 will provide them the stock for growth in the next few years. Even holding the most pessimistic economic forecasts, one can say that if Pan Am can weather the first half of the 1970s, after taking 1970, it should be entering a more settled phase, and instead the problem airlines will be TWA and United.

Judicious purchasing, the spacing of orders, deliveries and sales so as to minimise injurious financial fluctuations are some of the aims of airline management. One airline which has been more successful than most in this is Eastern, which under the sales guidance of Mr Breidenbach, has pursued a rigorous sales programme in conjunction with its purchasing policy. Since the re-equipment orders were made Eastern has sold and leased some $82 million worth of used aircraft, including 2 DL-8-50s, 13 DC-8-20s and 19 Electras. On the lease of 7 DC-8-61s to JAL substantial gains above book values were made. Others have been less fortunate. United's Caravelle's sales in 1971 realised losses of around $400,000 per aircraft. Other airlines having been moving their depreciation rates to cover drops in used market prices. BEA use a continuous market valuation in depreciating their stock, which means write-off losses in the long run will be more evenly spread over time. For instance, in 1969/70 BEA wrote off some £2.8m. Swissair in 1971 increased its write-off figure by nearly 25 per cent, while BOAC showed foresight by accelerating its write-off period back in 1967.

There are still wide differences in depreciation rates for the same aircraft, as is shown by a reading of the annual airline reports and the *CAB Aircraft Operating Cost and Performance Reports*. The depreciation range on long haul first generation jets is from 10 to 15 years write off and 0 to 15 per cent residual values. There is reason to believe that, except for the longer depreciation rates, the rates on average will be sufficient to accommodate the price drops. Table 8.8 shows the jets released from the stock of the leading US airlines plus BOAC up to mid 1971. Table 8.9 shows the desired jet unloadings of the jet reequipping airlines, some of which have stated publicly their intended sales. Those airlines which have not announced their plans have been estimated after examining the age of existing stock and the capacity on order. There is obviously some degree of judgment in these figures and, as we have suggested, sales are highly sensitive to misjudged demand forecasts.[22]

The general indication is, however, that the older long haul jets, the

Table 8.8

Jet aircraft sales
(US and UK airlines since 1966)

Airline	1967	1968	1969	1970	1971
American	2 CV-990A 2 Electras	10 CV-990A 12 Electras	2 BAC1-11 5 CV-990A 10 Electras		
United	2 V-700	9 B727-22 22 V-700	3 DC-8-10 21 V-700		1 B737-222 4 Caravelles
Pan Am		3 DC-8	9 DC-8	3 DC-8	8 B707-321
Eastern		4 Electras		15 B720-025 15 Electras	7 DC-9-14 1 DC-8-21
National Airlines				1 DC-8-61	
BOAC					7 B707-436

B707-320s, the DC-8-20s, the DC-8-50s and the Caravelle 6Ns will be in plentiful supply. As a proportion of existing stock these sales will be high, but from the point of view of predicting price changes, it is the percentage change in sales which is important. Using the results of estimates of price flexibility coefficients [23] one can expect the prices of long haul first generation jets to have fallen by something like 100 per cent by the end of 1973. By this date most of the jets in question will be over 10 years old, and most likely written down to their scrap value. Those airlines with the longer write off, however, may still be in difficulties. Table 8.10 shows the book values taken from the sources mentioned above, and expressed as a percentage of original cost. Similarly expressed prices are shown, with the approximate price range which, in certain instances, are quite wide.

Those which are over-valued and are likely to remain over-valued are the B707-120s, the DC-8-10s and the B720s. In the case of the latter, United are likely to suffer a loss on sales unless their depreciation rates are adjusted; in the case of the DC-8-50s, Delta have written off considerably more than Eastern. With the exception of the Electras, most short to medium range jets have kept above their book values. This could change, for the delivery of the wide bodied, short range jets in 1973 and 1974 could leave the DC-9 considerably over-valued. At present being depreciated over something like 10 to 15 years, the book values in 1974 will be around 35 per cent of original value. This may be too high in view of the

Table 8.9

Estimated* number of aircraft sales
1971–73

Aircraft make: Airline	Boeing 707	720	McDonnell Douglas DC 8	Others
American		22 Bs		
United		25 22s		
Eastern			2 50s	19 Electras
			13 20s	
Pan Am	25 320s			
TWA		17 131s		
Northwestern		16 051Bs		
BOAC	10 436s			
JAL		4 32s		
		7 53s		
KLM		6 32s		
Lufthansa	5 430s			
Delta			20 51s	
Braniff	4 227s	5 027s		
National			3 21s	
			6 51s	
Air Canada			11 42s	28 Viscounts
				12 Vanguards
Air France	18 328s			
Air India	5 437s			
Alitalia			13 43s	
El Al	2 420s		7 52s	
Iberian				
Irish Int.		2 048s		
SAS				16 Caravelle 3
Sabena				10 Caravelle 6N
S. African	2 344s			4 Viscount 800
Swissair				4 Caravelle 3
				3 Fokker Friendship
Totals	71	87	105	
Percentage of total stock in service	10	65	19	Vanguard 30 Viscount 15 Caravelle 10

* This assumes the aircraft on order in 1971 are not cancelled.

Table 8.10

Used aircraft market values and book values

Model	Used market price (mid 1971) as a percentage of original price	Value in the books percentage of original price
Viscount 700	1 – 2	5
Vanguard	12 – 20	30
Canadair (L-44)	23 – 30	15
CV-880	18 – 25	23
CV-990	20 – 30	30
Fokker F-27-100	60 – 70	23
*Fokker F-27-200	40 – 62	15
Comet IV	9 – 15	15
Trident 1E	60 – 75	58
*Lockheed Electra	25 – 40	25
DC-8-10	18 – 25	23
DC-8-60	55 – 60	58
DC-9	70 – 85	72
*B707-120	34 – 40	23
B707-320B	38 – 49	30
*B720	25 – 35	23
B720-B	30 – 34	30
B727-100	65 – 70	23
Caravelle 6	41 – 45	41

* Especially wide market.

Sources: *Flight* and Wold & Associates.

fact that Eastern and Delta, purchasers of the DC-10 and the L 1011, are among the largest operators of the DC-9. Braniff and Delta have prudently adopted 10 year write-offs which should see these airlines recovering their estimated 15 per cent residual values.

In summary, the débâcle of the early 1960s is unlikely to be repeated. The used market demand is wider with the growth of charter and supplementary carriers, although many of these are now more likely to buy first hand than they were 10 years ago. It is true the used market may only be able to absorb a limited number of used jets, forcing many airlines to scrap, but at least airlines will be obtaining scrap money roughly in line with the residual values in their books. The depreciation upsets of the early sixties were largely caused by the use of large propeller aircraft as stopgaps before jets were delivered. The 12 year gap between the two jet generations should be long enough for the prudent airline to accommodate steady write off programmes.

Notes

[1]   There have been some studies, however, including A.D. Little [1], Denver Research Institute [2] and the Ministry of Defence [3]. See also A. Phillips [18].

[2]   See [4] p. 266.

[3]   See [4] p. 259 where it is suggested that detailed specification from the buyer has been inimical to progress.

[4]   See Mansfield [5] p. 181–182. 'Almost all the innovators (in the railway industry) were among the ten largest firms, and about one-half were among the four largest. Moreover, although the largest firms accounted for about 32% of the Industry's ton miles, they account for 65% of the innovators.' For a recent study on technological change in the civil aviation industry in the USA see [17].

[5]   See Table 6. Chapter 1.

[6]   See for example E. Mansfield [8].

[7]   See [4] Chapter 8 for a discussion of the role and the effects of Government intervention in the introduction of new aircraft types.

[8]   See [9] for an essay on a similar replacement problem.

[9]   See Chapter 6 for an analysis of the airline purchasing behaviour.

[10]   See Chapter 1 for a discussion of the industry's pricing structure.

[11]   The situation with respect to depreciation in the US domestic market created considerable controversy in the 1950s. This is illustrated by the comments made on the 1957 CAB hearings in the Suspended Passenger Fare Increase Case reported in *Aviation Week*, 2 September 1957. The airlines were pushing for a 6 per cent emergency fare increase. The policy on depreciation recommended by the Bureau of Air Operations was one of a seven year life and 10 per cent or 15 per cent residual value. CAB witness H.H. Schneider testified: 'The depreciation allowance which the carriers have been charging for post war piston engines have borne little, if any, direct relationship to the actual depreciation expense . . . . . At the present time there is no indication that the market for modern piston engine aircraft will change significantly.'

[12]   See [4] Appendix B for depreciation details of propeller and jet aircraft on US routes.

[13]   The literature with respect to used commodities has so far been scarce. The following studies have dealt with the demand for used goods

in a general manner: [10], [11], [12] and study [13] dealt specifically with the used prices of motor vehicles but this was bedded in the larger study of car demand. In the case of air [14] has been the one major theoretical study.

[14] The number of one year old aircraft in 1968 will depend upon the number supplied in 1967 minus those that crashed.

[15] Of course if the commodities are similar it is possible to aggregate them together and to exclude differences in ages. However, an examination of the price data suggests quite marked differences in price according to age. Furthermore, such an aggregation would involve even more difficulties in index problems.

[16] See equation (8.1).

[17] See Chapter 4 for details on aircraft type histories.

[18] In making these estimated sales we performed the following exercise. We calculated the departure probability on those aircraft for which we had detailed data, related these estimated to the production data on types for which we had no detailed sales information and obtained the expected sales. These aggregate sales for the differing ages of aircraft were obtained for each year and the data on prices related to them. Unfortunately, time series estimates could not be calculated and instead cross-section estimates for 1962/3 and 1964 were obtained. These price flexibility coefficients after transformation (only price was included as an independent variable) yielded elasticities.

[19] See Chapter 6 for details.

[20] An income measure was not included because of data limitations. We would have required a measure of the income of 'second rank' airlines. Although this is available for the USA, the division of front and second rank airlines is not available in sufficient detail for the rest of the world.

[21] See [15] p. G 18 and Table G 13.

[22] See [16] for an examination of the impact of the supply of wide bodied jets on the US civil aviation industry.

[23] See Table 8.5.

References

1   A.D. Little Inc., *Transfer of Aerospace Technology in the U.S. A Critical Review.*

2   *Commercial Applications of U.S. Aerospace Technology*, Denver Research Institute, Colorado, 1962–63. Study carried out on a NASA contract.

3 *A Pilot Study on Technological Spillovers from Defence and Development Activities*. A report prepared for the Ministry of Defence in August, 1968.

4 R. Miller and D. Sawers, *The Technical Development of Modern Aviation*, Routledge & Kegan Paul, London, 1968.

5 E. Mansfield, 'Innovation and technical change in the railroad industry' contained in *Transport Economics. A Conference of the Universities*. The National Bureau Committee for Economic Research (NBER) 1965.

6 J.A. Schumpeter, *Capitalism, Socialism and Democracy*, Harper & Bros, 1942.

7 J.K. Galbraith, *American Capitalism, the Concept of Countervailing Power*, Penguin 1970.

8 E. Mansfield, 'Technical change and the rate of imitation', *Econometrica*, October, 1962.

9 M.H. Peston, *Public Utility Pricing: The Case of North Sea Gas*, Essays in honour of Lord Robbins (ed. B. Corry).

10 A.H. Fox, 'A theory of second hand markets', *Economica* (New Series), vol. 24, 1957.

11 H.L. Miller, 'A note of Fox's theory of second hand markets', *Economica*, August 1960.

12 K.J.W. Alexander, 'Markets in second hand goods', *Lloyds Bank Review*, July 1970.

13 M.J. Farrell, 'The demand for motor cars in the U.S.', *Journal of the Royal Statistical Society*, Series A, 1959.

14 S.P. Sabotka and C. Schnabel, 'Linear programming as a device for predicting market value: prices of used commercial aircraft 1959–65', *Journal of Business* 1961.

15 *The Market for Used Aircraft*. Undertaken by United Research Inc. September 1957 on behalf of the United States Air Force.

16 'Impact of new large jets on air transport system, 1970–73', *CAB*, November 1969.

17 W.M. Capron (ed.), *Technical Change in Regulated Industries* (Chapter by A. Phillips), Brookings, 1971.

18 A. Phillips, *A Study of the Aircraft Industry*, Heath Lexington Books, 1971.

9 The Overall Model

9.1 Policy objectives and performance

The economic and strategic importance of the civil aviation industry to the developed and under-developed countries, and its natural economic character, has meant close government surveillance.[1] Such an industry, subjected to mixed social, economic and military objectives is likely to suffer from confused and contradictory goals. Similarly, the policies of respective governments have differed, as shown in the frequent disputes at IATA and ICAO meetings. While policies have differed, the means have usually been the same. These have been to use national flag carriers to further the aims of the civil aviation industry, sometimes as a means of furthering economic development (e.g. stimulating tourism), promoting the civil aircraft industry ('buy British Aircraft') and sometimes by simply promoting national prestige.

The outcome has been the development of a structure of international regulations and controls which has to some extent found the common denominators of differing national policies. This structure has operated so as to regulate scheduled air fares, restrict entry and sometimes to control capacity. The result, as Chapter 2 illustrated, has been to stabilise fares, while other variables in the final passenger market such as load factors and profits, have fluctuated considerably; similarly with airline investment.

The industry's structure, as Chapter 1 illustrated, is one of rigid scheduled fares, constituting a value of service pricing structure with a large degree of cross-subsidisation, government restricted entry, bilaterally negotiated frequencies and revenue pools. The growth of non-scheduled operators has led to fighting fares, but the 'wars' that have occurred have been largely over promotional fares, and not standard scheduled fares. Non-price competition, state subsidised airlines and bilateral agreements have formed a market with many high cost operators, and much non-price competition. Stable fares and regular scheduled frequencies have been achieved and maintained, but at the cost of large fluctuations in investment, excess capacity and low profits. The question can only be effectively answered by isolating and evaluating the truly exogenous events, for if these are considerable, a high degree of instability can be expected whatever the market structures and its system of controls.

With this latter point firmly in mind, we have two purposes to fulfil in this chapter: to discover the impact of the industry's regulation on its stability, and to use this information to make conjectures as to the likely effects of introducing or removing certain regulations. The emphasis is on the dynamic aspects of the regulatory mechanism, and not the so-called static, resource allocation effects. The latter has been dealt with elsewhere, e.g. by Straszheim [2]. We shall use the model outlined in Chapter 2 and developed in subsequent chapters by exploring its stability. This will provide an information framework within which we can place possible policy changes.

9.2   The overall industry model

Chapter 2 outlined the various sections of the overall industry model, while subsequent chapters examined and estimated the constituent parts of the model. It is the task of this section to bring together these results, to fit them into the overall model, and to examine its stability.

Before proceeding to the model, a number of clarifying points should be made concerning the primary demand model. Chapters 3 and 4 developed and estimated demand models applicable largely to individual routes and route groups. The model constructed in this chapter concerns the world civil aviation industry. We are concerned with aggregate world demand and supply of aircraft services, changes in world orders for aircraft, etc. This global distinction has been upheld in that the demand relationships built into the model are estimated in this section rather than derived from Chapter 4. World scheduled industry data has been employed, using ICAO time series data on passenger flows, load factors and fares for the period 1955–1970.

Price regulation in the primary market raises the problem of equilibrium. How responsive are the regulated fares to deviations between demand and supply? This asks a question of the method by which fares are set. In an unrestricted market, when the demand for a service is high relative to the supply we expect the price to rise, the rate of rise being greater the greater the excess demand. Conversely, when demand is low relative to supply. In a market such as civil aviation where fares are fixed under unanimous agreement rules[2] and where capacity restrictions operate it is unlikely that the fares will exactly reach the equilibrium level. However, this level at which fares are fixed is likely to be influenced by the prevailing, or recently prevailing, differences between demand and supply. It seems possible, therefore, to postulate relationships between load factors

260

Table 9.1

World primary market demand model
Dependent variable price *(PT)*

(a) *Linear form*

Independent variables				R^2	D.W.
D	LF	Y	Constant		
–	+0.01	–	3.2	0.13	4.1
–	+0.03	−0.017	7.3	0.63	1.1
−0.003	−0.02	–	5.4	0.82	0.8
−0.007	+0.22	–	2.1	0.86	1.3
–	–	−0.007	4.5	0.42	0.6

(b) *Log form*

Independent variables				R^2	D.W.
D	LF	Y	Constant		
−0.06	−0.38	–	1.36	0.45	0.4
–	−0.04	−0.03	1.9	0.48	1.0
−0.07	−0.04	1.4	0.48	0.80	0.1
−0.004	–	−0.09	0.8	0.31	0.5
−0.02	–	–	0.6	0.32	0.4
–	0.13	–	0.36	0.13	0.3

PT = price of travel, the dependent variable
D = demand (thousand million passenger km per annum) and
Y = income defined as GNP *per capita.*
LF = load factor

and the fixed fares[3] to explain the level at which fares are fixed. A number of these relationships will be tested below.

These relationships between institutional fare fixing and market demand and supply have further implications for the model. If fixed prices are a function, say, of load factor (*LF*) 2 periods ago, and price (*PT*) enters the demand function, price is in effect a lagged endogenous variable. Correct model specification in effect leads to both demand and price predictions.

Examining the relationship between price and load factor, the results of Table 9.1 point to the equation

$$PT_t = 2.1 - 0.007D_t + 0.22LF_{t-1} \qquad (9.1)$$

261

as representing the probable pricing mechanism.

The passenger demand D_t is thus a function of price and, implicitly, of load factor. From this we can obtain the effect of supply changes on output passenger demand.

In Table 9.2 a number of proposed models suggests that either

$$D_t = 0.95 - 0.97D_{t-1} + 0.45Y_t - 33.1PT_t \qquad (9.2)$$

or

$$D_t = 5.70 + 0.91\,Y_t - 130.5PT_t \qquad (9.3)$$

are the most likely candidates to be included in the final model. We note that the demand data is annual rather than quarterly; it will be seen possible to derive approximate quarterly dynamic equations.

The most acceptable order model is given by equation (6.13) here repeated (here ^ indicates a forecasted quantity: 12 quarters lead time assumed.)

$$\log O_t' = 0.94 + 0.53 \log O_{t-1}' - 1.15 \log \hat{FV} - 0.868 \log \hat{PQ} + 1.5 \log \hat{K}$$

Models of less validity, yet with meaningful arguments to support them are:

$$\log O_t' = -0.72 + 0.54 \log O_{t-1}' - 0.64 \log \hat{FV}_t - 0.42 \log \hat{K}_t + 0.75 \log D_t$$

$$(9.5)$$

(this is equation 6.11)

and, possibly, as a linear investment model:

$$W_t = 6.7 + 1.5\,W_{t-1} - 0.39\,W_{t-2} - 1.4\,\hat{FV} \qquad (9.6)$$

$$O_t' = W_t - W_{t-1} \qquad (9.7)$$

In all these ordering models, the data O_t' is given in capacity units, and all variables are given as quarterly data. We include equations (9.5), (9.6) and (9.7) as secondary models for stability analysis.

The complete model in diagrammatic form is shown in Figure 9.1. The structure includes functional blocks, labelled 'forecast', which describe the aggregate method of forecasting used by the industry to derive $\hat{u}$ from variable u. We assume the equations

$$\hat{u}_{k+1} = y_k + mx_k \qquad (9.8)$$
$$y_{k+1} = 0.2u_k + 0.8(y_k + x_k) \qquad (9.9)$$

262

Table 9.2

World primary market demand model
Dependent variable passenger demand *(D)*

(a) *Linear form*

Independent variables				R^2	D.W.
D_{t-1}	Y_t	PT_t	Constant		
−8.25	5.1	−94.9	−8.25	0.65	2.11
−	0.91	−130.5	5.70	0.97	0.75
1.17	0.15	4.4	−35.9	0.99	1.88
0.97	0.45	−33.1	95.0	0.99	2.30

(b) *Log form*

Independent variables				R^2	D.W.
D_{t-1}	Y_t	PT_t	Constant		
0.02	1.3	1.1	2.06	0.1	0.45
−0.005	0.8	0.6	4.3	0.4	1.15

(c) *Linear difference* (ΔD)

Independent variables				R^2	D.W.
ΔD_{t-1}	ΔY_t	ΔPT_t	Constant		
−	5.2	0.95	−8.25	0.68	2.1
0.75	1.5	−31.06	−1.9	0.85	2.38

$$x_{k+1} = x_k + 0.05 \left[u_k - (y_k + x_k) \right] \qquad (9.10)$$

where u_k is the input data, y_k, x_k are estimates one period ahead of u_{k-1} and its difference, and $\hat{u}_{k+m}$ is the forecast m periods ahead.

It is convenient to write y_{k+1} as ∇y_k, using the shift (or delay) operator ∇; it is then found that the forecasting equations (9.8), (9.9) and (9.10) become:

$$\hat{u}_{k+m} = \frac{\{0.2 + m(0.05) - \nabla[0.15 + m(0.05)]\}\, u_k}{1 - 1.75\,\nabla + 0.8\nabla^2} \qquad (9.11)$$

or if $m = 12$

$$\hat{u}_{k+12} = \frac{(0.8 - 0.75\nabla)\, u_k}{1 - 1.75\nabla + 0.8\nabla^2} \qquad (9.12)$$

The diagram of Figure 9.1 also indicates scaling factors c, k which allow for alteration in capacity measure. The output demand model may be put in quarterly terms if the dynamics are appropriately adjusted. If this part of the model is linearised, the steady state relationships can be assumed to be constant.

9.2.1 Use of the model for forecasting

A recent study [1] (among many) on the future of London airports using slightly differing forms of growth trend equations, gave widely different figures for 1977. Thus, aggregate annual passengers for 1977 in thousands are shown in Table 9.3.

Although each of these models fits past and current data with acceptable R^2 (greater than 0.9), such a result emphasises the need for a behavioural model. The search for such models by automatic model building methods is currently of interest [2,3,4] but has clearly to be based on *a priori* economic considerations to be most efficient.

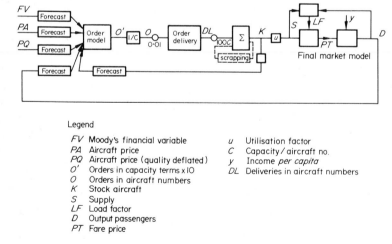

Legend

FV	Moody's financial variable	u	Utilisation factor
PA	Aircraft price	C	Capacity / aircraft no.
PQ	Aircraft price (quality deflated)	y	Income *per capita*
O'	Orders in capacity terms x 10	DL	Deliveries in aircraft numbers
O	Orders in aircraft numbers		
K	Stock aircraft		
S	Supply		
LF	Load factor		
D	Output passengers		
PT	Fare price		

Fig. 9.1   Final model

Table 9.3
Passenger forecasts for
London Airport 1977

Model	Passengers (annual in thousands)
Linear autoregressive	25,277
Log linear autoregressive	22,962
Linear trend	23,302
Semi-log trend	55,387
Semi-quadratic trend	12,470

The significant elements of the final model are the ordering mechanism and market demand models, respectively Figure 2.4 and Figure 2.5 in Chapter 2. The ordering mechanism in particular is unlikely to be predicted by any kind of simple exponential smoothing, although certain of its determinants, e.g. FV, PQ, etc., exhibit reasonably mild behaviour and can be approximated by straight line or first order smoothing. In fact, this produces a rough linear interpolation, for n quarters ahead of the base year 1969. Details are as follows:

$$\hat{K}_n = 50 + (42/24)n \tag{9.13a}$$

$$\hat{FV}_n = 5.5 + (8.5/24)n \tag{9.13b}$$

$$\hat{PA}_n = 182 + (10/24)n \tag{9.13c}$$

$$\hat{PQ}_n = 170 + (8/24)n \tag{9.13d}$$

For a diagrammatic representation see Figures 9.2a and 9.2b.

The seasonal variations, of course, are absent in these forecasts. Putting in appropriate values to determine future ordering activity (Equation 6.12) a much lower level from the peak of 1968 is obtained. In Chapter 6 it was suggested that the ordering process is highly sign sensitive to the slope of C^*, the equilibrium level, so that if O^* suddenly declines, then this is the signal for an upsurge of order placements. Perturbations in FV and PQ (Figure 9.3) yield a sensitivity measure of this effect. This appears to place emphasis, for current ordering forecasts, on accurate prediction of FV, PQ, etc. including all seasonal variations and transients. Thus, given the airline industry's structure, the problem is one of forecasting accurately the behaviour of aircraft prices and the performance of airline finances.

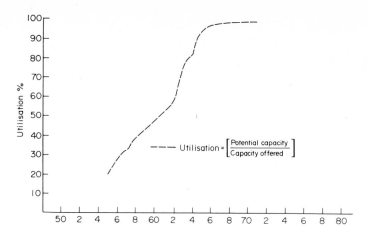

Fig. 9.2a   Forecast of order determinants: utilisation (1950–80)

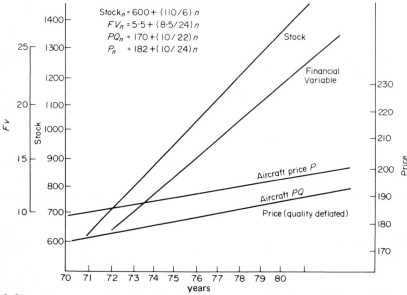

$$Stock_n = 600 + (110/6)\,n$$
$$FV_n = 5{\cdot}5 + (8{\cdot}5/24)\,n$$
$$PQ_n = 170 + (10/22)\,n$$
$$P_n = 182 + (10/24)\,n$$

Fig. 9.2b   Forecast of order determinants: stock, financial variables, aircraft price and quality changes (1970–80)

The market demand model, on the other hand, while clearly important is much more sluggish in response, even allowing for the yearly data. The order-delivery lag seems to match the fast ordering response to the slow demand model, and lessens the need for aggregated load factor, price and

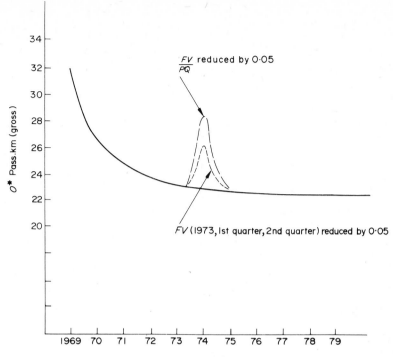

Fig. 9.3   Sensitivity of the order mechanism

passenger figures on a monthly or quarterly basis.

One should note that the second hand market (Chapter 5) has not been included in the final market, although it clearly has a meaningful bearing on the ordering mechanism.

9.2.2   *Stability and the civil aviation industry model*

The fluctuations within the industry may be ascribed to both the industry structure and also to the external forces. While a multiple looped system may be envisaged, whereby prices, load factors and passengers are all taken account of in the ordering process, the simplest and most viable approach is to take passenger seat miles sold as being the major (and for an initial survey, the sole) feedback variable. Thus, aircraft orders are assumed to be based upon passenger forecasts, together with certain exogenous factors. Orders lead to deliveries and aircraft stock relates to supply which further stimulates passenger demand and so on (Figure 2.4). It is of interest to examine the closed loop system from a stability point of view. We consider here not the simple 'constant proportionality of growth' meaning of stability, but also the 'fluctuation amplitude' growth. This is of interest because the *raison d'être* of many controls could be interpreted as based around supposed stabilisation of load factors and investment.

The stability analysis we introduce is based on linear system theory, so that in the event of logarithmic relationships, some linearisation is necessary. A delay operator ∇ is again introduced so that each model element may be related by a polynomial in which ∇ effectively replaces the difference equation. Coalescing the individual transfer functions, we obtain a composite expression. In the case of an ordering mechanism affected by demand, this relates the additional stimulation of demand by demand. In other words we examine the result of an initial change in demand causing an ordering perturbation to arise, hence causing an alteration to aircraft stock, which directly affects services and so on. If this expression is written as $p(\nabla)/q(\nabla)$ then the stability is governed by the roots of

$$1 - p(\nabla) \,/\, q(\nabla) = 0 \qquad\qquad (9.14)$$

If the roots lie inside, or on, the unit circle, the system is stable: if any lie outside the unit circle the system is unstable, to a degree dependent on the distance of that particular root from the origin. Since root solving routines are simply acquired, the task of formulation becomes one of collecting the elemental models into the form $p(\nabla)/q(\nabla)$.

As an example of this technique let us take a typical set of acceptable models, and hence illustrate the formulation for a stability analysis. Thus:

Order model

$$\log O_t = 0.54 \log O_{t-1} - 0.64 \log F\hat{V}_t - 0.42 \qquad (9.5)$$
$$\log \hat{K}_t + 0.75 \log \hat{D}_t - 0.72$$

(Note that D_t is quarterly data)

Order-delivery lag model

$$DL_t = \nabla^{12}\, O_t \qquad\qquad (9.15)$$

(This is a pure lead time approximation to the distributed lag)

Stock model

$$K_t = \frac{DL_t}{1 - \nabla} \qquad\qquad (9.16)$$

268

(Stock capacity is the summed capacity deliveries)

Output supply-demand model

$$S_t = K_t \qquad (9.17)$$

(Supply equals utilisation, here assumed 100 per cent)

$$PT_t = 2.1 - 0.007D_t + 0.022F_{t-1} \qquad (9.1)$$

$$D_t = 570 + 91Y_t - 130.5PT_t \qquad (9.3)$$

The forecasting formula, put into shift operator terms,

$$\hat{D}_t = \left[\frac{0.8 - 0.75\,\nabla}{1 - 1.75\nabla + 8\nabla^2} \right] D_t \qquad (9.18)$$

completes the model equations.

It is necessary to linearise the order and demand models, before putting into operator form. Equation (9.9) may be linearised via

$$\frac{\delta O_t'}{O_t'} = 0.54\,\frac{\delta O_{t-1}'}{O_{t-1}'} + 0.74\,\frac{\delta \hat{D}_t}{\hat{D}_t}$$

whence inserting 1972 figures for O_t, O_{t-1}, D_t, we obtain the transfer

$$\frac{O_t'}{\hat{D}_t} = \frac{0.06}{(1 - 0.54\nabla)}$$

By a similar method equations (9.1) and (9.3) give on an annual basis

$$\frac{\delta D_t}{\delta S_t} = \frac{0.203\,\nabla}{0.086 + 0.37\nabla}$$

while the interpolation to quarterly figures yields

$$\frac{\delta D_t}{\delta S_t} = \frac{0.203\nabla}{0.344 + 0.122\nabla}$$

The entire transfer function is shown in Figure 9.4a, exhibiting one major feedback loop, neglecting initially the K_t inner loop that arises in equation (9.5). The degree of stability is indicated in Figure 9.4 b(i)(ii) (iii) as a function of root location. Figure 9.4b (i) is the nominal linear model, while (ii) and (iii) represent hypothetical variations in forecasting in both positive and negative sense (see also Table 9.2). In order to be accurate, there shall be inserted into the transfer function diagram (Figure 6) the stock feedback loop that is evident in equation (9.5). This stock, rather than passenger demand, also is present in the major order model of equation (9.4). There is a suggestion made here that the determinant of orders is more likely to be current stock rather than passenger kilometres flown. This means that asymptotic stability is purely a function of the placing of orders and of the order-delivery lag, and that the final market

269

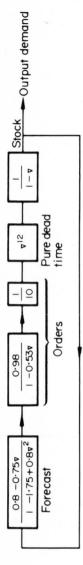

Fig. 9.4a   Stability according to the linearised order model

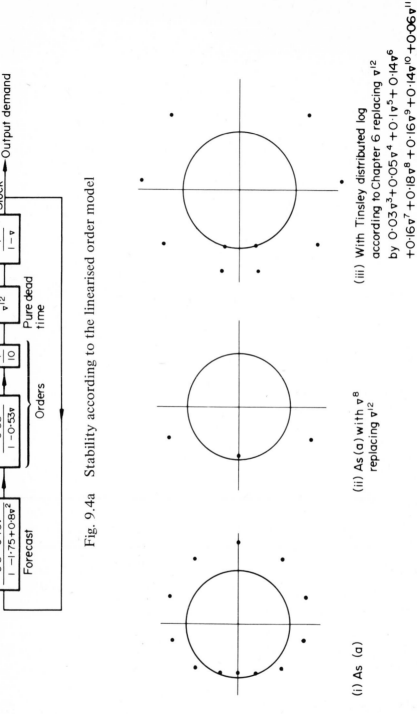

(i) As (a)

(ii) As (a) with ∇^8 replacing ∇^{12}

(iii) With Tinsley distributed log according to Chapter 6 replacing ∇^{12} by $0 \cdot 03\nabla^3 + 0 \cdot 05\nabla^4 + 0 \cdot 1\nabla^5 + 0 \cdot 14\nabla^6 + 0 \cdot 16\nabla^7 + 0 \cdot 18\nabla^8 + 0 \cdot 16\nabla^9 + 0 \cdot 14\nabla^{10} + 0 \cdot 06\nabla^{11}$

Fig. 9.4b   Roots of the transfer function closed loop

model has no contributory influence on the preceding causal mechanisms being inherently stable itself. The root location for both these further combinations is shown to be within the unit circle. Finally, the effect of a change in lag distribution completes the picture of stability of the linearised model.

This technique of evaluating system stability is useful in so far as the linearised system approximates to the actual system model [4, 5, 6]. More precise knowledge of the stability is given by purely moving the model, or models, forward in time. This is carried out in Chapter 10, where the use of the model for forecasting purposes is discussed. However, the main results arrived at are:

1 The system is slightly unstable, that is, there is a regenerative aspect that operates even when the order determinants are constant. Even under static economic conditions, there exists a propensity to order and stimulate passenger growth, a not surprising result in view of the relatively small proportion of people who travel by air.

2 This growth is essentially small and the demand for air travel is largely fostered by external variables such as variations in GNP.

3 A reduction in lead time, or an equivalent tendency in the form of distributed lag, enhances stability.

4 The system as a whole, retains the property of essential global stability, under price alterations based on load factors. Assuming a linear price of travel/lagged load factor relationship, a doubling or a halving of the proportionality still results in a linear system.

The result (4) leads to one major policy suggestion: if the removal or relaxing of price controls does not lead to a decreased stability, why retain such controls? This will be discussed further in the next section. However, the ordering mechanism, as discussed in Chapter 6, especially in the non-linear form remains a highly sensitive mechanism. Orders are placed both according to the market as in practice in a highly fluctuating manner, fortunately smoothed by the order-delivery lag and by the cumulative summation of delivered aircraft that form the stock. This means that the supply of aircraft in capacity terms grows reasonably smoothly, despite the highly transient origins of the eventual stock arrivals. There is no suitable analysis that determines this type of stability: instead simulation becomes necessary.

9.3 Alternative regulations

An appraisal of an industry's regulations is a difficult task. Essentially it involves comparing the net differences between its performance under regulation, and its possible performance under alternative regulations. The difficulty is threefold. To specify and to produce practical alternative policies, and to predict the effects of the alternative policies. Specification is often the easiest of the tasks, especially when supported by theoretical orthodoxy. Equate price to long run marginal cost . . ., remove price discrimination . . . . Even assuming the acceptance of static allocation efficiency, and leaving aside income distribution and second best problems, the practicalities in changing over to anything like a marginal cost pricing policy are likely to be considerable. Comparisons with the performance of industries subjected to different and prescribed regulation is a more fruitful approach. Finding such comparisons is difficult.

Our task is not to make normative evaluations of the civil aviation industry's performance. It is to use the model of the industry to predict the effects of changing certain of its present regulations. Stability of one or other variable is not deemed to be desirable; stability of profits or prices is not accepted as the unquestioned object of regulation. Instead the purpose is to give some prediction as to the likely outcome of changing the industry's regulations; of discovering whether removing price control leads to greater or less fluctuations in investment.

Section 9.2 dealt with the effects on stability of changing certain of the equation parameters. As we showed, such changes have significant meaning to the industry's performance. The example of reducing the time taken to produce civil aircraft and of changing demand coefficients have meaning for industrial and economic policies. These changes will, in certain areas, be complementary to the policy changes regarding regulations. With this in mind, our objective in this section is to isolate those changes in policy regulations which are practical and politically feasible, and then to examine their impact on the industry's stability.

Making a rough divide between those policies which affect the final passenger market and the factor input market, we can envisage something like the following regulations:

Final passenger market	*Factor market*
1 Removal of price control.	1 Constraint of orders by means order ceilings.
2 Removal of entry control.	
3 Introduction of capacity controls:	2 Selective financial policies imposed as a means of stimulating and constraining aircraft purchases.
(a) Without price control	
(b) With price control.	

This is far from being an exhaustive list, but it does contain some of the possible policies that have been proposed. Some of these, in part, already operate. For instance, in the US until recently, special concessions were granted to airlines purchasing American aircraft. Many markets have capacity controls in the form of bilateral agreements on equipment, frequencies of pool sharing schemes. Furthermore, there is no reason for all to be in operation at the same time: fare and entry controls removed along with order ceilings, capacity controls with no fare controls, etc.

The permutations are considerable, even with this small list. But what of the practical and political aspects? The industry is international, and agreement therefore difficult. Ceilings on orders are likely to be impossible to impose, and financial constraint likely only to pertain to individual countries. If changes are to be implemented, it is more likely to be in the final passenger market.

The removal of entry controls is unlikely in this scheduled market. North America, the United Kingdom and some West European countries possibly, but unlikely in the under-developed world. National prestige, economic requirements, even if spurious, are likely to lead to restrictions implementing capacity controls only in slump conditions, i.e. not permanent and not paramount through bilateral negotiations. The removal of price control is the most likely alternative. In a sense, the rigidity of the IATA price fixing in Western Europe and on the North Atlantic route, the removal of minimum price IT and liberal bilateral agreements on charter flights, reduced non-scheduled flights by bidding away the non-business traveller and winning substantial numbers of business travellers, have all forced the schedule airlines to introduce reduced promotional fares. As yet standard scheduled fares have not fallen in any significant amount in the face of this competition, yet it is movement in scheduled fares that is likely to follow from a removal of fare control.

In examining the removal of fare control, two questions have to be answered. Firstly, given the present structure of fare fixing, how could such a policy take place? Secondly, if an open fare situation takes place, what is the likely extent of the price variation that will follow?

Central to both answers are the governments of the respective airlines. Under present conditions, governments have the right of veto over air fares negotiated by their airlines at IATA meetings. The removal of landing rights is, of course, the means of enforcing this veto. This is a powerful veto, and can be used as a means of supporting IATA agreements—by means of barring a non-IATA airline – as well as rejecting them. An effective policy of fare competition would have to involve inter-government support for such a situation—a veto of IATA fares but freedom of fare fixing to competing airlines.

The extent of the variation in fares depends upon the structure of the airlines and the behaviour of the government. Freedom of charging could lead to considering price variation, differing over the day, year and with respect to equipment. Collusion is of course possible, but price competition could take place without any of the excessive instability suggested by some economists. Some of the competition could lead to large fare changes, particularly if the governments supported their airlines by means of substantial subsidies. This is a likely possibility, and substantial fare changes would follow. On certain routes, therefore, changes in fares would be more substantial than those implemented by the IATA agreements.

9.4   Conclusions

We can now state that according to the developed model, the removal of the IATA price regulations will not have a de-stabilising effect. Thus, immediately we can ask, since the reason behind the IATA fare fixing is the desire for stability, why not remove the controls? In practice it should be at least possible to have a more flexible form of pricing; the advantage to the airlines is that they then have an extra variable of decision making at their disposal.

However, extreme variations in the ordering pattern are likely to arise. The sensitivity of the 'desired' level of ordering for the industry to a combination of forecast passenger demand, financial variable, aircraft price and other determinants, gives rise to what may be termed instability. The uncertainty of forecasting plays the major role here, and will be discussed in the next chapter.

However, given a differing form of pricing policy it is highly likely that orders will not be placed according to the same premises. The order mechanism model developed may no longer become applicable. It is possible, for instance, that a more rational stock adjustment process may arise. From at least argumentative grounds, since the rivalrous intentions of airlines become blunted with variable pricing arrangements, the tendency to over-order will disappear, and the order pattern will present a less variable picture.

One is tempted to dwell upon limitations on ordering, new option clauses, governmental subsidies to expand manufacturing capacity and to reduce lead times. These do not represent feasible policies for the aggregate industry, although they may offer theoretical improvements in the dynamics of the individual industries. The major policy that could be implemented, a relaxation of fares policy, is suggested by the model.

How valuable has been the effort spent on examining different sections of this study? Where is the element in the model that most repays continued study? The answer is that the distributed lag and second hand market aspects are less important than the order mechanism and the output demand model. Both these latter two, therefore, are the prime areas of the industry to watch, in the future. They can be regarded as indicators that will reflect any future structural changes in the industry. Again, they are prominent in any discussion, such as now follows, of forecasting.

Notes

[1] See Chapter 1.
[2] See Chapter 1.
[3] The relationship between load factor and the normal market clearing mechanism in an unrestricted market is as follows:

In an unrestricted market price adjustment can be seen to be a function of

$$\frac{dP}{dt} = \alpha \frac{(\text{Demand}_t - \text{Supply}_t)}{\text{Supply}_t} 100$$

This is equivalent to $\alpha \left[\dfrac{D}{S} - 1 \right] 100$ where $\dfrac{D}{S}$ is load factor: variable LF = 100 load factor.

References

1   M. Desai, 'Forecasting airport passenger traffic: two approaches', BAA working paper, 1969.
2   J. Bray, 'Dynamic equations for economic forecasting with the GDP — unemployment relation and the growth of GDP in the United Kingdom as an example', *Journal of the Royal Statistical Society,* Series A (General), vol. 134, no. 2, 1971 (pp. 167–228).
3   K.D. Wall, A.J. Preston, J.W. Bray and M.H. Peston, *Estimates for a Simple Control Model of the UK Economy*, Conference on Modelling of the UK Economy, London Business School, 3–6 July 1972.
4   K. Hilton and D. Heathfield (eds), *The Econometric Study of the United Kingdom*, discussion C.R. Wymer and R.J. Ball, Macmillan, 1970 (p. 54).

5 A.W. Philips, 'Stabilisation policy in a closed economy', *The Economic Journal*, June 1954 (pp. 292–323).

6 A.W. Philips, 'Stabilisation policy and the time-forms of lagged responses', *The Economic Journal*, June 1957 (pp. 165–77).

7 D.C.C. Ho and M. Noron, 'A study of the alternative policies in the control of a national economy via dynamic programming', *Economica*, vol. 39, 1972 (pp. 135–59).

8 F.F. Kno, *Network Analysis and Synthesis*, Wiley, 1966 (pp. 365–412).

10 A Look Forward

10.1 Introduction

Forecasting the demand for travel is a central task of all sections of the aviation industry. Inaccurate demand forecasting leads to capacity problems, and consequently to revenue difficulties. One of the problems of the industry is the length of time ahead the forecasts have to be made. The development and gestation period of aircraft manufacture and airport construction have meant that, relative to other industries, the lead time in aviation is very long.[1] Airlines placing an order for an aircraft need to consider the demand from t periods ahead, t being determined by the time it takes to build the aircraft and deliver it into service. Aircraft manufacturers have to consider the time it takes to develop an aircraft prototype, and then the production run period of payoff for the investment in the project. As Mr J. de Lagarde of Sud Aviation[2] has written: 'The manufacturer is interested in the trend over at least the next three years, ten years and over if we add up the time it takes to produce a prototype, taking as point of reference the middle of their operational life.'

Airlines generally have a shorter forecasting horizon. Mr C. Tillinghast of TWA[3] suggests that his airline draws up a 5 year plan, in which adaptive, short term forecasts of demand play a central role.

In the case of airports, Roskill's forecasts for the third London airport extend 15 years into the future, although the total construction time for such an airport was estimated as seven years.[4] The aim here was to plan an airport, i.e. to obtain an idea of the time ahead when the airport capacity was likely to fail to meet the requirements demanded of it. This meant, of course, a longer forecast than if the project forecast was for a period just long enough to cover the construction time. The social externalities in building an airport have necessitated much detailed, long term forecasting, in order that the accepted plan can be implemented.

These are all long time horizons,[5] the longest probably faces the airport planner, then the aircraft manufacturer and then the airlines. It is not surprising, therefore, that the long range forecasts have been dominated by the airports (e.g. The Port of New York Authority) and the aircraft manufacturers (particularly the US manufacturers). In section 10.2 we shall examine some of the passenger forecasts made by these bodies. Passenger demand forecasts are central to all sectors of the industry, and it is therefore appropriate that we examine these forecasts. The main purpose, however, is to evaluate past forecasting methods, in order to come to some general conclusions as to forecasting technique. Such arguments will be presented in section 10.2 while sections 10.3 and 10.4 deal with aircraft demand forecasting.

10.2   Passenger demand forecasts: a retrospective look

The mid 1950s, the threshold of the jet age, was a period of considerable interest in the future growth of civil aviation. Forecasts proliferated, but as the future turned into the present with the passing of time most of them were shown to be widely inaccurate. The majority turned out to be under-estimates, suggesting that the evaluations of technological and economic changes were inaccurate.

To give reasons why forecasts were inaccurate might at first appear to be a straightforward task. With conditional forecasts, the forecast conditions can be related to what actually occurred, and some explanation can be built up as to the divergence between the predicted and the actual. With other forecasts, such as trend extrapolation unaccompanied by any economic or technological explanation, such evaluation is not possible. Instead, comment is concentrated on the importance of the base year, and the length and character of the fitted time series. The outcome of these evaluations, however, is not to offer some best forecasting method, but rather to detail the properties of a good forecast, and to illustrate the need for clearly stated and testable explanations of the assumptions underlying the forecast.

Dealing with the accuracy of the forecasts first of all, we have chosen two markets, the world (ICAO) scheduled and the US domestic. Most of the published forecasts in these markets are trend forecasts, in which (say) x per cent growth for the next n years is postulated. Sometimes these forecasts are based on economic reasoning, e.g. growth is expected to be 6 per cent because income elasticity is 2 and growth in income is expected to grow at 3 per cent per annum. Others are just straight extrapolations of past trends. We have distinguished these methods of forecasting from what we have termed econometric forecasts, in that the latter state explicitly the model, its variable, coefficients and the expected growth in the independent variables. The latter will be examined in the last half of this section.

Predictive accuracy can be measured in a number of ways. We have chosen three tests:

1   The accuracy of point estimates.
2   The ability of the forecast to foresee turning points.
3   The test of mean square prediction error.

The mean square prediction error has been applied to only two of the

Table 10.1

World forecasts: passenger miles (thousand millions)

Forecaster	Base year	Forecast	Point accuracy*	Forecaster	Base year	Forecast	Point accuracy*
Boeing [24]				*T.P. Wright* [23]			
	1958				1956		
1960		72.6	+0.70	1960			
1965		145.4	+0.18	1965		70.0	+0.03
1970		235.9	−0.01	1970		155.0	+0.26
Canadair [22]				*ICAO*†			
	1956				1960		
1960		67.8	0.00	1960		69.0	+0.02
1965		105.3	+0.01	1965		100.0	−0.18
1970		147.2	−0.38	1970		137.0	−0.23
Convair				*ICAO*†			
	1957				1965		
1960		67.0	0.00	1970		414	+0.07
1965		110.2	−0.10	*ICAO*†			
1970		156.2	−0.34		1968		
Douglas						366	−0.05
	1957						
1960				*Boeing*			
1965		63.8	−0.05		1966		
1970		87.5	−0.28			268	+0.11

* This is obtained by the following calculation:

$$\left[\frac{\text{Forecast} - \text{Actual}}{\text{Actual}}\right] \times 100$$

† Nearest estimate of range taken

forecasts, the point estimates being preferred as a measure of accuracy. This is because most of the forecasts suggest constant growth rates, their purpose being not to forecast the cycle, but to be accurate for a specific date in the future. The constant growth factor of many of the forecasts means, of course, they are unable to deal with the possibility of turning points of inflexion in the growth of demand. Nevertheless, this aspect of the forecast shall be examined, for it is relevant to some of the forecasts which postulate changing growth rates.

Table 10.2

US domestic market forecasts: passenger miles (thousand millions)

Forecaster	Base year	Forecast	Point accuracy
Curtis [25]	1956		
1960			
1965		42.0	−0.18
1970		51.7	−0.48
Boeing	1958		
1960			
1965		46.3	−0.10
1970		61.9	−0.38
Convair	1957		
1960			
1965		50.7	−0.02
1970		65.4	−0.34
CAB	1956		
1960		34.1	+0.16
1965		49.0	−0.05
1970		73.8	−0.26
T.P. Wright	1956		
1960		35.0	+0.19
1965		64.5	+0.24
United	1958		
1965		42.0	−0.18
1970		51.7	−0.48
Boeing	1965		
1970		100.5	−0.06

Table 10.3

Yearly percentage increase
in passenger miles

Calendar year	US domestic trunk		ICAO world	
1956	12.7		16.0	
1957	13.2		15.0	
1958	−0.3	D	4.0	D
1959	15.1	U	15.0	U
1960	3.9	D	11.0	D
1961	1.0		7.0	
1962	7.8	U	11.0	U
1963	14.3		13.0	
1964	14.5		16.0	
1965	17.6		16.0	
1966	15.4		16.0	
1967	24.0		19.0	
1968	16.0	D	14.0	D
1969	9.0		13.0	
1970	4.8		11.0	

D – downturn
U – upturn

An examination of Tables 10.1 and 10.2, relating passenger miles forecasts in the world and USA markets, shows the preponderance of under-
estimates. The negative signs indicate under-estimates, the positive sign
over-estimates.[6] This is particularly the case with the older forecasts, although the exception to this is T.P.Wright's forecast [23] which generally
gives an over-estimate. Clearly, in these largely trend forecasts the base year[7]
of forecasting is important, for a trend projection, giving greater weight to
the near past, is likely to be considerably influenced by the growth in the
base year. Table 10.3 sets out the growth rates in the two markets, indicating also the points of inflexion in the market's growth. Take for instance 1958, when a business slump arrested the growth of the aviation
market, possibly causing forecasts with 1958 as the base to postulate a
lower growth rate. We see from Table 10.3 the number of undulations the
growth path has followed. On the whole, the points of inflexion forecasted
have not been accurate, due largely to their inability to predict economic
fluctuations rather than their inability to predict technological innovations.
T. P. Wright, for instance, chose a growth rate of 12 per cent between
1955–1960, and an upturn in 1960 to 13 per cent. As we can see from

Table 10.3, 1960 marked a downturn in the market, and the onset of the business slump in the US. United Research predicted a downturn in 1965 from 15 to 12 per cent growth per annum, yet this year marked an upturn in the market. In an attempt to deal with the important problem of forecasting turning points, Boeing[8] have introduced a forecasting model specially designed for this purpose. As Table 10.4 shows, Boeing's 1966 forecast has been accurate, predicting the upturn of 1967, and the downturn from 1968 onwards. Although relatively little time has passed to test the forecast, it would appear that more disaggregated models, dealing specifically with technological and economic variables, can lead to more promising results.

Another test of a forecast is to compare its predictive accuracy for every year of the forecast. In this way its performance over the whole of the period covered is measured, rather than for, say, some terminal year. One convenient method of obtaining such a measure is to take the actual figures, take away the forecast figure and represent as a percentage, square the result, take the products for all years and divide by the number of years. This measure, known as the mean square prediction error,[9] was performed on two forecasts of the US domestic market, Boeing's 1961 forecast and Larsson's 1956 forecast for Canadair [22]. The mean square prediction errors were 138 and 46 respectively, again suggesting that the base year was crucial in the forecast.

The base year, the form of the smoothing, the expected behaviour of the independent variables all affects the accuracy of the forecasts. The useful aspect of econometric forecasts is that the forecasted independent

Table 10.4

Boeing's forecast of
the US domestic and world's 'turning points'

Growth rates (Percentage per annum)

| | USA | | World | |
	Forecast	Actual	Forecast	Actual
1966	16.0	15.9	17.1	16
1967	15.5	24.0	19.9	19
1968	14.9	16.0	14.5	14
1969	9.6	9.0	13.6	13
1970	4.2	4.8	10.8	11

Source: [21]

Table 10.5

Details of some econometric forecasts

1 FAA	Base 1965
	Source: [11]

Time series 1950–1965
Model: $\log Q = 1.0 \log Y - 1.5 \log F - 0.6 \log S$
where Q = *per capita* revenue passenger miles
Y = excess income, i.e. incomes \$7,500/annum/US population
F = average fare deflated by consumer price index
S = average travel time

2 CAB	Base 1965
	Source: [27]

$\Delta\log Q = 0.085 - 1.28 \, \Delta\log F + 1.16 \log Y - 0.04 \log T$
Q = revenue passenger miles
F = fare/passenger miles
T = time trend
Y = *per capita* income deflated by consumer price index

3 Houthakker and Taylor: [26]

US domestic inter-city air expenditures
Model $q_t = 0.95 \, q_{t-1} + 0.00025 \, x_t - 0.0012 \, p_t + 0.27 \, z_t$
q_t = *per capita* personal consumption expenditure on air
p_t = relative price
x_t = total *per capita* personal consumption expenditure
z_t = three dummy variables
Assumptions: 4 and 5 per cent full employment equilibrium rate of growth in aggregate GNP between 1961–1970

Forecast:	Budget share (in actual prices) of inter-city air expenditure 1970	0.0027
Actual:	Budget share (in actual prices) of inter-city air expenditure 1969	0.0036

variables can be tested against the actual outcome. In order to illustrate this aspect of econometric forecasts we have taken forecasts of the US domestic market, two of which forecast future passenger miles and one, by Houthakker and Taylor, which forecasts air travel expenditure.

As Tables 10.6 and 10.7 show, all three have been off the mark by varying degrees. The interesting point, however, is the degree to which these forecasts have erred due to an incorrect forecasting of the indepen-

Table 10.6

Econometric forecasts
of the US domestic market

Forecaster	Base	Forecast	Point accuracy
FAA	1965	90	−0.10
CAB	1965	75	−0.25

Table 10.7

Recalculated US forecasts

Variable	Actual average change between 1965–70	Average per annum Forecast change 1965–70	
		by FAA	CAB Houthakker
Population	+ 0.011 per annum		
Consumer price index	+55% per annum		+1.5
Air fares	− 0.015 per annum	−0.02	−0.011
Air time	− 0.06 per annum	−0.001	
GNP *per capita* (red)	+ 0.32 per annum	+0.015	
Current disposable income *per capita*	+ 0.03		+0.019

Revised forecasts	1970	Point accuracy
CAB	83.26	−0.17
FAA	99.3	−0.01

dent variables. As a means of testing these models, we have re-run them, fitting in the correct data for the independent variables. This information and the recalculated forecasts are contained in Table 10.7, showing the improved accuracy resulting from accurate independent variable forecasts. The original assumptions are displayed in Table 10.5.

Comparing the FAA with the CAB forecasts, we see that the trend item in the former was insufficient to account for all the considerable qualitative changes in the market. The FAA forecast explicitly treated the speed variable, but projected a low value for the changes in speed, but nevertheless sufficient to give it the edge over the CAB forecast. Houthakker and Taylor's study forecast much lower expenditure on inter-city air travel than realised but this would appear to be due to the inappropriateness of the predicting model rather than to the inaccurate independent variable forecast.

The above three are all time series studies, and as such suffer from the usual statistical problems such as multi-collinearity, serial correlation, etc. Cross-section estimates, while being subjected to their own particular statistical problems, are often useful means of calculating income elasticities.

In the field of civil aviation, one of the most extensive cross-section studies has been undertaken by the Port of New York Authority. The method employed in their 1957 forecast was to obtain propensities to travel for differing characteristics of travellers, stratified according to income, age, occupation, etc., and then to predict the expected change in propensity to travel by air by predicting income and demographic changes. Table 10.8 sets out the forecast and the assumptions, being the 1957 forecast. It is interesting to note the relative accuracy of its forecasts compared with others undertaken at the same time (see Table 10.2). The approach of this forecast was to concentrate on the determinants of the long run changes in demand—in other words on the determinants of the trend. At the expense of forecasting market turning points, such long run trend forecasts based on cross-sectional information appear to have given more accurate forecasts.[10]

In the earlier chapters we have explored a number of forecasting techniques such as trend projections and autogressive models. The technique adopted in presenting aircraft order forecasts (see 10.3) has been to project forward to 1980 the various exogenous variables used in the aircraft order model (see equation 9.4). It uses a short term forecasting method employed by Harrison [28]. Before examining these forecasts, a caution is required. It will be recalled (see 6.3 and 9.2) that the aircraft ordering mechanism is extremely sensitive to movements in exogenous variables, and so it follows that the forecasts will only give rough guides to the future expected order series. This should remembered when interpreting the results of the forecasts.

10.3   Model forecasts

In Chapter 6.3 we developed and estimated an aircraft order model (see equation 9.4), which we subsequently employed in Chapter 9.2. in the overall industry stabilisation exercise. Equation 9.4 forms the basis of the forecasts presented graphically in Figures 10.1 and in tabular form in Appendix 10A.2.

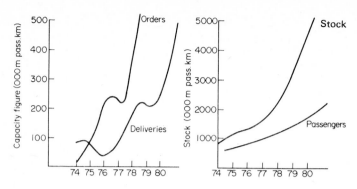

Fig. 10.1a   Forecasted variables from model (8 quarters lead time assumed) (1974–80)

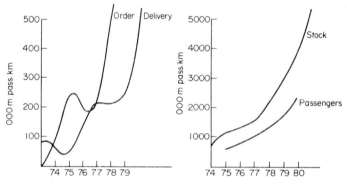

Fig. 10.1b   Forecasted variables for 30 per cent variation in $\left[\dfrac{\text{Price}}{\text{Load factor}}\right]$ (from 1974)

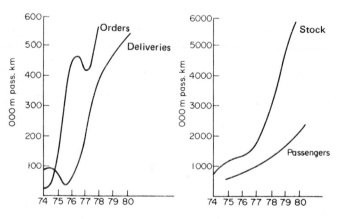

Fig. 10.1c   Forecasted variables from model (12 quarters lead time assumed) (1974–80)

Three forecasts have been made, each subjected to a different assumption. However, one common feature of the forecasts is that two of the independent variables, $(\hat{F}V)$ and the quality variable $(\hat{P}Q)$, have been extrapolated forward by means of a short term forecasting technique, such as the one used by Harrison [28]. The same forecasts of these two variables have been employed in all three forecasts. Figure 10.1a illustrates the forecasted orders and deliveries assuming an eight quarters lead time, while Figure 10.1c depicts the forecasts under the assumption of a twelve quarters lead time. Figure 10.1b illustrates the impact of the removal of price controls on aircraft orders. The effect of such a development on aircraft orders is via changes in passenger demand (see Figure 9.1). Figure 10.1b produces the forecasted changes resulting from a 30 per cent change in the price/load factor relationship. This was considered a large change, sufficient to encompass any likely change in schedule fares. We do not append probability figures on these projections, because of the non-linear characteristic of the order placing process.

An interesting result of the three forecasts is the timing of the downturn in aircraft orders. Both Figures 10.1a and 10.1c predict a downturn in orders in the fourth quarter of 1976. The forecast illustrated by Figure 10.1a has the shorter trough, the upturn occurring in the second quarter of 1977, the third quarter of 1977 being the predicted upturn of Figure 10.1c. The forecast represented by Figure 10.1b is the interesting one, for the downturn in orders is later, the second quarter of 1977 extending for the rest of 1977. The forecast figures of these forecasts are contained in Appendix 10A.2.

We do not here ring the permutations of the model with quantitative but hypothetical policies. We have merely demonstrated the major features of the industry, and shown that if fare fixing is removed, then no great instability will ensue. The strong likelihood is that the change will be beneficial to the civil aviation industry, and to the airline passenger.

10.4 1980—as seen by the planemakers

Civil aviation is an industry in which decisions taken in the sixties can shape the future of the seventies. The forthcoming decade will be that of the wide bodied jets and of supersonic transport. The design and technological development making possible these aircraft took place in the fifties and sixties, the decisions to order in the late sixties. The question to ask, however, is what picture of the future was held by the airlines and the aircraft manufacturers in the late sixties when the designs were transformed into orders? This is an important question, for the future view of the

Table 10.8

Cross section forecast:
Port of New York Authority 1957
forecast of US domestic air passenger market
1965−75

Base	1955		Actual	Point estimate
Forecast	1965	90m	95	−0.05
	1975	167m		

Assumptions

1   Population will grow at the projection A of the Bureau of Census forecast.
2   Employment by occupation and industry in 1965 and 1975 will con-
form to the preliminary estimates of the Bureau of Labour Statistics.
3   National Income will increase at 3 per cent per annum for 1955−65
and at an annual rate of 3 to 4 per cent for 1965−75.
4   Distribution of income will be constant at the 1939 level.
5   The rate at which non-fliers become fliers will be at a constant rate.
6   Air trips per thousand of the population will increase in accordance
with the estimated trend from 1935 to 1955.

market as held by the aircraft producers was crucial in setting the course
of the world's civil aerospace industries. Unprecedented capital sums
were allocated to development projects from private and public sources.
The difference between the realised picture and the one painted by the
aerospace producers emerges as the seventies roll on. Obviously only in
1980 will an historical account be possible. The task here is to assess the
likelihood of the aerospace producer's pictures being realised. This is a
two part task. This section will deal with the detailed forecasts of the
aerospace industries, and section 10.5 with our own aircraft forecasts
drawn from models developed earlier in the text.

   To an expensive research industry like civil aviation, future forecasts of
potential markets are subject not only to the unknown caprices of the
future, but also to political pressures derived from their heavy financial
requirements. There is temptation to work from estimates of development
costs by calculating the potential market share—which is in effect the
break-even sales numbers plus profitable extras. The forecasting task is
then effectively one of accurately forecasting development costs. The past
has shown the planemakers to be most fallible in such forecasts. This has
been particularly so when the finance has come from government sour-

ces. The awareness that the potential market is unlikely to be realised sets off a barrage of economic chauvinism. If we do not build, the foreigners will, and we will have to suffer heavy balance of payments deficits. The development costs are unlikely to be covered, but the external benefits (the spinoffs) more than compensate for the loss. If we do not build, the skilled labour force will be dismissed, and never be replaced.

Some of these arguments have some validity, as Plowden pointed out, although few have sound statistical support.[12] They only tend to enter, however, when private sources are unable to finance the project. Central to the future assessment, upon which governments and private financial enquiry is concentrated, is the purchasing behaviour of the airlines as predicted by the planemakers. The deviation between the actual and the planemakers' desired aircraft sales is where the crucial gap lies.

Most of us are myopic when looking at a future which lies some 10 years ahead. The immediate foreground obscures too much of our vision. Unfortunately, there are no correcting spectacles to put the picture right. What we can do is to enquire what others can see, and try to evaluate the reliability of their white sticks.

The picture as seen by the planemakers of their own future, and of their rivals', is shown in Table 10.9. Lockheed [10], for instance, predict wide bodied jets to be providing 74 per cent of the world's revenue passenger mileage by 1980, divided among long range trijets (22 per cent), B747 (18 per cent) medium range trijets (23 per cent) and short range wide bodied jets (11 per cent). These projected sales of wide bodied jets leaves the remaining 36 per cent of the market to be shared by narrow bodied and supersonic transports. Perhaps, not unnaturally, the manufacturers tend to see a more favourable future for their own aircraft than those of their rivals—Lockheed for instance give themselves a larger share of the medium trijet market than Douglas, while the American IDA study [11] into the demand for SST aircraft gave much higher forecasts for the US SST than for Concorde.

However, a glance at the order books as they stand in 1972 (see Table 10.9) indicates the forecast figures were optimistic. Apart from temptations induced by state financing, two possible reasons for this optimism lie firstly with the economic climate in which the original forecasts were made, and the nature of the markets the new aircraft were aiming at.

The market forecasts were calculated in the late sixties, when the airline industry, particularly in the USA, was growing at record levels. Not surprisingly the forecast growths in traffic were large and close together. The limits which the annual growth in traffic lay were within 10 and 11

Table 10.9

Summary of aircraft forecasts
for the year 1980

Forecaster	Aircraft	Type	Number in 1980	Aircraft type share of the market	Situation at 31 January 1973	
					Orders[g]	Deliveries
Douglas[a]	DC-10	Medium/Long	1,300[b] – 30%	715	206	104
Lockheed	L-1011	Medium	775	409	117	37
Lockheed	L-10011-8	Long	600	400	–	
Boeing	B-747	Long			233	210
Lockheed	B-747	Long		400	233	210
IDA[b]	B-747	Long	489[c]		233	210
			576[d]		233	210
			572[e]		233	210
			616[f]		233	210
Lockheed	A-300B	Short	700	920	16	–
Hawker Siddeley	A-300B	Short	1,100		16	–
BAC	Concorde	Long		250	9	–
IDA			90[c]		9	–
			37[d]		9	–
			349[e]		9	–
			123[f]		9	–

[a] These figures include the DC-10 and DC-10-30, i.e. the medium and long haul versions.
[b] The assumptions made in these calculations were: the SST price would be $40 million; the passenger value of time would be valued at the wage rate; the fares were based on a 30 per cent flyaway price.
[c] No sonic boom restrictions.
[d] Sonic boom restrictions.
[e] No SST project, no sonic restrictions.
[f] No SST, sonic boom restrictions.
[g] The figure includes optional as well as firm orders.

per cent. Lockheed and ICAO forecasted the lowest growth figures, 10 per cent for world scheduled traffic, 10 per cent and 10.2 per cent respectively for US domestic. The upper figure of 11 per cent was advocated by the American Air Transport Association[13] which undertook an extensive survey of airline, airport and aircraft manufacturers' forecasts.

The growth in traffic has also been in line with these forecasts, at least in the world market, where passenger kilometres flown on scheduled services grew by 11 per cent in 1969/70 and 13 per cent in the previous year. In the USA growth has slowed down to 6 per cent in 1969/70 after having been 11 per cent for 1968/69 and 12 per cent for 1967/68. In the fourth quarter of 1971 the market, particularly in the USA, picked up its rate of growth. Economic recovery in election year occurred as predicted and it looks as if the forecast growth rates will be on target. But why the lack of orders?

The short run — i.e. 1969/71 — has been affected by the downturn in the US economy. The advent of the B747 during this fall in demand led to falling load factors, but mainly on long haul routes. The DC-10-10 and Tristars and A-300'3s, of course, are medium/short haul aircraft, whose potential operators are the medium route operating airlines in the USA and European international airlines. Such airlines have been affected by the fall in demand, but have not suffered the massive excess capacity the long haul airlines have experienced.

It is likely these airlines are holding back their firm commitments until demand starts to grow again, and the uncertainties surrounding performance, prices, etc. are cleared. Central to any explanation, however, is the simple fact that it is the airlines, and not the aircraft producers, who make the ordering decisions. Even though the aircraft manufacturers and airlines, as we have seen, have made very similar forecasts of the future market, the weighting given to the future lies with the airlines. The aircraft producers recognised this by examining the main aircraft purchasing airlines — monitoring their markets, equipment and expansion plans. Such a micro-approach has its limitations, for ultimately the manufacturer has to judge the airlines' future growth and the response this will have on its purchasing behaviour. Nevertheless, it does give a lead into a method of enquiry into future orders. The long run questions, then, are what are the markets the new aircraft are aiming at, and what are the present conditions of the operating airlines?

The bulk of current orders are for wide bodied short, medium and long haul jets. In capacity terms, of secondary importance are supersonic transport aircraft. The problems of forecasting the latter market is the price customers are willing to pay to go faster, the price at which they value time saved by travelling by supersonic transport. There is here also an important problem of how far the airlines can be induced to change the present air fare structure to accommodate these faster aircraft. Uncertainties on both these problems are central to the economic problem surrounding supersonic forecasting. In the case of medium haul large bodied jets, the problems are not so much forecasting overall market requirements as in forecasting the market shares going to each aircraft producer. Uncertainties surround the viability of Lockheed's Tristar, while both the DC-10 and Tristar are under strong competition from the shorter range version of the B747. This is causing some anxiety among potential airline customers. Finally, the airbus project hinges on the extent of the non-scheduled European operators. The question is whether this market will be long enough to support the airbus project. We shall deal with each of these market details in turn.

10.4.1 *Medium/long haul wide bodied jet market*

The development of wide bodied civilian jets was largely the result of advances made in military design. In 1965 General Electric won the C-5A power plant competition to build a 10,000 lb static thrust engine to power a large military transport. Lockheed, in close competition with Boeing and Douglas, won the airframe contract with their design of the C-5A Galaxy. The losers, however, lost little time in turning their research into the civilian market. Boeing, by January 1966, had completed designs of their B747, and obtained orders in the following April. A $500 million development programme was initiated, such that by December 1969 the first versions were being delivered to Pan Am. Boeing was out on its own with the long range B747 (although, later versions were in effect short/ medium range models), the intense competition being between Douglas and Lockheed over sales for the medium haul routes.

Lockheed, having lost the SST order in 1966 to Boeing, re-entered the civilian market with what eventually became known as their Tristar (the L1011). Initially designed to satisfy American airlines' need for a twin engine 250 passenger carrier over US domestic routes, the aircraft was redesigned with three engines in order to appeal to a wider number of airlines. The competition from Douglas was considerable, for the latter, amalgamating with McDonnell in 1967 in order to build up the necessary financial resources for their DC-10 project, were powerful and experienced civil aircraft producers. Spending something like $1,200 million[14] on development Douglas drew heavily on their advanced versions of their DC-9s. The DC-10-10 was attractively priced, somewhat cheaper than the

Tristar, and with sufficient promise to tempt American airlines to switch their order from Lockheed to Douglas in early 1968. A large order from United Airlines for the DC-10 stipulated the inclusion of the General Electric's LF6 engine. The latter were in close competition with Rolls Royce for both aircraft engine orders. Lockheed, however, chose Rolls Royce, who then embarked on what turned out to be a disastrous application of carbon fibre technology to their engine design. This failure, and the alternative use of titanium, was largely the cause of Rolls Royce's financial fall in 1971.

In this medium range market Douglas are winning. Having kept their customers warm with their DC-8-30s and DC-9s, Douglas have had the experience of the sixties behind them in their sales drive, a factor with which Lockheed could not compete, for their last civilian aircraft, the Electra, was built over a decade ago. As Table 10.9 shows, in the medium haul market the DC-10-10 has nearly 100 more orders than the Tristar, plus the added advantage of having delivered the first models to United in the autumn of 1971. Comparing their sales forecasts, see Table 10.9, both are way behind their expectations, for Lockheed's projections hope for a sales total of 400 plus by 1980. To achieve these sales they will have to more than double (their present orders) over the next 8 years. Lockheed's forecast of the DC-10 share of this market is perhaps naturally smaller than their own, 264, a figure which Douglas is only halfway to achieving. Examining Table 10.9, and comparing the sales pattern so far, Douglas have been more successful in the US market, Lockheed in the foreign market. Delta's switch to DC-10s in 1972 underlies Douglas's present superiority in this market. The threat to both producers' sales, however, comes from Boeing with their short range B747 SR. The attraction here to the airlines is that they are already flying big brother B747. In consequence, the Japanese and Australian markets have been captured by Boeing while strong competition will have to be faced in the European market from the longer range European A-300.

In the long range market Boeing have returned to the forefront after the depression of 1971/72, when they did not sell a single aircraft. Leading their challenge is the 'special performance' B74SP. This carries 100 fewer passengers than the operating 747s, with a range of just under 7000 miles. This means that with a full load it can fly non stop from New York to Tokyo or Tehran. Clearly it offers a serious challenge to Concorde.

Table 10.10
Aircraft orders, January 1972

Airline	Long range wide bodied		Medium range wide bodied		SST aircraft
	DC-10-30s	B747	L-1011-1	DC-10-10	Concorde
National	2			9	
NW	14 + (14)				
ONA	3 + (3)				
TIA	3 + (1)				
World	3				
American		3		20 + (20)	6
Braniff		1			3
Continental		3		16	3
Delta		2	24	8	
Eastern			25 + (25)		6
United		9		37	
PSA			5		
Hans Turner			2		
TWA			22 + 22		
Air Holdings			29		
Air Jamaica			2		
Air France		3	3		8
Air Canada		1	19		
Air India					2
Alitalia	4 + (6)				
BOAC		6			8
El Al		2			
Iberia		1			
Japan		10			3
KLM	6 + (6)	4			
Quantas		5			4
SAS	8	1			
Sabena	2				2
SAS		5			
Swissair	6 + (5)				
TAP		2			
Condor Flych		1			
Air Afrique	3 + (2)				
Air NZ	3 + (1)				
UTA	4 + (4)				
Lufthansa	4	3			3
Pan Am		4			
MEA					2
Court			2 + (3)		
Iran Air					3
China					3
Totals	116	70	178	110	56

Note: brackets refers to options.
Note also the drop in Concorde orders since this date.

10.4.2   Short range wide bodied market

The short range, wide bodied jet owes its market potential to the saturated use of short haul routes by narrow bodied jets. This is particularly the case in Europe, where the returns to increased frequencies have diminished almost to zero, owing to the delay times at congested airports. To carry more people and to meet the growing demands, the required aircraft are those which are fast and of high capacity. Europe is the key market, with its short, dense air routes, and short/medium tourist trips from North to Southern Europe.

The consortium of European companies, known as Airbus Industries, is in the lead in this market, having spent some $546m (£228m) in building two prototypes of the A300B. Built in France, Germany, Holland and the UK, it has government financial support from the first three, Hawker Siddeley in the UK supporting its own wing construction contribution to the project.

The aggregate market forecasts in the short haul market have been around the 1,000 mark, with Hawker Siddeley projecting 1000 of which they hope to win 920. This forecast was made in 1968 [13]; the current estimate has been reduced to around 600. This target is aimed at with three Airbus types: the A-300 B1, the standard version, handling routes of 900–1,000 km. The A-300 B3 is the long range version for routes around 3,600 km, and directed at the US domestic and longer European routes, while the A-300 B7 was a version aimed at BEA. Its increased capacity (30 to 40 more seats) and range being thought more suitable for some of BEA's longer Eastern Mediterranean routes.

Priced at around $13m the estimated break-even number of sales is

Table 10.11

Projected air bus sales

Airline	Break-even number	Eventual sales
Air France	40	
Lufthansa	20	Europe 200–290
Sabena, Alitalia, Iberia & TAP	20	USA 160–360
European charters	80	Oceana 50
BEA	40	
American airlines	20	700
S. America }	50	
Oceana and Australia }		
British charters	80	

around 360, which, it is hoped will be reached by 1982. The break-down of the hoped for sales is as shown in Table 10.11. Aircraft orders (including options) at the beginning of 1972 is shown in Table 10.10. This gives some idea of the spread of orders among the world's airlines.

The major questions concern the US and European charter markets. The US market has always been a difficult market for European producers to penetrate, and there is strong competition from the short range Tristar and DC-10s. Furthermore, the B747 SR, a threat to the Tristar and the DC-10, is also a strong competitor.

The European charter market, however, is the market segment of largest projected sales. The difficulty here is the interdependence between the European scheduled carriers and the charters. Although the charters are starting now to buy direct from the factory, the bulk of their services are performed in narrow bodied aircraft. The potential sales in fact hinge on whether the scheduled carriers who buy the A-300B can unload their B727s, DC-9s, DC-8s, B707s and Caravelles on the charter market. To the latter, a low priced used B727 could be a more commercial proposition than a $13m Airbus in a market with large seasonal peaks. As Table 10.12 shows, the scheduled airline unloading of the above mentioned aircraft looks like being heavy, a fact which suggests direct sales of the Airbus to schedule carriers will be over a protracted period of time.

The sales to scheduled carriers in Europe will be most likely made to the so-called ATLAS Group (Lufthansa, Air France, Sabena, Iberia and Alitalia), the KSSU group (KLM, SAS, UTA and Swissair) having already moved for the DC-10. While the Airbus has captured the Spanish and Portuguese markets,[15] its most sought after customer was BEA. The latter's requirement was for a longer range type than the standard A-300B, hence the bespoke fitting of the A-300B7. With a longer range and payload it is virtually a medium range jet, and it faced strong competition from Lockheed's Tristar. This competition proved to be too strong, for in 1972 BEA ordered 5 Tristars.

As for the other markets, the South American is likely to be the most successful. The widespread use of the successful Caravelle has built up commercial confidence in European aircraft. It also facilitates financially attractive trade-ins. The Japanese and Australian markets, as mentioned earlier, are likely to be won over completely by Boeing. The major flag carriers have plunged heavily for the B747s, a factor of some importance in Australia[16] where Ansett and Qantas work under joint investment supervision.

Table 10.12

World (excluding North America) market
for short-haul large-bodied jets

	No. of aircraft in stock, December 1971			
	European charters	European schedule	Central and South America	South Africa and Australia
B707	18	48	18	8
Electra		2		3
BAC 1-11	54	18		
VC-10	4			
B-320	1			
B-720	3			
B-727	3	44	10	19
B-737	12	26	6	6
B-747	1	13		
CV-880/990	7			
DC-8	11	36	1	
DC-9	11	67		17
Caravelle	26	81	13	
F27/28	21	24		25
HS748	1		27	3
Trident	2	41		
CV-640	2			
Britannia	4			
Vanguard		19		
Viscount 800/700	4	24		9
Comet IV		2	4	
NAMC YS-11A			8	
Propeller	46		14	14
Medium short range	27		70	34

Airlines

European schedule: Air France, Lufthansa, Sabena, Alitalia, Iberia and TAP and BEA.

Central and South American: Aerolineas Argentinas, Cruyeiro, Lan Chile, Varig.

South Africa and Australian: TAA, Ansett and SAA.

European charter: Atlantia, Autair, Balair, Bavarian, Branthens, Britannia, British Caledonian, Channel, Condor, Danair, Donaldsons, Itavia, Laker, Lloyds, Luytransport, Martinair, SAM, Scanair, Skyways, Spantax, Sterling, TAE, Transair Sweden, Transavia Holland, Trek.

10.4.3 *The supersonic market*

Supersonic transport forecasts began confidently at the start of the sixties, ICAO [14] forecasting 158 mach 2s by 1967, while in 1962 the sales of Concorde were predicted to be 400 by 1980. In 1969, BAC's forecasts had dropped to a modest 250, while recent French statements indicate a figure of around 200 by 1980. Such downward adjustments were inevitable in view of the very real threat of overland banning because of the sonic boom, the widespread use of B747s on long haul routes, and the recent fall in air travel demand, causing considerable excess capacity.

The most detailed published forecast of SST was undertaken by IDA in the USA in 1967 [11]. Concerned with forecasting the demand for supersonic transports, they concentrated on route lengths exceeding 700 miles, considering this to be the minimum distance which supersonics would operate. The forecasting model was a sophisticated one, involving a number of interlocking sub-models. A final model, using econometric time series estimates was used to make conditional forecasts of passenger demand for all air travel up to 1990. A modal choice model was calibrated, in which travellers were assumed to chose between subsonic and supersonic services by comparing the cost of time saved (by supersonic travel) to their value of time.

It was then assumed that the differential costs of operating aircraft producing different services over the same route would be passed on to the passengers in the form of fare differentials. By asserting such a competitive structure, the analysists could assume that the rates of return on competing planes would be equal. In this way differing prices of aircraft could be fed into model, related to the trip fares and hence to the deter-

Table 10.13
IDA's forecasts
of aircraft fleet mix in 1980

	No sonic boom restrictions	Sonic boom restrictions	No SST No sonic boom restrictions	No SST Sonic boom restrictions
SST	254	107	0	0
Concorde	90	37	349	123
B747	489	576	572	616
DC-8-63	308	397	419	455
B-707	488	538	488	538

Source: IDA's Demand Study for SST [11] Tables 18 and 19

mination of the modal split. The final model was that which converted passenger flows into aircraft types. This was achieved by using two techniques, a straightforward model using assumptions as to airline size, utilisation and load factor, and a more sophisticated linear programming model.

The assumption that fares are directly related to long run marginal costs of the most efficient airline is one which is open to question, as Chapter 1 has illustrated. The advantage of such an assumption, of course, is the flexibility it allows in examining differing aircraft prices. Details of IDA's forecasts are contained in Table 10.12. Given the assumed growth of demand and the behavioural assumptions outlined above, the figures contained in Table 10.13 make three major assumptions. Firstly, that the price of SST is $40 million, secondly that passengers value time at their earnings rate, and thirdly that fares are derived from an assumed 30 per cent rate of return on the flyaway price of the aircraft. Two further assumptions are considered, namely the effect of sonic boom causing the restriction of overland travel, and the possibility of the suspension of the American SST project. Certainly, the latter has occurred, and the former is highly likely. In the circumstances, the forecast figures of 123 Concordes by 1980 can only be described as low, only the figure of 349 (without sonic boom restrictions) is anywhere near the BAC Concorde forecasts.

BAC's forecasts [15] seem to have adopted the reasonable approach of estimating the number of sales they require to make the project viable—which appears to be around 250—and then to work back to the fare structure needed to achieve this sales figure. In order to sell 250 Concordes by 1980, they calculate they must capture 20–25 per cent of the long haul traffic. Concorde, it is suggested, can capture 100 per cent of the available market for first class travel and 15 per cent of the present economy class.

In order to achieve this division they suggest the optimum fare for Concorde to be 35 per cent above present economy fares, but at this rate, this means being 15 per cent below the present first class level. In this way BAC hope to capture the business first class users and, very importantly, business travellers in the economy class. Without the latter, this project is unlikely to achieve its 250 sales objective, hence the lower fares.

The method adopted by BAC was to calculate the time savings, dividing by the price differences (first minus economy fare), and where the business wage was greater, assumed the traveller would divert to the Concorde. In this model, the wage rate is assumed to equal the value of time, and where the price of time saved using Concorde is less than this value, the diversion to Concorde will be made. Given the number of potential passengers with the given wage rate, obtained from income distribution data, the potential market is calculated.

The surcharge enters into the discussion when airlines do not want to switch to the specialist class of transportation, i.e. first class by Concorde and economy class by subsonic. During the transitional period, such a differential charge for Concorde over the existing first class subsonic fares is likely. This is the source of the airline interest, for they are unsure as to the return on such a mixed fleet. Concorde's forecast in fact lies with whether the proposed institutional fare changes will be adopted or rejected. These are the really important conditional factors in the forecast.

Even assuming the adoption of the desired fare structure, caution must be exercised when using the underlying behavioural assumptions. The IDA study showed that the forecasts were highly sensitive to changes in the assumed value of time and changes in the growth of income. The study indicated that if the value of passenger time is halved, aircraft demand would fall by more than 70 per cent,[17] while an increase in the growth of income from 2 to 3 per cent would result in an increase in demand (by 1980) of over 40 per cent.[18] Demand, not unexpectedly, was shown to be sensitive to changes in the assumed supersonic surcharge.[19]

On the evidence of the IDA study, Concorde's forecasts are highly sensitive to changing economic conditions. In consequence, we can expect a wide margin of error.

10.5   Aircraft forecasts for 1980

Ex post analysis of the deviations between forecast and observed results are dangerous for the scope it gives to rationalisations. As we have indicated, it is often difficult to discern why a forecast deviates from the actual outcome. Even if we think we have the causes correctly weighted in their importance, such information is not necessarily of much use when the next forecast of the future comes to be made. We have pointed out in earlier chapters the importance of economic fluctuations in the determination of passenger demand, and the impact of technological change in the form of the introduction of a new aircraft type, on the demand for aircraft. To pinpoint the source of the industry's fluctuations is essential, but unless we can place the timing and magnitude of such changes in these 'variables', we will not have a very accurate prediction of the future. This point has been brought out in Chapter 9. In this section we shall develop this aspect, introducing our own notions of likely outcomes and so presenting a framework within which long range forecasts can be analysed.

300

One of the reasons for observing and explaining the past behaviour and performance of the industry was to provide a basis for predicting and evaluating the outcome of alternative market structures. The results of this research showed the interdependence of the industry, the links between government financing and aircraft development, the relationship between government approval and international fare fixing and between aggregate economic fluctuations and passenger demand. The importance of these findings for forecasting in general is that they bring into sharper focus the relationships between the conditional and the dependent relationship in the forecast.

The forecasting problem, as such, depends on who is forecasting and the variables they have under their control. Governments have considerable influence on the pace of technological development by the control they exercise over research and development expenditure. The government's objectives could be viewed as allocating scarce R & D expenditure against the return from aerospace advancement. As for the aerospace industries, it is in their interest to outline the economic viability of proposed investment, and to pursue those which they can manage with their own resources. In the past, civil projects have precariously rested on cross-subsidisation from other aerospace projects and from generous government subsidies. This gives governments enormous control over the industry, for in controlling investment, they control technological change and consequently one of the largest sources of the industry's fluctuations. Although airlines are the purchasers of aircraft, their control over technological change has been lightly constrained by government pressures. Direct subsidies and the need for government sanctioned fares leaves the airlines with few variables over which they have direct control. Control over fares, for instance, could add considerably to their forecasting accuracy, particularly on individual routes. Indeed, in trying to achieve efficient and accurate forecasts, it is most important, and perhaps more productive than using statistical relationships, to show the control over variables which could improve the forecasters' results.

The course of this argument leads directly into policy questions, such as whether civil aircraft projects should be as heavily subsidised (as they have been in the past), whether air fares should be decontrolled, etc. Some of these questions have been examined in other chapters, and at this stage we shall accept the conditions under which various sections of the industry undertake their forecasts. Given this institutional structure, the forecaster is faced with two main problems. Firstly, what will be the course of economic and technical change – the two main sources of the industry's fluctuations – and, secondly, the timing of substantial changes in these conditions. We have chosen 1980 as a time horizon because it is sufficiently long enough to illustrate these two aspects of aviation forecasting.

Forecasting of income changes, particularly the turning points in the trade cycle, is important to an industry, such as civil aviation, whose product is highly income elastic. The predominance of the US market in civil aviation, and its likely dominance at least until the end of the decade, mean that accurate forecasts will depend upon accurate forecasts of the behaviour of the US economy. Boeing,[20] for instance, recognise the importance of upturns and downturns in economic activity. For the US economy, they have forecast a strong economic recovery during 1972,[21] with a moderate downturn anticipated during 1973-74. It is assumed that this will be followed again by a recovery, and so continuing the cyclical characteristics of the economy in the past. This is a difficult task, and one which few forecasts attempt, relying instead upon trend extrapolation of past behaviour. Ultimately, however, both approaches depend upon the accuracy of aggregate macro-forecasts. The aviation forecaster, in other words, has to rely upon macro-forecasts often produced by organisations other than civil aviation bodies. In evaluating these forecasts, importance should be given to the forecast's turning points, of the upturn and downturn in the economy, because it is these points which mark changes in aviation activity.

Similarly, with the advent of technological change in whatever guise it appears. The large order fluctuations, as we have seen, were initiated by the advent of new aircraft. What of the likely developments in the next decade?

Given the present direction of development, technological changes in the next decade are likely to centre around the redesign of aircraft such that weight is reduced, and the utilisation of metals which will allow flights at higher temperatures and thus at higher speeds.

Limits to carrying capacity are set by weight problems, for weight and lifting forces vary in proportion to the cube of the linear change of scale, which varies as to the square. Important in the all-up weight are fuel (approximately 50 per cent) and payload (10 per cent). Hence the concentrated development on improved structures to reduced all-up weight and fuels which are of higher calorific value but lighter than the present kerosene.

In the case of structures, new composite materials, such as carbon reinforced plastic offer advances, but temperatures at high speeds present problems. Temperatures rise at supersonic speeds due to the compression of air. This pushes surface temperatures up, affecting surface finish and aerodynamic flow. At the moment, Concorde is flying at the limit of aluminium alloys. On the other hand the SST offered considerable advances with the use of titanium. Even with the full developments of these metals, it seems to be considered[22] that the problem of heat will limit winged passenger travel to the mach 3 to 4 range.

Technological fuel developments are essential if payload is to be increased. There are a number of fuels, such as liquid hydrogen and methane, which are superior to the presently used kerosene, but the latter has a higher density, and takes up far less space than its rivals. Liquid methane is perhaps the likeliest successor, for it is reputed to be[23] 20 to 30 per cent cheaper than kerosene but its potential weight saving compared with kerosene is only 13 per cent.

Developments in large capacity, short haul markets (50–300 miles) appear to be slim. Although the STOL still appears to be superior[24] to VTOL, the cost and thus the viable pricing of such services are still too high to attempt sizeable shifts from surface transport. Certainly up to 1980, such developments are likely to have little impact.

Such a brief survey shows the nature of the likely advances, or rather the direction in which most effort is being placed and is likely to be placed. It is in developing faster, bigger aircraft, areas of development which have been the unquestioned yardstick of the industry's development. In financing the direction of such research, governments have the obligation to ask is the public (as distinct from the flying public) best served by resources spent on producing faster, bigger and in all likelihood, noisier aircraft?

There is an institutional bias[25] in research directed to problems the industry has pursued in the past, such as speed and size, directions which are in a large part, the combined impact of defence priorities and the passenger market structure which has minimised price competition and placed a premium on product differentiation. This is not to deny the enormous advances that have followed from the advent of faster and larger aircraft. The point is, however, that the returns to development expenditures in these directions should be compared with viable alternatives, such as the development of quieter engines (even at the expense of speed), and the improvements of safety by advancing navigational aids. The important role of the government is not just in controlling technological advancement by directing finance, it is in seeing that technical advances are transmitted quickly and accurately to the market in the form of costs and prices which truly reflect the cost in achieving and producing the services. Only by creating such a final market structure will the government know whether the flying public is able to support the research pushed into its development.

It is likely, however, that for the near future, aerospace investment will be determined by a range of political reasons, among which economic rationale will have little say. In consequence, forecasting the change and timing of aeronautical technology remains highly hazardous.

APPENDICES

10A.1   Technical appendix

We have defined in Chapter 10 what we mean by econometric forecasts — namely those forecasts which are derived from explicitly stated economic reasoning.

Here we shall set down a simple demand forecast in order to bring out the nature of the forecasting variance and the problems that follow from this incorrect specification of autoregressive models (as developed in Chapter 4).

10A.1.1   *Variance of prediction error of econometric forecasts*

Treated more formally, we can express the build up of a forecast from a statistically estimated demand relationship in the following way:

Suppose our objective is to forecast demand (y) changes in the next year. Our simple theory is that demand is simply a function of price (x_1). Hence:

$$\Delta y_t = \beta \, \Delta x_t + u_t \tag{10A.1}$$

where u_t is the disturbance term. Assume that the β coefficient is estimated from time series, and that x_t is given — i.e. we know with certainty the the price of the goods. Thus Δx_{t+1} is assumed known, but β and u_{t+1} are unknown.

In order to obtain information on the latter we shall make the following assumptions:

(a)   The disturbance $u \ldots u_{t+1}$ are all independent, random variables with zero mean and variance σ^2.
(b)   The coefficient β is nonstochastic, and is fixed.
(c)   The disturbances are all normally distributed.

Using least squares regression to estimate β, the conditional point prediction of Δy_{t+1}, given Δx_{t+1} is:

$$\Delta \hat{y}_{t+1} = b \, \Delta x_{t+1} \qquad\qquad (10A.2)$$

The interval prediction is simply (10A.2) minus (10A.1)

$$\Delta \hat{y}_{t+1} - \Delta y_{t+1} = (b - \beta) \, \Delta x_{t+1} - u_{t+1} \qquad (10A.3)$$

The L.H.S. is the prediction error, the R.H.S. contains the error in estimating β.

All disturbances have zero mean, and hence the prediction error has zero mean, which implies that $\Delta \hat{y}_{t+1}$ is an unbiased prediction.

Squaring both sides of 10A.3 and taking the expectation, we obtain the variance of the prediction error:

$$(\Delta \hat{y}_{t+1} = \Delta y_{t+1})^2 = (\Delta x_{t+1})^2 \, E(b-\beta)^2 + E \, u^2{}_{t+1}$$
$$-\Delta x_{t+1} \, E[(b - \beta) \, u_{t+1}] \qquad (10A.4)$$

The variance of the prediction error takes the following value:

$$E(\Delta \hat{y}_{t+1} - \Delta y_{t+1})^2 = \frac{\sigma^2 \, (\Delta x_{t+1})^2 + \sigma^2 = v^2}{\Sigma \, (\Delta x_t)^2} \qquad (10A.5)$$

Assumption (10A.3) is that the disturbances are normally distributed, which implies that the prediction error (being a linear combination of these disturbances), is normally distributed with expectation zero and variance v^2. We are thus able to produce an interval containing Δy_{t+1} to be predicted with a predetermined probability.

For instance, the interval $(b\Delta x_{t+1} - 1.96v, \; b\Delta x_{t+1} + 1.96v)$ will contain Δy_{t+1} with a probability 0.95.

Notice that it follows from (10A.5) that the variance of the prediction error takes its minimum value (σ^2) when $\Delta x_{t+1} = 0$ and that this variance becomes indefinitely large when Δx_{t+1} becomes larger and larger in absolute value.

Returning to our field of application, this last point implies that supposing we know with certainty the behaviour of the independent variables over time, the further ahead we forecast, the larger the variance of the prediction error becomes. Assuming these conditions held in the aviation industry, the accuracy of predictions in ascending order would be found in the airport, aircraft manufacturing and airline sectors. As we have shown in Chapters 6 and 7, the forecasting horizons in the civil aviation industry are longer than the average for industry, hence we can expect larger than average forecasting errors in this sector of the economy.

For further reading on this subject see H. Theil [29].

10A.1.2 *Problems of serial correlation in autocorrelated models*

In Chapters 3 and 4 we developed and estimated air passenger demand models which included an autoregressive term. There are a number of statistical problems involved in using these models, here we shall deal with one of them, the problem of incorrect specification of the source of serial correlation.

Suppose we estimate the following model:

$$y_t = b\,x_t + c\,y_{t-1} = v_t \tag{10A.6}$$

However, suppose (10A.6) is not the 'true' form of the relationship, but is instead represented by (10A.7):

$$y_t = \beta x_t + e_t \tag{10A.7}$$

$$e_t = \phi\,e_{t-1} + w_t \tag{10A.8}$$

where x_t is a nonstochastic variable and e_t and w_t are random variables with zero expectations and variances σ^2 and $\sigma^2\,(1 - \phi^2)$ respectively.

We go ahead and estimate (10A.6), perhaps on the assumption that the serial correlation (10A.8) is due to a distributed lag model. Now assume the 'true' equation to be the combination of (10A.6) and (10A.7),

$$y_t = \beta x_t + \phi\,e_{t-1} + w_t \tag{10A.9}$$

The specification error is clearly the substitution of y_{t-1} for e_{t-1}. The expected value of c is zero (given by the 'true' coefficient of y_{t-1}) plus the coefficient of the omitted variable e_{t-1}, which is ϕ times the coefficient of y_{t-1} in the regression of e_{t-1} on x_t and y_{t-1}, the regression of the omitted variable.

$$E_c = \phi\,E(b\,c_{t-1}\,y_{t-1}\,x_t) \tag{10A.10}$$

Since $E\,e_{t-1}, x_t = 0$, and assuming x_t to be serially correlated

$$E\ x_t\ y_{t-1} = 0 \text{ and } E\ b\ e_{t-1}\ y_{t-1}\ x_t = E\ B\ e_{t-1}, y_{t-1}$$

$$= \frac{E\ e_{t-1}, y_{t-1}}{\sigma^2\ y_{t-1}} = \frac{\sigma^2}{\sigma^2\ y}$$

Then $\qquad E\ c = \phi\ \dfrac{\sigma^2}{\sigma y} = \phi\ (1 - r^2\ y_t\ x_t)$

Thus, even though the true structural coefficient of y_{t-1} is zero, so long as $\phi > 0$ and x_t does not account for a very large part of the variation

Table 10A.1

Statistical details of Figure 10.1a

Year		Orders	Deliveries	Stock	Passengers
1974	1	15	85	800	404
	2	22	87	919	457
	3	30	90	1020	510
	4	57	87	1084	552
1975	1	80	85	1150	577
	2	111	60	1181	594
	3	145	45	1200	608
	4	171	43	1247	623
1976	1	205	40	1300	652
	2	218	44	1349	674
	3	239	50	1460	696
	4	233	68	1453	720
1977	1	225	90	1500	746
	2	229	112	1719	841
	3	240	135	1950	961
	4	286	168	2013	994
1978	1	340	195	2150	1066
	2	403	204	2376	1113
	3	465	210	2600	1268
	4	—	208	2890	1443
1979	1	—	205	3200	1586
	2	—	269	3444	1685
	3	—	215	3710	1807
	4	—	230	4051	2029
1980	1	—	250	4600	2245
	2				
	3				
	4				

Units: '000 million passenger kilometres

in y the estimates are likely to show positive and 'significant' coefficients for the lagged dependent variable.

The incorrectly specified model therefore, gives the illusion of working. Hence, specification of the source of the serial correlation is all important.

For further details of autocorrelation, and means of overcoming it by such methods as instrument variables, see Z. Griliches [30].

Table 10A.2

Statistical details of Figure 10.1b

Year		Orders	Deliveries	Stock	Passengers
1974	1	—	80	800	405
	2	20	83	910	457
	3	30	76	990	486
	4	65	70	1030	492
1975	1	94	55	1070	537
	2	118	44	1110	555
	3	165	46	1160	573
	4	196	47	1260	629
1976	1	225	52	1260	633
	2	242	63	1310	648
	3	237	79	1350	667
	4	224	100	1400	691
1977	1	206	140	1470	730
	2	195	155	1600	776
	3	192	192	1750	870
	4	196	206	1880	916
1978	1	201	208	2000	992
	2	204	210	2250	1100
	3	257	211	2500	1190
	4	310	209	2750	1360
1979	1	368	207	3000	1478
	2	450	204	3250	1599
	3	505	208	3500	1695
	4	560	215	3750	1864
1980	1	—	240	4000	1950
	2	—	266	4300	2119
	3	—	291	4600	2200
	4	—	303	4950	2416

Units: '000 million passenger kilometres

10A.2 Aircraft order model

This section contains the statistical data illustrated by Figure 10.1.

The three tables illustrate the results of varying the magnitude of the independent variables, the finance variable (FV), and the quality variable. For details of the development of this equation consult 6.3. Two of the

Table 10A.3

Statistical details of Figure 10.1c

Year		Orders	Deliveries	Stock	Passengers
1974	1	25	80	800	405
	2	29	85	921	461
	3	35	90	1007	503
	4	70	80	1036	516
1975	1	140	65	1070	520
	2	200	43	1139	564
	3	300	30	1200	594
	4	365	39	1388	639
1976	1	430	50	1400	699
	2	440	69	1446	721
	3	450	110	1500	746
	4	421	164	1604	801
1977	1	400	220	1700	837
	2	415	253	1992	979
	3	450	301	2300	1142
	4	481	348	2710	1262
1978	1	520	375	3005	1485
	2		399	3464	1693
	3		420	3960	1908
	4		435	4411	2156
1979	1		450	4900	2306
	2		472	5193	2490
	3		490	5500	2650
	4		505	5757	2774
1980	1		520	6000	2840
	2				
	3				
	4				

Units: '000 million passenger kilometres

independent variables, the finance variable (FV), and the quality variable (PQ) have been extrapolated forward by means of a short term forecasting technique, such as the one used by Harrison [28]. The forecasts inputs of these two variables are common to the three forecasts illustrated in this appendix.

Table 10A.1, represented graphically by Figure 10.1a, forecasts orders and deliveries assuming an eight quarters lead time. Table 10A.2 (see Fig. 10.1b) introduces the possibility of large changes in passengers' fares, as a result say of the removal of price controls in the scheduled market. The effect of such a development on aircraft orders is via changes in passenger demand. Table 10A.2 produces the forecasted changes resulting from a 30 per cent change in the price/load factor relationship. The explanation of the relationship between aircraft orders, passenger demand and passenger fares, is developed in 9.2 (see also Figure 9.1). Table 10A.3 shows the impact on orders and deliveries of assuming a twelve quarters lead time. These figures are illustrated by Figure 10.1.c.

Notes

1 Lead time can be defined as the time period commencing with the placing of an order to add to stock, and terminating when the order is delivered into the stock. See Chapter 6 for inter-industry comparisons.

2 See J. de Lagarde, ITA Symposium, Paris, 24–25 November 1966 [1].

3 C. Tillinghast and A.F. Mukendi, ITA Symposium, Paris, November 1966 [2] p. 4: 'In projecting the future course of corporate activities, TWA uses a five year plan. This is revised annually, in each case with a projection one more year into the future than in the previous plan, and with a refinement of estimate between planning and research and other departments of the Airline, so that plans are not drawn up in vacuum, but on the basis of correct information and realistic projections.'

4 The Roskill Report [3] Para. 5.4, p. 24: 'The B.A.A. suggested that the planning and the detailed design of a third London Airport would take two years and its construction a further five . . . the weight of the evidence supported the authorities estimate of the total period involved and we accepted that estimate.'

5 See section 10A.1 for a discussion of the relationship between length of forecast and standard errors involved in forecasting.

6 The measure in the third column equals

$$\frac{Forecast - Actual}{Actual} \times 100$$

[7] Note that it is not the base year figure which is important, of far more importance is the chosen rate of growth. However, the behaviour of the industry during the making of the forecast can have effects on the growth rate chosen. Hence it is the effect of the base year on the rate that is important.

[8] See W.M. Wallace and J.G. Moore: Boeing's 'Calling the Turns' May 1968 [21]. This model is described in greater detail in Appendix III to Chapter 4.

[9] Mean square prediction error $= \dfrac{\sum\limits_{1}^{n} \left(\dfrac{Actual - Forecast}{Actual}\right)^2}{n}$

where n = number of years.

[10] Other forecasts using the cross-sectional approach on US data are: Stanford Research Institute Forecasts [4] and the Port of New York Authority 1965 [5].

[11] For further discussion of autoregressive forecasting techniques see Bray [6] and Box and Jenkins [7].

[12] An exception to this is the study of industrial innovation undertaken on Concorde [9]. See also [20].

[13] See [12] for a summary and discussion of the US industry's forecasts for the seventies.

[14] See *Interavia* April 1971. The 9 months financial statement issued by McDonnell Douglas in 1971, showed that of its backlog of $3.44 million, 67 per cent was commercial. Of this $2.3 million, most was committed to the DC-10.

[15] See *Interavia* April 1971 where it is suggested that export/import bank facilities are being used so that 0.85 per cent of the price of the aircraft is loaned and payable over 10 years with a rate of interest of 6-7 per cent. Iberian were attracted by the joint production agreement made with the Spanish Government in October 1971.

[16] For a discussion of this point, see Chapter 1, section II.

[17] See p. 53 [11].

[18] See Table 23 [11].

[19] See Table 24 [11].

[20] For the recent Boeing forecasts, see *Flight International*, 24 June 1971, p. 916–17.

[21] See the footnote to Table 10.4.

[22] See N.W. Boorer: *The Future of Civil Aviation* [17].

[23] See L.G. Dawson and J.B. Holliday: 'Looking ahead in aeronautics propulsion' [18].

[24] See *An Economic Analysis of Commercial VTOL and STOL Trans-*

port Aircraft [16]. Stating the requirement needs of such aircraft as a capacity of 60-70 seats, cruising speeds of 400 mph and range of 50 miles, the study concluded that the US domestic market in 1980 would support about 55 VTOL and 85 STOL aircraft. For a more up to date view of the Airlines see K.G. Wilkinson, 'STOL – UK to Europe', *Flight*, 13 January 1972.

[25] It must be remembered, however, that the aerospace industries are a large employer of skilled manpower. As such, whether for the right reason or not, governments have sought to maintain employment in this sector. See for instance M.H. Spiro, *The Impact of Government Procurement on Employment in the Aircraft Industry* [19] where he conducted a time series estimates on quarterly data 1948–60 for the USA Aerospace industries. Using financial data, he discovered that the total net change in employment resulting from increase of $1 million in government obligations is about 35–40 workers. The estimated average lag between obligation and expenditures was about 13 months, and the estimated total lag was about 20 months.

References

1   J. de Lagarde, *The Aircraft Industry and Conjecture of Air Transport*, ITA Symposium, Paris, 24–25 November 1966.
2   C. Tillinghast and A.K. Mukendi, *The Air Transport Operator and Conjectures on Air Transport*, ITA Symposium, Paris, November 1966.
3   Commission on the Third London Airport, 1971.
4   W.H. Chartener, *Economic Trends to 1975: Long Range Planning*, Stanford Research Institute.
5   Port of New York Authority, Aviation Economics Division, *Travel Patterns and Characteristics of Air Passengers originating in New York*, 1965.
6   J. Bray, 'Dynamic equations for economic forecasting with the GDP', *Royal Statistical Society*, Series A (General), vol. 134, no. 2. 1971.
7   G.E.P. Box and G.M. Jenkins, *Time Series Analysis, Forecasting and Control*, Holden Day, 1970.
8   F. Fisher, *A priori Information and Time Series Analysis*, N. Holland, 1962.
9   Centre for the Study of Industrial Innovation, *Aspects of Spin Off: A Study of the impact of Concorde on the Advanced Passenger Train*, 1971.
10   Lockheed, *The Market for Wide Bodied Transport Aircraft 1970–80*, CMP/1392, May 1971.

11   N.J. Asher *et al., Demand Analysis for Air Travel by Supersonic Travel*, Institute for Defence Analysis, Contract FA 55–66–14, December 1966.

12   D.W. Bluestone, 'US airline business will soar in the seventies', *Airline Management*, January 1970.

13   'The A 300B Airbus', *Hawker Siddeley Review*, vol. 6, no. 2.

14   *Technical, Economic* and *Social Consequences of the Introduction into Commercial Service of the Supersonic Aircraft – Preliminary Study*, (Doc. 8087 – C/925) ICAO, August 1960.

15   BAC, *Concorde: The Effect of Single Class Operation on Airline Profitability. International.*

16   *An Economic Analysis of Commercial VTOL and STOL Transport Aircraft*, FAA contract no. FA 64 WA 4997, 1965.

17   N.W. Boorer, 'The future of civil aviation', *Futures*, March 1969.

18   L.G. Dawson and J.B. Holliday, 'Looking ahead in aeronautics propulsion', *Royal Aeronautical Society Journal*, vol. 72, 1968.

19   M.H. Spiro, 'The impact of government on employment in the aircraft industry' in *Studies in Economic Stabilization* (ed. A. Ando *et al.*), The Brookings Institute, 1968.

20   P.K. Woolley, 'Cost-benefit analysis of Concorde', *Transport Economics and Policy*, September 1972, vol. VI, no.3.

21   W.M. Wallace and J.G. Moore, *Calling the Turns*, Boeing, May 1968.

22   K.H. Larsson, *A Critical Review of Earlier Forecasts of Air Traffic and a New Approach*, Canadair Ltd, 1960.

23   T.P. Wright, 'Some economic factors in air transport', *Aeronautical Engineering Review*, June 1966.

24   L. Hanson, *Mathematics and Forecasting*, Boeing, August 1958.

25   *National Requirements for Aviation Facilities 1956 to 1975* by the Aeronautical Research Foundation for Mr E.P. Curtiss, special assistant to the President for Aviation Facilities Planning, June 1957.

26   H.S. Houthakker and L.D. Taylor, *Consumer Demand in the US, 1929 to 1970*, Harvard, Cambridge Mass., 1966.

27   CAB, *Forecasts of Passenger Traffic 1965–75*, Staff Research Report no. 5, 1965.

28   P.J. Harrison, 'Short-term sales forecasting', *Applied Statistics*, vol. 14, 1965.

29   H. Theil, *Applied Economic Forecasting*, North Holland, 1966.

30   Z. Griliches, 'A note on serial correlation bias in estimates of distributed lags', *Econometrica*, vol. 29, January 1961.

11 Conclusions

The technological achievements of the civil aviation industry over the last 20 years have been astounding. Its growth has been considerable. The particular interest of the study, however, has been the fluctuations about these growth trends. Two questions have been central. Firstly, have the industry cycles been caused primarily by influences external to the airlines or by the response of the airlines to these forces? Secondly, what would be the effect on the stability of the airline industry by the alteration of present controls?

The simplified answer to the first question is that the airline industry's fluctuations have been caused by rapid developments in aeronautical technology and by sharp changes in economic growth. The rigid fare fixing of scheduled services and the resulting emphasis on qualitative competition has contributed to the industry's instability, but so too has eccentric management.[1] These have been very much secondary to the instability caused by technological and economic change.

Technological change, often stimulated by the close relationship between military and civil aircraft production,[2] brought with it considerable economies. The jet, despite some initial doubts, proved to be much more economical than its longer range propeller rivals. This was reflected in its rapid and wholesale adoption on long haul routes. The second surge was for the short haul jets, a result largely of pent up demand. The knowledge of future jet developments kept some airlines from purchasing short haul propeller aircraft, and instead employing depreciated long haul propeller types. In consequence the availability of the short haul jets met with rapid and heavy demands. The wide bodied jets were economically superior to their first generation jets, as well as being available at a time of rapid economic growth in the North American economy. Retrospectively, some airline purchases seem to have been excessive to their requirements, but on the whole, the two major troughs in the industry, at the start of the sixties and seventies, were due to unexpected downturns in the US economy, occurring at the time of aircraft deliveries. Long aircraft lead times and the difficulties of forecasting economic change were partly the cause of many airline problems, but so too were inadequate airline forecasting departments.

A third and important factor in the industry trough of the the early

1970s has been the incursion into the scheduled market of charter operators. The scheduled operators were faced with a declining share of a
slowing market. The rigid scheduled fare structure and the increased freedom given to non-scheduled operators were the cause of this share change.
In this sense, the rigid fare structure of the scheduled airline industry has
been partly responsible for the excess capacity among the scheduled
operators, and for the slow rate at which this has been absorbed.

The answer to the second question is that price controls have not been
the cause of the industry's instabilities, nor will their removal cause any
significant instability in investment or operating profits. An open,
competitive industry would be one in which airlines made their own
pricing decisions and in which there are no restrictive pooling agreements
on capacity, revenue or costs. The effect on the market would depend
upon the route groups. The larger routes would attract a number of operators, providing a diverse range of variously priced services. Thinner routes
are likely to be served by two operators. In general, the services provided
would indicate the heterogeneous nature of the particular markets. The
prices charged would reflect this heterogeneity, in contrast to the rather
false division that has arisen under the present controls between scheduled
and non-scheduled services. The increased choice, at least on the denser
routes, and the removal of the more glaring price differentiation would be
obvious advantages to the customer. As for the airlines, there is no evidence that such a structure would lead to excessive industry instability.
Past evidence of open competition,[3] analysis based on the industry's
structure[4] and the dynamic analysis of the present study refute the suggestion that excess industry instability would ensue.

One problem would remain, the possibility of international subsidy
wars. The higher cost airlines are likely to have flights subsidised by their
respective governments. During certain periods the customer could gain by
the lowering fares. The major difficulty concerns the behaviour of the
North American airlines. They are not state supported, and to change such
a policy is likely to prove very difficult.

The practicalities of introducing a competitive structure are that fares
on the whole are set unilaterally, while capacity is restricted bilaterally.
The point is that open competition would have to to be achieved largely
by changing bilateral agreements. The present situation is further complicated by the fact that non-scheduled services, unlike scheduled services,
are not regulated by bilateral agreements. Authorisation is left to the
discretion of the countries concerned, with the result that many differing
regulations have ensued.[5] This is important because the scheduled operators have responded to the increasing challenge of the non-scheduled

operators by advocating greater controls to be placed on their rivals. Two recent studies[6] of this problem have recognised this danger. They advocate the placing of scheduled and non-scheduled traffic within more liberal bilateral agreements.

A characteristic of other policy proposals recently forwarded[7] is a desire to afford some protection to scheduled services and at the same time to bring fares more directly into line with costs. The difficulty here is finding and implementing the set of controls to achieve such objects. Open competition and the granting of direct subsidies from central government funds has the advantage of reducing implicit internal cross-subsidisation. Such a policy, however, is unlikely to be accepted on international services.

All these sets of policy proposals need government approval. This is a difficult task. Even partial acceptance of changes in the present set of controls is unlikely to be forthcoming from many governments. However, the pressures for change are considerable, and these are in fact coming from within the scheduled industry. This is shown by the recent history of IATA price agreements. The North Atlantic Conference has shown that considerable divergencies in interest exist, with the 'fighting' concessional fares proposed by some airlines have been unacceptable to others. Continued disagreement is likely in such a heterogeneous market. In consequence, the unanimity rule is likely to go. The introduction of a majority rule seems likely. This will be a considerable step, for it will grant greater competitive power to the lower cost airlines. IATA regulation 0-45, concerning the pricing of non-scheduled services, has also been steadily broken by many governments. This has strengthened the competition challenge of the non-scheduled airlines, and has been instrumental in the pressure to bring down scheduled fares.

The reduction of scheduled fares by differentiating the market and charging lower fares for forward booking, off-peak trips, etc. has brought problems for the airlines. Price dilution has occurred, while non-scheduled carriers have continued to expand their share. Complicated fare structures are likely to be accepted by the customer if it means a selection of cheaper fares. The difficulty is that scheduled operators are likely to press for greater controls to be imposed on non-scheduled services. This should be resisted, for the freedom granted to non-scheduled operators has been, and will continue to be, the means by which technological advantages are passed on to the customer in the form of lower fares. Government policy should be concerned with strengthening the structure of the non-scheduled sector and not at devising protection for the scheduled operators.

The strict enforcement of safety regulations and the protection of the customer from fraudulent operators will be necessary in the future. Restrictive controls on the competitive freedom of the non-scheduled operators should be avoided. The consolidation and concentration of ownership in the North American and European non-scheduled market argues well for their competitive strength. It is the task of the scheduled carriers to adjust to this challenge without government protection.

The structure of the industry is likely to change considerably over the next 10 years. The growing importance of non-scheduled carriers suggests that they will become important first hand buyers of aircraft, particularly of short and medium haul wide bodied jets. This will serve to widen the base of first hand buyers, and so reduce some of the instability which has ensued from buyer concentration.

In the manufacturing sector, trends indicate that technical advances will be very expensive, stretching to the limit firm's ability to raise money from the market. The past history of the industry has shown governments the risks involved in investing in projects which the private capital market has rejected. Perhaps Concorde's and SST's lasting contribution to the industry is that they will remind governments of the risks of investing in future aviation technology. The next big battle among the manufacturers will be over the production of a short haul wide bodied jet. This is the growth market in the industrialised countries, but again there are dangers for the manufacturers. Speed of delivery will be important, and it seems likely one of the big three USA air frame producers will be forced to amalgamate with one of the other two.

The problems of the industry over the last 20 years have sprung largely from the need to adjust to the very rapid changes in aircraft technology. The future problems of the industry will be to adjust to its own growth. The problems are seen already in the crowded airports, the long ground delays and aircraft noise. Here are the problem areas to which a mature aviation industry should be directing its considerable inventiveness.

Notes

¹ For example, the aircraft purchasing plans of TWA under Howard Hughes and the jet buying sprees of Pan Am can both, in part, be explained by the eccentric ways the airlines were managed.
² See Philips [1] for a thorough study of the relationship between technological change and military projects.
³ See A.P. Ellison [2] pages 486—7 for a study of the effects of open competition in the UK airline industry in the 1930s.

⁴ See H.M. Cooper [4] and Doganis [3].

⁵ See Doganis [3] p. 117—18 for an analysis of the regulations concerning non-scheduled traffic.

⁶ See Doganis [3] pages 130—133 and Cooper and Maynard [4] p. 51.

⁷ See the Edwards Report [5].

References

1   A. Phillips, *Technology and Market Structure: A Study of the Aircraft Industry*, Heath Lexington Books 1971.

2   A.P. Ellison, 'The Edwards Report and civil aviation in the 1970s', *The Aeronatical Journal*, vol. 74, no. 714, June 1970.

3   R. Doganis, 'Air transport: a case study in international regulation', Journal of Transport Economics and Policy, vol. VII, May, 1973.

4   M.H. Cooper and A.K. Maynard, *The Price of Air Travel*, Hobart Paper 53, Institute of Economic Affairs, 1971.

5   *British Air Transport in the Seventies*, Report of the Committee of Inquiry into Civil Air Transport, Chairman Prof. Sir R. Edwards, Cmnd. 4018, HMSO, May 1969.

Select Bibliography

The following books and articles have been arranged very roughly into various topics of interest. Specialisation has centred upon economic studies. Abbreviations used in the text descriptions are as follows:

JRAS   : *Journal of the Royal Aeronatucial Society.*
EJ   : *Economic Journal.*
JPE   : *Journal of Political Economy.*
JTE & P : *Journal of Transport Economics and Policy.*
F Int   : *Flight International.*
JAL & C : *Journal of Air Law and Commerce.*
TR   : *Transportation Research.*
AER   : *American Economic Review.*
FAA   : Federal Aviation Authority.
CAB   : Civil Aeronautics Board.
QJE   : *Quarterly Journal of Economics.*
ITA   : Institut du Transport Aerien.
ICAO   : International Civil Aviation Organisation.

Useful statistical and contemporary commentaries can be found in the following: *Flight International, Interavia, Flight, Airline Management* and the *Economist.*

Bodies producing regular series of statistical information:

Transportation Association of America
Bureau of Census (US)
Ente Nazionoli per il Turismo (Italy)
Federal Aviation Agency
International Civil Aviation Organization
      Series AT, Airport traffic
      Series F, Financial data
      Series F, Traffic
      Series F.T., Traffic flow.
Department of Trade and Industry (formally the Board of Trade):
Annual passenger surveys
British Travel Association
Bureau pour L'Étude des Marches Touristiques Internationaux

Central Bureau Voor de Statisticks
Commissariat Général pour Tourisme
Divo Institut
Institut National de la Statistique et des Etudes Economiques (INSEE-France)
The Port of New York Authority
Statistiches Bundesamt
European Air Research Bureau (EARB)

General studies

Aldcroft, D., 'Railways and air transport: 1933–39', *SJ of PE*, June 1965.

Anderson, T.W., K. Arrow and J.E. Walsh, 'A mathematical model of an air transportation system' RM 224, The Rand Corporation 26 August 1949.

Barry, W.S., *Airline Management*, Allen & Unwin Ltd., London 1965.

Bluestone, D.W., 'The problem of competition among domestic trunk airlines' (unpub. Ph.D. American Univ., 1954).

Brancher, S.S.W., 'International aids for air navigation', *JTE & P*, vol. 2, no. 2, 1968.

Brooks, P.W., 'The development of air transport', *JTE & P*, vol. 2, 1967.

Brown, R.T., *Transport and the Economic Integration of South America*, Transport Research Programme, Brookings Inst., 1966.

Buergenthal, T., *Law Making in the International Civil Aviation Organisation*, Syracuse Univ. Press, 1969.

CAB, *Charter Travel and Economic Opportunities*, Washington DC., June 1969.

Cartaino, T.F., *Air Transportation in the 1970s. Problems and Opportunities*, Memorandum RM-5268-Pr, Rand Corporation, January 1968.

Caves, R.E., *Air Transport and Its Regulators*, Harvard University Press, Cambridge, Mass., 1962.

Civil Aviation Policy, Cmnd. 4213, HMSO, November 1969.

Cheng, Bin, *The Law of International Air Transport*, Stevens & Sons Ltd., London 1962.

Cohen, R.S., *IATA: The First Three Decades*, IATA, *Montreal* 1959.

Council of Europe, *Certain Financial and Economic Aspects of Air Transport Operations,* Strasbourg, 1964 (The Duynstee Report).

Davies, R.E.G., *A History of the World's Airlines*, Oxford University Press, London 1964.

Doganis, R., 'Air transport – a case study in international regulations', JTE & P, May 1973.

Doganis, R., 'How safe are air charters?', *JTE & P*, vol. 2, January 1968.

The Edwards Committee Report, *British Air Transport in the Seventies*, Cmnd. 4018, HMSO, May 1969.

Elle, B.J., *Issues and Prospects in Interurban Air Transport*, Almquist & Wickell, Stockholm, 1968.

Ellison, A.P., 'The Edwards Report and civil aviation in the 1970s', *JRAS*, vol. 74, June 1970.

Elstub, *Productivity of the National Aircraft Effort*, Report of a Committee appointed by the Minister of Technology and the President of the Society of British Aerospace Companies under the chairmanship of Mr St. John Elstub, HMSO, 1969.

Foldes, L., 'Domestic air transport policy I & II', *Economica*, May and August 1961.

Gill, F.W., and G.L. Bates, *Airline Competition*, Harvard University, Graduate School of Business Administration, Boston 1949.

Hudson, K., *Air Travel: A Social History*, Adams & Dart, London 1973.

Jackson, R.R.P., and P.A. Longton, 'Operational research and aviation management: an introduction to operational research', *JRAS*, vol. 69, Aug. 1965.

Mornton, R.L., *International Airlines and Politics*, Michigan Institute of Business Studies, University of Michigan, 1970.

Peck, M.J., and J.R. Meyer, 'The determination of a fair return on investment for regulated industries', *Transportation Economics*, Colombia University Press, 1965.

Penrose, H.J., *British Aviation*, Putman & Co., 1969.

Plowden Report, *Report of the Committee of Inquiry into the Aircraft Industry*, HMSO, 1965.

Richmond, S.B., *Regulation and Competition in Air Transportation*, Colombia University Press, 1961.

Schriever, B.A., and W.W. Seifert, *Air Transportation 1975 and Beyond. A Systems Approach*, MIT Press, 1968.

Sealy, K.R., *The Geography of Air Transport*, Hutchinson, 1966 (3rd ed.).

Spears, R. Dixon, *et al.*, *The Magnitude and Economic Impact of General Aviation*, Washington DC., 1968 (prepared for the Utility Airplane Council).

Spears, R. Dixon, *Technical Aspects of Air Transport Management,* McGraw-Hill, 1955.

Stanford Research Institute, *Air Transport Development and Coordina-*

tion in Latin America: A Study of Economic Factors, SRI, for the Organisation of American Studies, 1961.

Startford, A.H., *Air Transport Economics in this supersonic era*, Macmillan, 1973.

Straszheim, M.R., *The International Airline Industry*, Brookings Institute, 1969.

Sundberg, J.W., *Air Charter*, P.A. Norstedt & Söner, Stockholm 1961.

Taffe, E.J., 'A map analysis of airline competition', *JAL & C*, vol. XXV, 1958.

Verploeg, E.A., *The Road Towards a European Common Air Market*, Utrecht NV, 1963.

Wheatcroft, S., *The Economics of European Air Transport*, Manchester University Press, 1956.

Wheatcroft, S., *Airline Competition in Canada: A Study of the Desirability and Economic Consequences of Competition in Canadian Transcontinental Air Services*, prepared for the Minister of Transport, G. Hess, Ottawa, 1958.

Wheatcroft, S., *Air Transport Policy*, Michael Joseph, London 1964.

Whitehead, A.H., 'Effects of competition and changes in route structures on the growth of air travel', *JAL & C* vol. XXII, 1951

Aircraft and the aircraft industry

Asher, H., *Cost-Quantity Relationships in the Airframe Industry*, The Rand Corporation, 1956.

Booze, Allen and Hamilton Inc., *Supersonic Transport Financial Planning Studies*, F.A.A. contract FA-55-66-23 AD652314, May 1967.

Breckner, N.V., 'Efficiency and the military "buyer seller" device', *JPE* October 1960.

Capron, W.M., *Technical Change in Regulated Industries,* Brookings Institute, 1971.

Cartaino, T.F., *Technological Aspects of Contemporary and Future Civil Aircraft for the World's Less Developed Areas*, Rand Corporation, Santa Monica, July 1962.

Centre for the Study of Industrial Innovation (UK), *Aspects of Spin-Off: A Study of the Impact of Concorde and the Advanced Passenger Train*, London, October 1971.

Commission of the European Community, *The Aeronautical and Space Industries of the Community Compared with those of the UK and US*, 5 vols, 1971.

Davis, J., *The Concorde Affair*, L. Frewin, London 1969.

Denver Research Institute, Colorado, *The Commercial Applications of US Aerospace Technology*, 1962/63.

Edwards, C.B., *Concorde, A Study in Cost Benefit Analysis* (Anti-Concorde Project 2971).

Ellis, E.M., *The Interaction between the Aero Engine Industry and the Growth of Air Transport*, ITA, Paris 1966.

Ellison, A.P., 'Used Airliner Market − A Look Forward', *Flight International* 23 September, 1971.

Ellison, A.P., 'The civil aircraft market: an examination of the replacement order cycle of the used aircraft market', *JRAS*, vol. 75, July 1971.

Ellison, A.P., and E.M. Stafford, 'How many aircraft? ', *Shell Aviation News*, 405, 1972.

Ellison, A.P., and E.M. Stafford, 'The order delivery lag in the world's civil aircraft industry', *Journal of Applied Economics*, April 1973.

Ellison, A.P., and E.M. Stafford, 'Concorde cuckoo', *New Society* 8 June 1972.

Enke, S., 'Government industry development of a commercial SST', *American Economic Review*, vol. 57, 1967. Papers and proceedings.

ESSO Air World, 'Turbine engine fleets of the world's airlines' (annual survey, issued usually in July).

Fromm, G., *Civil Aviation Expenditure: Measuring Benefits of Government Investment*, ed. R. Dorfman, Washington DC, 1965.

FAA, *Technical and Economic Evalustion of Aricraft for Intercity Short Haul Transportation*, FAA.-ADS. 74, 2, 1966.

Galgher, H., and E. Granlich, 'A technique for forecasting defence expenditure', *Review of Economics and Statistics*, May 1968.

Gellman, A., 'The effect of regulation on aircraft choice' (unpublished Ph.D.,MIT 1968).

Mon Lin Lee, 'Impact pattern and duration of new orders', *Econometrica*, vol. 33, January 1965.

ICAO, *The Technical, Economic and Social Consequences of the Introduction into Commercial Service of Supersonic Transport*, 1960.

Leontief, W.F., and M. Hoffenberg, 'The economic effects of disarmament', *Scientific America* vol. 240, no. 4, April 1961.

Levenson, G.S., and S.M. Barro, *Cost-Estimating Relationships for Aircraft Airframes*, Rand Corporation RM-4845, May 1965.

Longton, P.A., and A.T. Williams, 'Operational research and aviation management: procurement and capital investment programmes', *JRAS*, vol. 69. September 1965.

Lockheed: California Company, *The Market for Wide Body Transport Aircraft, 1970−80*, CMP/1392, 20 May 1971.

Lungberg, B., 'Pros and cons of supersonic aviation — related to gains and losses in the combined time comfort considerations', *JRAS*, vol. 68, September 1964.

Miller, R., and D. Sawers, *Technical Development of Modern Aviation*, Routledge & Kegan Paul, London 1968.

Phillips, A., *Technology and Market Structures: A Study of the Aircraft Industry*, Heath Lexington 1971.

Reed, A., *Britain's Aircraft Industry*, Dent, London 1973.

Rolls Royce, *World Demand for Civil Passenger and Cargo Aircraft. 1967–1980*, May 1967.

Sabotka, S.B., and C. Schnabel, 'Linear programming as a device for predicting market value and prices of used commercial aircraft, 1959–65', *Journal of Business*, 1961.

Society of British Aerospace Companies, *A Future Plan for Britain's Aerospace Industry*, January 1972.

Spiro, M.H., 'The impact of government procurement on employment — the aircraft industry', *Studies in Economic Stabilization* (ed. A. Ando *et al.*), Brookings Studies in Government, Washington 1968.

Sturmey, S.G., 'Cost curves and pricing — aircraft production', *EJ* December 1964.

Summerfield, J.R., *A Model for Evaluating Fleets of Aircraft*, Proceedings of the Second Int. Conf. of Operations and Research, 1960.

Swanborough, G., *World Airliner Registration*, Ian Allan, London 1972.

United Research Inc., *The Market for Used Aircraft*, US Airforce, September 1957.

Watts, A.F., *Aircraft Turbine Engines — Development and Procurement Costs*, Rand Corporation RM–4670. PR, November 1965.

Wiggs, R., *Concorde — the Case Against Supersonic Transport*, Pan Books, 1971.

Wooley, P.K., 'Cost-benefit analysis of concorde', *JTE & P*, vol. 6, September 1972.

Air transport: demand studies

Air Transport Association of America, *Airline Airport Demand Forecast, Industry Report and Execution Summary*, July 1969.

Alcoly, R.E., 'The demand for air travel: studies in travel demands', *Mathematica*, Princeton University, 1964.

Asher, N.S., *et al*, *Demand Analysis for Air Travel by Supersonic Transport*, IDA, report no. R–118, contract FA 33–66–14, December 1966.

326

Askari, H., 'Demand for package tours', *JTE & P*, vol. 5, no. 1, 1971.

Bartlette, H.C., *The Demand for Passenger Air Transportation 1947–62*, unpub. Ph.D., University of Michigan 1965.

Beckerman, M.J., 'Decision and team problems in airline reservations', *Econometrica*, vol. 26, 1958.

Beckerman, M.J., and F. Bobkoski, 'Airline demand: an analysis of some frequency disturbances', *Naval Research Logics Quarterly*, vol. 5, no. 1, March 1968.

Bieber, A., *Model Evolution of Intercity Travel Demand – A Markovian Analysis*, Univ. of California. Institute of Transportation and Traffic Engineering, 1966.

Belmont, D.W., 'A study of airline intersection traffic', *JAL & C*, vol. 25, 1958.

Boeing Corporation (USA):

   T.F. Cornick and W.M. Wallace, *Domestic Air Traffic Forecasts*, 1961.

   J.G. Moore and W.M. Wallace, *Calling the Turns: The Forecasting Problem in the Schedule US Domestic Trunk Line Industry*, A-3648 May 1968.

   G. Sukovaty *et al*, *International Air Traffic Forecasts*, ISR. 1093, 1966.

   W.M. Wallace, *The Demand for Airline Travel, A Study of the Price Elasticity of Demand for Airline Travel*, 1964.

Brown, S.L., 'Measuring the elasticity of air travel' presented at the 125th Annual meeting of the American Statistical Association, September 1965.

CAB:

   Forecasts of Airline Passenger Traffic in the US, 1959–65, Washington DC, December 1959.

   Forecasts of Passenger Traffic of the Domestic Trunk Carriers: domestic Operation: Schedule Services, 1965–1975, Washington DC, September 1965.

   Forecasts of Schedule Domestic Air Passenger Traffic for the Eleven Trunk Carriers 1968–77, I. Sagivier, 1967.

   Measuring the Elasticity of Air Passenger Demand: A Cross Section Study of Air Travel and its Determinants in 300 City Pairs in 1960 and 1964, Washington 1966.

   Measuring the Elasticity of Air Passenger Demand: A Study of Changes over Time from 1953 to 1964, Washington D.C., February 1966.

   Traffic, Fares and Competition on the Los Angeles–San Francisco Air Travel Corridor, Staff Report no. 4., Washington D.C., 1965.

Doganis, R., 'Traffic forecasting and the gravity model', *Flight International*, 28, September 1966.

Douglas Aircraft Division, *Effect of Selected Demographic Characteristics on US Citizens' Travel Abroad*, California 1957.

Douglas, McDonnell

The European Charter Airlines, Long Beach, Calif., November 1970.

The Transpacific Air Travel Market — Reservoir of Dynamic Growth, Calif. 1967.

Measuring the 1970's — Air Travel Market Analysis, Calif. 1966.

The Economist Intelligence Unit, *International Tourism*, London 1970.

Ellison, A.P., 'Air Transport Demand Estimates for UK Domestic and International Routes': I 'Demand Models', *A.J.*, vol. 76, no. 736, April 1972; II 'Estimates', *A.J.*, vol. 76, no. 737, May 1972.

Ellison, A.P., 'Forecasting passenger air demand', *Flight International*, 8 July 1971.

European Air Research Bureau, *Detailed Forecasts of Intra-European Air Traffic 1961–70*, ARB/291, B. Björkman, 1963.

Falkson, L.M., 'Airline overbooking: some comments', *JTE & P*, vol. 3, September 1969.

FAA:

A Survey and Assessment of Air Travel Forecasting, J.D. Kiernan, FAA-IDA-P-540, April 1970.

A Survey of the Dynamics of Mode Choice Decisions, the Needs and Desires of Travellers in the N.E. Corridor, FAA Doc. 9-0048, February 1970.

An Analysis of Intercity Passenger Traffic Movement within the Californian Corridor through 1980, W. Metzger and H.R. Ross, 1966.

Gamey, R.K., *Long Range Forecasting and International Boarding of Passengers at Canadian Airports by Multiple Regression Analysis*. M.A. University of British Columbia, 1969.

Gerakis, A.S., *Effects of Exchange Rate Devaluations and Revaluations on Receipts from Tourism*, IMF Papers, 1965.

Gronau, R., *The Value of Time in Passenger Transportation: The Demand for Air Travel*, NBER Occasional Paper 109, N.Y. Columbia Press, 1970.

Guthrie, H.W., 'An economic analysis of revenue from tourism', *Ekonomi Dan Keunagan* (Imtongesie), January/February 1960.

Guthrie, H.W., 'Demand for tourist goods and services in a world market', *Papers and Proceedings* of the Regional Science Association, vol. 7, 1961.

Hamnier, C., and F.C. Ikle, 'Intercity telephone and airline traffic related to distance and propensity to interact', *Sociometry*, vol. 20, Dec. 1957.

ICAO, *Traffic Forecasts on North Atlantic Routes*, Circular no. 77, 1966.

ITA:

    Demand Elasticities in Air Transport, 12–13 November 1964.

    Methodes d'Etude du Marche dans le transport Aerien, G. Desmas, 69/22, 1964.

Joung Pyo Joun, *The Demand for Air Travel*, unpublished Ph.D., University of Washington, 1966.

Kestler, D.S., *Relationships between Intercity Air Passengers and Economic Demographic Factors – A Multiple Regression Analysis*, M.Sc. Thesis, Princeton 1965.

Lansing, J.B., *The Travel Market 1964–65*, Survey Research Centre, Institute for Social Research, Ann Arbor, Michigan, University of Michigan, 1964.

Lansing, J.B., *et al*, *The Travel Market, 1961–67*, Michigan 1963.

Lansing, J.B., *et al*, *The Travel Market 1958, 59–60*, Michigan 1963.

Lansing, J.B., and E. Libienstein, *The Travel Market 1955*, Michigan 1956.

Lansing, J.B., Jung Chao Lui and D.B. Suits, 'An analysis of inter-urban air travel, QJE, February 1961.

Lansing, J.B., and H.E. Neil, Jr, 'An analysis of non-business rail travel', *Land Economics*, May 1959.

Long, W.H., 'Intercity airline service and demand', *JTE & P*, vol. 3, September 1969.

Marshe, R., and B. Flaven, *Passenger Air Travel: Characteristics and Forecasts of Demand in Europe: Aeroport de Paris*. Société d'Etudes Techniques et Economiques (SETEC) March 1968.

Peters, M., *International Tourism*, Hutchinson, London 1969.

Port of New York Authority (Aviation Dept., New York):

    Air Traffic Forecasts 1950–80, 1950.

    Forecasts of the Overseas Air Passenger Market through N.Y. 1965–75, 1958.

    New York Air Travellers, 1955.

    New York's Domestic Air Passenger Market; April 1963 through March 1964, 1965.

Quandt, R.E., and W.J. Baumol 'The demand for abstract travel modes: theory and measurement', *Journal of Regional Science*, vol. 6, no. 2, 1966.

Richmond, S.B., 'Forecasting air passenger traffic by multiple regression analysis', *JAL & C*, vol. XXII, Autumn 1955.

Richmond, S.B., 'Interspatial relationships affecting air travel', *Land Economics*, February 1957.

Rothstein, M., 'Airline overbooking: the state of the art', *JTE & P*, vol. 5, January 1971.

Simon. J.L., 'An almost practical solution to airline overbooking', *JTE & P*, vol. 2, May 1968.

Simon, J.L., 'Airline overbooking: a rejoinder', *JTE & P*, vol. 4, May 1970.

System Analysis and Research Corporation: [Boston. Mass.]:
  Demand for Intercity Passenger Travel in the Washington Boston Corridor, 1963.
  Feasibility of Developing Dollar Values for Increments of Time Saved by Air Travellers, 1966.

Taff, E.J., 'Trends in airline passenger traffic: a geographical case study', *Annals*, IL, 1959.

Turner, F., *Price Elasticity and Income Elasticity of Domestic Schedule Air Travel in the USA, 1947–1960*, SAAB, 1 June 1962.

Vickrey, W., 'Airline overbooking: some further solutions', *JTE & P*, vol. 6, September 1972.

Wright, T.P., 'Some economic factors in air transport', *Aeronautical Engineering Review*, April 1957.

Yance, S.V., 'A flight choice model', *JTE & P*, vol. 4, May 1970.

Airports

Armstrong, W.H., 'Airport accessibility network', *STE & P*, vol. VI; September 1973.

Baltimore Regional Planning Council, *The General Aviation Airport System: A Locational Analysis Process*, Baltimore, Maryland, 1968.

Baron, P., 'A simulation analysis of airport terminal operations', *TR*, vol. 3, December 1969.

Beese, G., *World Airport Passenger Traffic: A Tentative Analytic Survey*, ITA Studies 63/16 E, 1963.

Brown, J.F., 'Airport accessibility affects passenger development', *Journal of Aerospace Transport*, Division of American Civil Engineering, April 1965.

Buckley, J.C., 'The effects of airport distance on traffic generation', *Journal of Aerospace Transport*, Division of American Civil Engineering, May 1956

Corbin, A., and R.E. Pack 'A model of long delays at busy airports', *JTE & P*, January 1970.

Corbin, A., and R.E. Pack 'Marginal cost pricing of airport runway capacity', *AER*, June 1970.

Corbin, A., and R.E. Pack, *The Efficient Use of Airport Runway Capacity in a Time of Scarcity*, Rand Corporation, RM-5817-PA, Santa Monica Calif., August 1969.

Conoley, K., *Airlines, Airports and You*, Longmans, London 1969.

Crawley, R.W., 'A case study of the effects of an airport on land values', *JTE & P*, May 1973.

Doganis, R., *A National Airport Plan*, Fabian Tract 377, Fabian Society, 1967.

FAA:

   Airborne Instruments Laboratory: Airport Capacity, Deer Park N.Y., June 1963.

   The Airport − Its Influence on the Community Economy, Government Printing Office 1967.

   United Research Inc., *A Method for Determining the Economic Value of Air Traffic Improvements and Applications to All Weather Landings Systems.*

Feldman, P., 'On the optimal use of airports in Washington DC', *Socio-Economic Planning Sciences*, vol. no. 1, 1967.

Forsyth, P.J., 'The timing of investments in airport capacity', *JTE & P*, vol. 6, Jan. 1972.

Grampp, W.D., 'An economic remedy for airport congestion: the case of flexible pricing', *Business Horizons*, vol. XI, October 1968.

Hooton, E.N., H.P. Galliher *et al.*, *Operational Evaluation of Airport Runway Design and Capacity*, Airborne Instruments Laboratory Report 7601-6, Deer Park N.Y., January 1963.

IATA, *Major Airports and Terminal Area Problems*, Montreal 1967.

ICAO, *Conference on Charges for Airports and Route Navigational Facilities*, Report, Doc. 8675, CARF, 1967.

Little, I.D.M., and K.M. McLeod, 'New pricing policy for British airports' *JTE & P*, vol. 6, May 1972.

Mourer, R., and R. Peladon, 'Terminal transport and other reasons for ground delays in air transport', *ITA*, Study 67/6 E, 1967.

Mishan, E.J., 'What is Wrong with Roskill?', *JTE & P*, vol. 4, September 1970.

Nwaniri, V.C., 'Equity in cost benefit analysis: a case study of the third London airport' *STE & P*, vol. IV, September 1970.

Oily, J.G., 'Cost-benefit analysis of airports', *JTE & P* vol. 3, September 1969.

Port of New York Authority, *Report on the Airport Requirements and Sites in the Metropolitan New York − New Jersey Region*, 1961.

Roskill: Commission on the Third London Airport. Particularly: *Proposed Research Methodology*, 1969; *Papers and Proceedings*, vol. VII, 1970.

Stage III, *Research and Investigation. Assessment of Short Listed Sites*, HMSO 1970.

Stratford, A., 'Airports and air transport. Growth and transformation', *JRAS*, May 1969.

Thompson, G.F., 'Airport cost and pricing with particular reference to the West Midlands', unpublished Ph.D., University of Birmingham, 1971.

Woods, D.F., 'Determining general aviation airport system benefits', *JTE & P*, vol. 5, September 1971.

Yance, J.V., 'Movement time as a cost in airport operations', *JTE & P*, vol. 6, September 1972.

Yance, J.V., 'Airline demand for use of the airport and airport rents', *TR*, vol. 5, December 1971.

Air transport: costs

Air Transport Association of America, *Standard Method of Estimating Comparative Direct Operating Costs of Transport Aircraft*, 1960.

Derkin, B.M., and T. Seward, *Productivity in Transports. A Study of Employment, Capital, Output, Productivity and Technical Change*, University of Cambridge, Department of Applied Economics, Occasional Paper 17, Cambridge University Press, 1969.

Dickser, R.D., 'Airline service abandonment and consolidation', *JAL & C*, Autumn 1966.

FAA, *Direct Operating Costs and Other Performance Characteristics of Transport Aircraft-Airline Service*, annual series.

Gordon, R.J., *Airline Cost and Managerial Efficiency*, BNER Special Conference on Transport Economics, Columbia University Press, N.Y. and London 1965.

Harbeson, R.W., 'Economic status of local service airlines', *JTE & P* vol. 4, September 1970.

ITA Research Paper No. 33, *The Cost of Introducing the Jets in Terms of Additional Airlines Investment*, 1960.

ICAO, *Air Transport Operating Costs*, circular 77-AT.

Kahn, A.E., *The Economics of Regulation*, vols. I and II, J. Wiley & Sons, 1970.

Koontz, H.D., 'Economic and managerial factors underlying subsidy needs of domestic trunk line carriers, *JAL & C*, vol. 18, Spring 1951.

Kraft, G., *The Role of Advertising Costs in the Airline Industry*, NBER Special Conf. 17, Columbia University Press, N.Y. and London, 1965.

Lawrence, D.S., 'The initial decisions to build this supersonic transport',

American Journal of Economy and Sociology, October 1971.

Meyer, J., and G. Kraft, 'The evaluation of statistical costing techniques as applied in the transportation industry', *AER*, vol. 51, May 1971.

Meyer, J.R., *et al*, *The Economics of Competition – the Transport Industries*, Harvard University Press, 1959 (Chapter 3).

Proctor, J.W., and J.S. Duncan, 'A regression analysis of airline costs', *JAL & C*, vol. 21, Summer 1954.

Slocksfisch, J.A., and D.J. Edwards, *The Blending of Public and Private Enterprise. The SST as a Case in Point. The Public Interest*, Winter 1969.

Spurgeon, R.B., 'Subsidy in air transport', *Journal of the Institute of Transport*, 1956.

Walgrien, J.W., *et al*, 'The economics of the U.S. supersonic transport', *JTE & P*, May 1973.

Air transport: pricing

ABC Airway Guide, Thomas & Skinner, London.

Beckerman, M., 'The pricing of fixed services subject to a random demand', *Economica Internationale*, May 1956.

Brancker, J.W., 'Fares in air transport', *Review de la Federation Internationale*.

CAB, *A Study of the Domestic Passenger Air Fare Structure*, as prepared by the Research and Statistical Division of the Bureau of Accounts and Statistics, Washington 1968.

Cherington, P.W., *Airline Price Policy,* University Graduate School of Business Administration, Harvard, Boston.

Cooper, M.H., and A.K. Maynard, 'The effect of regulated competition on schedule fares', *JTE & P*, vol. 6, May 1972.

Cooper, M.H., and A.K. Maynard, *The Price of Air Travel*, Hobart Paper 53, Institute of Economic Affairs, London 1971.

Desmas, G., *Air Transport Passenger Fares*, ITA Studies 62/63, Paris 1963.

Fox, A.H., 'Fare fixing in air transport', *Three Banks Review*, 1957.

Gwilliam, K.M., 'Domestic air transport fares', *JTE & P*, vol. 2, May 1968.

Gwilliam, K.M., 'The regulation of air transport', *Yorkshire Bulletin*, vol. 18, May 1966.

IATA, *Agreeing Fares and Rates: A Study of the Methods and Procedures used by the member Airlines of I.A.T.A.*, IATA, Montreal, January 1973.

Mercier, J., *Differential Fares for Differential Air Services*, ITA, Doc. 66/6E, 1966.

Pilloi, K.G.J., *The Air Net*, Grossman, NY, 1969.

Rosenberg, A., *Air travel within Europe*, The National Swedish Consumers Council Stockholm, Kungl. Boklyckerial, 1970.

Schary, P., and R.E. Williams, 'Airline fare policy and public investment', *Transportation J.*, vol. VIII (Fall 1967).

Wheatcroft, S., 'In defence of I.A.T.A.', *Aeronautics*, May 1957.

Appendix 4A.3   Summary of selected transport demand studies

Air

Author(s)	Date and publication	Data	Description of study	Elasticities
L.J. Paradiso and E. Winston	'Consumer expenditure-income problems', *Survey of Current Business* XXV, September 1955, p. 29.	USA time series	This was a regression study on annual air traffic for the whole of the USA domestic market	Income elasticity for air +2.7. Inter-city bus travel income elast. 0.0. Inter-city rail travel income elast. −0.6.
United Research Incorporated	Study performed for the operations analysis directorate of the Federal Aviation Agency.	USA time series	This covered the Years 1947-57, and consisted of the total passenger air market in the USA. A quarterly time series model was employed, using dummies for the seasons.	Air own price elasticities −1.23
S.L. Brown and W.S. Watkins	'The demand for air travel, regression study of time series and cross-sectional data in the US domestic market.' *Highway Research Record* no. 213.	USA time series	Time series model. All domestic flights. All routes 1948-1966. Annual. *Model form* $\Delta \log T = \alpha_0 + \alpha_1 \Delta \log F + \alpha_2 \Delta \log Y + \alpha_3 \log t + u$ T = passenger miles/head F = average fares/mile (in real dollars) Y = real disposable income/head t = time	Income elasticity +1.119. Own fare elasticity −1.30.

Author(s)	Date and publication	Data	Description of study	Elasticities
M.R. Straszheim	*The International Airline Industry*	USA time series	Time series Model 1948-65 annual data use of 'Bayesian model' in which price elasticity −2.0 and income elasticity 1.17.	Elasticity with straight forward income and price elasticities NY/Montreal price −0.8; Income 0.39 Chicago/Toronto price −0.7; Income 5.3
R.K. Gamey	*Long Range Forecasting and International Boarding Passengers at Canadian Airports by Multiple Regression Analysis*, M.A. Univ. of Brit. Columbia, 1969	Canadian time series 1956-66	Used an autoregressive component of airline boardings. $B_t = a_0 + a_1 B_{t-1} + a_2 \text{GNP}_t + a_3 Y_t$ B_t = air boarding *per capita* GNP = gross national product y = average yield revenue/passenger mile	$B_1 = 0.29 + 1.05 B_{t-1}$ $+ 0.00006 \text{GNP}_t - 0.0072Y$
G. Sukovaty K. Okawa S.L. Durfee D.I. Wallace	The Boeing Company (Commercial Airplane Division Renton Washington) January 1966.	Time series on aggregate world routes.	To quote from the study 'Various techniques were used in developing this forecast. While it is difficult to predict the world's airline traffic by means of any formula, statistical correlation analysis were considered in portions of the forecast. Results of various travel surveys have also been incorporated, as were a number of airline estimates.'	'Free World Traffic is expected to more than quintuple in the next 20 years. Foreign and US International Airlines are expected to fly 4339 billion passenger miles in 1985, representing 59% of the total world traffic.'

Air

Author(s)	Date and publication	Data	Description of study	Elasticities
J.G. Moore W.M. Wallace	*Calling the turns* (the forecasting problem in the schedule US domestic trunk airline industry) Boeing 1968.	US time series 1949-68	The model was developed after long experience, as a means of forecasting US domestic air traffic. Specifically the model attempted to explain the occurrence of turning points in air's growth. Instead of just including fare, time and income, an attempt was made to include 'quality variables' which were themselves quantifiable. By multiple regression methods they found the following elasticities: 0.3 on *speed* 1.25 on *quality* (they then distributed this coefficient on to the various items of quality on an *a priori* basis and used it as a basis for forecasting) *yield elasticity* (revenue ÷ revenue passenger miles and deflated) of +2.0 when yield decreased and −1.0 when yield increased	$\% \Delta$ (RPM) = $\%$ quality + EY $\%$ Δ yield + residual $\%$ quality = 0.25% Δ (seat departures) + 0.10% Δ (airline scheduling) + 0.10% Δ (schedule reliability) + 0.10% Δ (schedule cancellations) + 0.05% Δ (CAB5500) + 0.30% Δ (flight time) + 0.15% Δ (noise) + 0.05% Δ (space) + 0.15% Δ (ride) *RPM* = revenue passenger miles *CAB* = measure of passenger service *Ey* = yield elasticity

Air

Author(s)	Date and publication	Data	Description of study	Elasticities	
H.S. Houthakker and L.D. Taylor	*Consumer Demand in the US 1929-70* Cambridge, Mass. 1966.	Time series 1929-64 US domestic inter-city	Distribution of income was tried in the static model and the result indicated a meaningful propensity to consume of the upper income groups which was higher than for lower income groups. In another model, inter-city rail price was found to be important along with total expenditure and own price elasticity. '*Per capita* stocks of automobile were insignificant.'	Short run price elasticity	−0.05
				Long run price elasticity	−2.3
				Lagged endogenous	+0.95
				Expenditure variable	1.96
				elasticity	
Roger Marche and B. Flaven	*Characteristics and Forecast of Demand in Europe*, Aeroport de Paris, Société d'Etudes Techniques et Economiques (ISETECI), Paris March 1968	Cross-section and time series estimates	Examination made of journey purpose. The size of coefficients for business and non business travel in Europe examined. Comparison made with earlier studies conducted in Europe. Income elasticities obtained from detailed cross section analysis.	Income elasticity (aggregate)	2.0
				Income elasticity (non-business) W. Europeans	1.5
				Price elasticities (business)	1.0
				Average for European travel	1.5
(See 'publication' and 'data' column)	*Demand Elasticities in Air Transport*, ITA International Symposium, Paris,	Three lectures by Bjorkman, Lansing and	Bjorkman quoted a time series study by Turner conducted for SAAB. This examined US domestic market. Time series study 1947-60.	*USA* Income elasticity	1.67
				Price elasticity *Paris to Mediterranean*	−1.15

338

Air

Author(s)	Date and publication	Data	Description of study	Elasticities
	12-13 November 1964	Desmar. Mainly discussion of problems and limitations of elasticity estimates	Time series studies on Europe and trans-atlantic traffic were also surveyed.	*Area* Price elasticity −1.6 *Domestic Scandinavian services* Price elasticity −2.0 *North Atlantic* Cross-section income elasticity 1.0 - 3.0
N.J. Asher W.F. Baxter W.A. Cox R.F. Muth W. Oi	'Demand analysis for air travel by supersonic transport.' Institute for Defence Analysis Report no. R-118 Contract FA-33-66-14, December 1966	Annual time series 1950-62	These estimates were part of a study into the prospects of supersonic transport. Data was largely taken from the US market using time series and cross-section budget information from the *Survey of Current Business*. Some of the methods were obtained from S.L. Brown (see above), particularly the use of the excess income variable. This variable was obtained by taking the incomes exceeding $7,500 per annum and dividing by the number of households with incomes exceeding that figure. Evidence for this figure was obtained from the *Survey of Current Business* budget surveys.	 <table><tr><td></td><td>Domestic</td><td colspan="2">International: US residents</td><td>International: Foreign</td></tr><tr><td>Excess income</td><td>1.0</td><td colspan="2">1.0</td><td>1.0</td></tr><tr><td>Fare</td><td>−1.5</td><td colspan="2">−1.5</td><td>−1.3</td></tr><tr><td>Speed</td><td>−0.6</td><td colspan="2">−0.6</td><td>−0.6</td></tr></table> The above are the co-efficients adopted by the authors from the many estimates and model forms they used. They also discovered that the price elasticities of business and non-business travel trips were of a similar size.

Air/Rail

Author(s)	Date and publication	Data	Description of study	Elasticities		
				Route	Price elasticity	Income elasticity
G.F. Thompson	'Airport costs and pricing, with particular reference to the West Midlands' unpublished Ph.D. thesis, University of Birmingham, 1971.	UK Monthly time series 1960-68	This study examines scheduled passenger flights from Birmingham airport. The dependent variable consisted of monthly time series from 1960-68. The feature of the estimates was the attempt to capture short run responses to price and income changes. A number of transforms were performed, including the taking of first differences. Other characteristics of the estimates were: 1 Prices were not deflated. 2 Dummies were used for January owing to the short fall in traffic. 3 The Birmingham/Glasgow route was split into two seasons: Winter (November-May) and Summer (June-October). 4 Rail and car costs were introduced to reflect substitute prices. Both found to be insignificant. Sea travel was not considered.	Birmingham/Glasgow Ordinary linear regression Winter Logs of monthly data 1960-68 Summer First differences. Ordinary linear Summer First differences. Ordinary linear Birmingham/Belfast First differences. Ordinary linear Birmingham/Dublin Log linear regression	-0.26 -0.22 -0.97 -0.90 -1.53 -1.58	$+1.60$ $+1.64$ $+2.2$ $+2.6$ $+3.4$ $+4.33$
E.J. Broster	'Railway passenger receipts and fares policy', *Economic Journal* 1937, p. 451-64.	UK 1932-1936 time series	This study used aggregate passenger data, with the exclusion only of London. He manufactured his own series of passenger miles for a number of the years, owing to lack of data. Trends were accounted for by income changes, and they were re-	Rail own price elasticity -1.17		

Rail

Author(s)	Date and publication	Data	Description of study	Elasticities
W.J. Dixon	Unpublished Ph.D. thesis (Yale 1941): 'The Elasticity of Demand for Railroad Passenger Transportation'	USA time series data 1935-1940	Regression study on the New York, New Haven shoreline.	Fisher describes 'own price elasticity' as 'elastic'
F.M. Fisher	'The survival of the passenger train: the demands for rail road passenger transport between Boston and New York', chapter 6 of *A Priori Information and Time Analysis: Essays in Economic Theory and Measurement* N. Holland, 1966	USA time series study Boston-New York Passenger (Rail) Route 1929-34 and 1952-56	He used a model which removed the trend by taking rail passenger figures and then taking the first differences of logs. The R value was 0.916. The income elasticity was significant at the 1% level, the own price elasticity was also significant, but the remaining variables were not. *Short run model* $\Delta \log D_t = \alpha_0 + \alpha_1 \, \Delta \log Y_t + \alpha_2 \, \Delta \log P_t + \alpha_3 \, \Delta \, \Delta B_t + \alpha \Delta_4 \log A_t$ where D_t = rail demand, Y_t = real personal income/head, P_t = real one way rail fare, B_t = real one way bus fare, A_t = real one way air fare moved from the data. He then attempted to compare two years, 1933 and 1935, in which passenger receipts had been due solely to rail pricing policies, and not due to changes in real income.	Rail own price elasticity −0.37 Income elasticity +0.282 Bus cross price elasticity +0.290 Air cross price elasticity +0.191

Rail/Bus

Author(s)	Date and publication	Data	Description of study	Elasticities
	BTC Passenger Charges Scheme, 1951, 1953 and 1957	UK expected yearly change in revenue resulting from a fare charge.	During the hearing of the BTC, evidence was sometimes produced to show the expected changes in revenue. The authors used this information to calculate the implicit rail price elasticity in these studies, with special reference to the calculation of 1957, which was based on evidence provided by Mr E. Dickson of the BR questions 490-500, p. 39, 30 May 1957. Select Committee on Nationalised Industries 1959.	1951 Ordinary monthly return −0.206 / monthly return −0.153 1953 Early morning season ticket −0.15 1957 Ordinary fare −0.16
H.H. Houthakker and L.D. Taylor	*Consumer Demand in the US, 1920-1970*, Cambridge Mass., 1966	Time series 1929-64	This used a dynamic model developed in the study and related variables, including a lagged endogenous variable, to consumers expenditure. Total expenditure was used instead of income expenditure.	*Inter city rail* Short run (own) price elasticity −1.2 Long run (own) price elasticity −2.7 Lagged endogenous variable +0.80 *Inter city bus* Price elasticity insignificant, expenditure coefficient 0.0007

Index

Indexer's note: In this Index the terms Aircraft and Aviation imply the word Civil. The various kinds of aircraft appear as follows: Jets: under Aircraft, kinds of, Jet. Others will be found under the maker's name (e.g. DC 3 or Viscount) or under the general headings of Piston-engined, Turbojet, and Turboprop.

Institute of Defence Analysis (US–IDA) 289–90, 298–300
Intercontinental Hotels Corporation 36
International Air Transport Association (IATA) 7–8, 9, 21, 47–9, 316; *see also under* IATA
International Civil Aviation Organisation (ICAO) 6, 8, 14–15, 55, 65, 279
IPEX fares (Immediate Purchase Excursion) 48
Iran Air 294
Irish International 253
ISETECI study (of French airports) 104, 108, 127
IT and ITX fares 11, 27, 43

JAL (airline) 181, 248, 251, 253, 294
Jet aircraft, introduction of 9, 21, 233–42, 239–42;
    stock surviving annually 164–5;
    see also aircraft
Jets, wide-bodied 292–7
Jumbo jets 35, 181

KLM (airline) 16, 180, 253, 294, 296
KSSU group 296

Lag, order-delivery, *see* order-delivery lag
Laker Airways 23, 48
Learning curve 36
Leasing 35
Life of aircraft frames 154–63
Load factors 168–70, 172
Lockheed 1, 38, 42, 60–1, 180, 183, 289–90, 292–3, 296
Long range aircraft, orders for, (tabled) Jan. 1972 294
Lufthansa (airline) 29–30, 49, 181, 248, 253, 294–6

McDonnell Douglas 38, 40, 60–1, 179, 183, 279, 289–3
MacNamara policy 42
Malinvaud, E. 131
Mansfield, E. 237
Market concentration 17–20
Market for the Used Aircraft, The, (USAF Study) 247
Market:
    structures 12–36;
    values of used aircraft 254
MATRA (France) 40
Maw, Lin-lee 214–16

Mayer, I.T., and Sonnenblum A. 215
MBB (German) 40
Measures and Interrelations in model development of Aviation Industry 61–9
Medium range aircraft, orders for, (tabled) Jan. 1972 294
Middle East Airlines 294
Miller R., and Sawyer, D. 168, 184, 233, 240
Mincer, J. 129
Model, the overall 259–75:
    policy objectives and performance 259–60;
    industry 260–4;
    forecasting, use of, for 264–7;
    stability and the aviation industry model 267–71;
    alternative regulations 271–4
Models for domestic and international air traffic 87–90
Mogridge, M.J.H. 106
Mohawk 41, 180
Moore and Wallace 127
Motoren and Furbinen-Union Group (Germany) 40

Nasher, A.J. *et al.* 289
National (airline) 252–3, 294
National Travel Survey (1965) 96
Nerlove, M., and Balestre, P. 101
New aircraft price index 183–4
Nicholson, R.J. 106
Nobay, A.R. 214–15
Non-scheduled services 9–12, 15
Nord 262 235
North American Aviation Group 61
North Atlantic fare battle, *see* Atlantic fares
North Western (airline) 16, 17, 253, 294

Off-peak fares 84, 114
ONA (airline) 294
Operating and depreciation expenses 243
Optimum size, what is, of an airline? 18–19
Order-delivery lag 211–30:
    engineering processes 212–17;
    exploratory model fitting 217–21;
    accurate distributed model derivation 221–9
Ordering of aircraft 179–207
Overall model, *see* model, the overall
Ozark (airline) 180